ARCTIC OCEAN

GSKII

67° 18' N Lat.

CAPE
SERDTSE
KAMEN

EAST
CAPE

CHUKOTSK
PENINSULA

BERING STRAIT

DIOMEDE IS.

ALASKA

KRESTA
BAY

CAPE
PRINCE
OF WALES

GULF OF
ANADYR

CAPE
CHUKOTSKII

Yukon R.

ST. ELIAS
(KAYAK) IS.

ING

A

AN ISLANDS

SHUMAGIN IS.

FIC OCEAN

N. L. DIAZ - 1974

EX LIBRIS

UNIVERSITATIS SANCTI JOANNIS

BERING'S VOYAGES

BERING'S VOYAGES

Whither and Why

RAYMOND H. FISHER

UNIVERSITY OF WASHINGTON PRESS
SEATTLE AND LONDON

Library of Congress Cataloging in Publication Data

Fisher, Raymond Henry, 1907–
  Bering's voyages.

  Bibliography: p.
  Includes index.
    1. Bering, Vitus Jonassen, 1681–1741.   2.   Bering's
Expedition, 1st, 1725–1730.   3.   Bering's Expedition,
2nd, 1733–1743.   I.   Title.
G296.B4F57   910'.92'4   [B]   77-73307
ISBN 0-295-95562-7

To my two Mary's

Contents

Maps

Author's Note

SINCE I HAVE CHOSEN to explain the purpose of this study in the first chapter, I will give here only recognition of assistance received and notice of certain practices followed.

Unless otherwise indicated, the translations from Russian into English are my own. Too often I found that existing English translations of Russian documents used in this study are deficient or inaccurate in crucial passages, so whenever the Russian original was available, I made my own translation. In many instances, of course, there was no choice because no English translations existed. I owe much to my valued friend the late Professor Oleg Maslenikov, of the Department of Slavic Languages at the University of California, Berkeley, for assistance given in establishing accurate rendering of obsolete words and syntax and sometimes ungrammatical writing. I found his knowledge of the Russian language, both of today and of the seventeenth and eighteenth centuries, to be invaluable. Professor Anatole G. Mazour of the Department of History at Stanford University has also helped me in the pursuit of accuracy of translation, as have some of my colleagues in the Department of Slavic Languages at UCLA. I might add that accuracy more often than not dictated a literal translation instead of a graceful rendering into English.

A certain amount of financial outlay—photoduplication of scarce materials, travel to other libraries, cartographic work, and the like—was called for by this study. These expenses were underwritten by the Research Committee of the Academic Senate at UCLA, and I express my thanks for its financial support of this undertaking.

A word or two about the maps. In most cases the maps are adaptations and simplifications of the originals; details not relevant to this study are omitted, and inscriptions and names are sometimes supplied. Many of the maps are parts or "details" from larger ones, and even in some cases a detail from a previous detail. The maps were prepared by Mr. Noel L. Diaz, cartographer in the Department of Geography at UCLA.

In the notes I have adopted a system of citation more common in scientific and anthropological works than in historical works. In the interest of conciseness I have, with a few exceptions, identified a book or article by the last name of the author or editor and the date of publication, in first as well as subsequent citations. When more than one title published in the same year by an author is cited, a letter (a, b, c, and so on) has been added to give unique identification. A full description of the work or article is given in "Works and Articles Cited" at the end of this study. In the case of authors, more than one of whose writings have been cited, his works are listed under his name in the order of dates or publication. In a few instances I have used other forms of abbreviation to identify certain titles, and in a few cases no abbreviations at all. In the bibliography no attempt has been made to differentiate between primary and secondary sources, official and unofficial publications, and such.

For reasons of production costs cross references within the text have been kept to a minimum. Where possible, references have been made to chapter and note numbers. In other instances the index may serve as a substitute.

Nearly all the dates found in this study are Old Style, i.e., according to the Julian calendar, which in the eighteenth century was eleven days behind the western or Gregorian calendar. I have, with some exceptions, followed the system of transliteration from the Cyrillic alphabet used at the Library of Congress.

The final typescript was prepared by Mrs. Ivy Tunick in the Central Stenographic Bureau at UCLA. The tedious task of proofreading was shared with my late wife Mary, whose moral support of this undertaking goes almost without saying, but should not go without recognition. She knew that this book was destined for publication; would that she could have seen it in finished form.

R. H. F.
University of California, Los Angeles

1977

Abbreviations

Atlas	*Atlas geograficheskikh otkrytii v Sibiri i v severo-zapadnoi Amerike XVII–XVIII vv.* (see bibliographical entry)
DAI	*Dopolnenia k aktam istoricheskim* (see Russia, Arkheograficheskaia kommissiia)
EB	*Ekspeditsiia Beringa: Sbornik dokumentov* (see bibliographical entry)
PSI	*Pamiatniki sibirskoi istorii XVIII v.* (see Russia, Arkheograficheskaia kommissiia)
PSZ	*Polnoe sobranie zakonov* (see Russia, Sobstvennaia ego imperatorskago velichestva kantseliariia)
TsGADA	Tsentral'nyi gosudarstvennyi arkhiv drevnikh aktov (see Grimsted 1926, "Glossary of Archival Terms," pp. 385–91)
TsGA VMG	Tsentral'nyi gosudarstvennyi arkhiv Voenno-morskogo flota
d.	*delo* (item, unit)
f.	*fond* (fond, collection)
kn.	*kniga* (book)
l., ll.	*list, listy* (folio, leaf, sheet)
ob.	*oborotnaia storona* (verso)
op.	*opis'* (inventory, shelf-list)
razr.	*razriad* (section, division)

BERING'S VOYAGES

1

Why This Study?

Vitus J. Bering, the Danish naval officer who served in the imperial navy of Peter the Great of Russia, rising finally to the rank of captain commander, made two voyages in the eighteenth century in the North Pacific Ocean. On the first voyage, in the summer of 1728, he sailed through the strait between the Seward Peninsula of Alaska and the Chukotsk Peninsula, the easternmost part of Asia, through the strait to which his name was later given.[1] On the second voyage, in the summer of 1741, Bering sailed eastward across the North Pacific at the head of an expedition of two vessels, one commanded by himself and the other by the Russian, Captain Aleksei I. Chirikov. Though the two vessels became separated in midocean, never to rejoin, Bering and Chirikov each discovered the northwest coast of America, first sighting land at points between 55° and 59° north latitude, along the panhandle of Alaska. Each turned northward, then west and southwestward, making his way along the Aleutian Islands. Chirikov returned to Avacha Bay in Kamchatka in October. Bering's ship was cast ashore in November on Bering Island, some four hundred miles short of Avacha Bay, and there in the following month he succumbed to exhaustion and disease. It was these voyages that established Bering as the discoverer of Bering Strait, and with Chirikov as the codiscoverer of Alaska.

Contemporaneously with the first voyage, the belief arose that Peter wanted to determine whether the continents of Asia and America are joined or separated, whether a northeast passage to the Far East was feasible. This view of the purpose of the voyage—to settle this geographical problem—is the one that became widespread and that has endured down to the present. Most of those who have examined or narrated Bering's voyages, Russians and

1. Comte de Redern appears to have been the first to apply Bering's name to the strait, in 1762, but it was not until Johann R. Forster, the German traveler and naturalist who accompanied Captain Cook on his second voyage to the Pacific, urged this designation of the strait that Bering was so honored permanently (Breitfuss 1939, p. 87; cf. p. 96; Baer 1872; pp. 141–42; Forster 1786, pp. 402–3).

non-Russians alike, have taken this purpose for granted and have not questioned it. In recent decades, however, Soviet scholars have given considerable attention to Russian geographical exploration and discovery, and Bering's voyages have come in for their share of attention. With this attention has developed a growing skepticism regarding the traditional view of the purpose of Bering's first voyage.

There is more than one reason why one might come to question this traditional view. My own initial reason for doing so differs from those of modern Soviet scholars. In 1648 Fedot Alekseev, the agent of a Moscow merchant, and Semen Ivanovich Dezhnev, a Siberian cossack commander, organized a party of cossacks and *promyshlenniki* on the Kolyma River to sail to the Anadyr River, which they understood lay somewhere east of that river and which was reported to have an abundance of sables and walrus ivory. In June 1648 this party, which numbered ninety men, departed from the Kolyma River in seven boats called *kochi* and headed eastward along the Arctic coast of northeastern Siberia. By the time this flotilla reached the eastern end or southeastern coast of the Chukotsk Peninsula, four of the boats had been lost. A fifth was wrecked on the peninsula. The two remaining boats, one commanded by Dezhnev, the other by Alekseev, became separated in a storm. Dezhnev's boat was thrown ashore on 1 October somewhere south of the mouth of the Anadyr River. Alekseev's boat allegedly reached Kamchatka, after which all but one of its occupants, the native concubine of Alekseev, perished. Dezhnev and twelve of his companions survived the harsh winter, and in the spring they established an outpost some distance up the Anadyr River. Seven years later Dezhnev sent two reports to the officials at Iakutsk, the administrative center of northeastern Siberia, in which he described his service of more than a decade and narrated briefly his voyage from the Kolyma to the Anadyr. Later, on the occasion of a visit to Moscow in 1662, he reported the voyage in petitions to the Siberian Department for payment of accrued salary.[2]

This voyage, its actuality having been established beyond a reasonable doubt,[3] raises the question, Why did Peter send Bering to determine whether Asia and America are joined or separated when the separation had already been demonstrated some eighty years before? Four possible answers

---

2. The most extensive treatment of this voyage is that of Mikhail I. Belov 1948, 1949, 1955, and 1973. An earlier account (1945) by Samoilov is also useful. The originals of Dezhnev's reports, long believed to be lost and containing important differences from the copies made by Gerhard F. Müller, were recovered in 1951 and have been published in Belov, ed. 1964, pp. 130–43. Meanwhile, Boris P. Polevoi has added much to our knowledge of the background of the voyage and has cleared up several of the controversial matters connected with the voyage, e.g., 1962a, 1962b, 1964c, 1965a, 1965d, 1970b, 1970c.

3. Golder (1914, chap. 3) contends that Dezhnev could not have made the voyage as claimed for him by Müller (1758a, pp. 7–20 and 1758b, 7:8–21). For an answer to Golder see my articles 1956, pp. 281–92 and 1973, pp. 7–26.

come to mind: (1) Peter knew of the voyage, but wanted better proof of the separation than the reports of an illiterate cossack; (2) the voyage was known, perhaps vaguely, but the significance of Dezhnev's reports to Iakutsk and petitions in Moscow were not understood there or in St. Petersburg, which became the capital of Russia in 1713; (3) by Peter's time, knowledge of the voyage had disappeared; or (4) Peter had something other than settlement of the geographical question in mind.

No evidence has been found from which one can conclude with any confidence that Peter or his officials knew of Dezhnev's voyage, with or without his name associated with it. Knowledge of the voyage in Moscow and European Russia seems to have disappeared by the end of the seventeenth century. It was known, on the other hand, in Siberia in Peter's time, but in a garbled form. It did not, so far as can be ascertained, have any influence on the planning in St. Petersburg of Bering's voyage. The voyage no doubt had been heard of in Moscow and in northern Russia in the 1660s when the Dutchman, Nicolaas C. Witsen, later burgomeister of Amsterdam, visited Moscow, but in the distorted version preserved in Siberia. The one hint that the significance of the voyage had become understood is the fact that several Russian maps of northeastern Siberia made in Peter's time show the Chukotsk Peninsula surrounded by water on three sides and unconnected with any land mass other than Asia. But those who made these maps may well have been unaware of Dezhnev's voyage and of it as the possible source of this conception of the northeastern corner of Asia.[4]

These findings rule out the first possible answer and leave the second and third ones, that is, the virtual ignorance of the voyage in St. Petersburg and Moscow, as viable explanations of the duplication of Dezhnev's voyage, unless, of course, the fourth possible answer can be shown to be the correct one. In that case the first three all become irrelevant, and one can discard them. Or to put it differently, to answer the question regarding this duplication of effort, the validity or invalidity of the fourth possible answer should first be established. This is the first of my reasons for undertaking this examination.

My inquiry into the purpose of Bering's second voyage stems from considerations both similar to and different from that for the first. As a concomitant to the traditional view of the purpose of the first voyage, some of its proponents have advanced the explanation that Bering proposed his second voyage and the exploration of Russia's Arctic coast in order to establish beyond reasonable scientific doubt the separation of the two continents, something he had not done by his first voyage to the satisfaction of his critics in St. Petersburg. On the other hand, the majority of the proponents of the tradi-

---

4. See the discussion of Russian cartography of eastern Siberia in the late seventeenth and early eighteenth centuries in chapter 3, section II (cf. Grekov 1960, p. 334, n. 5).

tional view see the objective of the second voyage as finding America, and
they either ignore or, at the most, tenuously express the idea that the voyage
was intended to give a better answer to the geographical question that the
first voyage supposedly was to answer. In the literature on the two voyages
there is ambiguity about the connection between them. Thus, even though
the view that the purpose of the second voyage was the search for America
rests on firm evidence, the existence of the concomitant view and the ambiguity about the connection between the two voyages invite another look at
the purpose of the second as well.

These do not, however, exhaust my reasons for examining the purpose of
the second voyage. In 1931 Robert J. Kerner, a student of Russian eastward
expansion, advanced the novel and, if true, revolutionizing thesis that Bering's second voyage had as its main, but secret objective the recovery for
Russia of the left bank of the Amur River, returned to China in 1689 (Kerner
1931, pp. 111–14). This thesis has not come in for much notice, but it was
advanced, and it has not, until recently, been critically examined.[5] Such a
critique, however, would not be complete without an examination of the
standard explanation of the purpose of the second voyage.

Still another question presented itself after I had begun my
examination. As I read the literature on the two voyages, I became increasingly aware that whereas scholars have devoted considerable attention to the
preparation and organization of the voyages (the logistics posed formidable
problems), the courses of the voyages, and the scientific data obtained, very
little attention has been given to the purposes of the voyages. This is due
mainly to the greater availability of data on the former matters, about which
the Russian officials were willing to divulge information, whereas Peter and
his successors had reason to confine knowledge of the real purposes of the
voyages to an inner circle that with a few exceptions excluded the foreigners
in Russia. Even so, such evidence as we do have about this aspect of the
voyages has not been examined with as much penetration and meticulous-
ness as it could be, nor has as much indirect evidence been utilized as is
available. This is not said in deprecation of Russian or Soviet scholarship. On
the contrary, Soviet scholars in particular have made a strong beginning in
an effort to penetrate the obscurity surrounding the question of purpose.
They have made available some new data from the archives; they have
provided much new cartographical information; and they have begun a close
analysis of some of the key documents. In fact, it was the analysis by Vadim I.
Grekov (1960, pp. 20–22) of the instructions of Peter the Great to Bering that
alerted me to the kind of results achievable through a close scrutiny of the

---

5. Indeed, it was with a critical scrutiny of Kerner's thesis that I began this inquiry. Most, but
not all, of my critique appears in my 1969, pp. 397–407. It is repeated in abridged form, with
some revisions and additions, in chapter 7, section VI.

documents. Without the contributions of Soviet scholars, the results of this examination would have been inconclusive at best. But more could be learned about the purposes of the voyages, I became convinced, from the available data than had been learned so far. Thus, I found that I had another good reason for undertaking this examination.

2

The Traditional View of
the First Voyage

THE COMMONLY ACCEPTED view that Peter the Great sent Bering on his first voyage to find out whether Asia and America are separated or joined, to determine the feasibility of an Arctic–Pacific water passage—in fact to do what Bering did do—is not a view derived from explicit written statements by Peter (*EB*, p. 11). It is based, rather, on indirect evidence and on the statements and opinions of several of his close associates and certain contemporaries. Once established, the view became widespread and was first seriously challenged only in the second quarter of this century.

I

This traditional view was born of the great interest of statesmen, merchants, and academicians in a northeast passage around Eurasia to eastern Asia as well as a northwest passage around North America (Müller 1758a, p. 1; 1758b, 7:3–4). Unless the two continents were in fact separated, as many did believe, there was no point in continuing efforts to find either a northeast or a northwest passage—efforts which were begun early in the sixteenth century by the Dutch and the English, who sought to find in the north sea-routes to Japan, China, and India comparable to, or shorter than, those in the south dominated by the Portuguese and the Spanish. The voyages of Sir Hugh Willoughby, Richard Chancellor, Stephen Borough, Willem Barents, and others attest this interest.[1] In Russia too there was interest in this matter. Dmitrii Gerasimov, emissary of Vasilii III to Pope Clement VII at Rome, was one of the first, in 1525, to advance the idea of a northeast passage to the Pacific (Belov 1956, pp. 40–45; Ianikov 1949, p. 8), though his suggestion did not lead to any Russian search for that route. However, western Europeans

1. See Burney 1819, chap. 2; and Nordenskiöld 1881, vol. 1, chap. 5 for accounts of the search for a northeast passage.

did undertake to push eastward along Russia's Arctic coast to such an extent that officials in Moscow, by an edict in 1619, barred foreigners from passage east of the Iamal Peninsula lest they invade the Russian monopoly of the Siberian fur trade (Fisher 1943, p. 78, n. 2; Belov 1956, pp. 116, 118–19; Andreev 1943a, p. 4). Thereafter, information on the Arctic coast of Asia was gathered by Siberian cossacks and promyshlenniki, much of it being made known in Europe by the Dutchman Witsen.

At the beginning of the eighteenth century, the questions of a northeast and a northwest passage and the essential corollary, the question of the separation of Asia and America, remained very much alive in Europe. During his reign Peter was importuned from several directions to make the effort to answer the questions, since he was the monarch who could most readily do this. Most of northeastern Asia fell under his jurisdiction, and foreigners were excluded from the Russian Arctic. Most persistent was the German mathematician-philosopher Gottfried W. Leibnitz, who evinced great interest in Peter's reforms and advanced many recommendations concerning them. Over a twenty-year period from 1697 to 1716, the year of Leibnitz's death, on at least five occasions, he addressed communications to Peter in which he mentioned the importance of finding an answer to the question of a connection between Asia and America and the glory to be achieved by doing so, pointing out that the only place where the boundary of Asia relative to America was still unknown lay within his dominions.[2] It has commonly been believed too, but not confirmed, that shortly after Leibnitz's death a similar request came from France. In 1717 Peter visited Paris, where he talked with members of the French Royal Academy of Science, of which he claimed thereafter to be a member. The members of the academy, in light of France's territorial holdings in Canada, were interested in a northwest passage and therefore in the question of the separation of Asia and America, which was related also to the problem of the origin of the aboriginal population of America. The academy members proposed to Peter that they be allowed to send an expedition across Russia and Siberia to investigate the matter. Peter would not consent to the admission of a foreign expedition into Russia and Siberia, but he indicated that he might organize such an expedition himself.[3] Meanwhile, Peter had also discussed the situation with informed people in Holland who expressed their interest in the question and its solution.

2. Berg 1946, pp. 7–9; Ger'e 1870, January: 14, 18 and 1870, April: 336–37, 377, 379, 384. Efimov (1950, p. 235) writes that there is no firm assurance that any of Leibnitz's proposals on this matter reached Peter. None of them has been found among Peter's papers.

3. Belov 1956, p. 250; Gmelin 1751, pp. 1–2; Efimov 1950, p. 289; Waxell 1940, p. 23, 1952, p. 47. Andreev (Waxell 1940, p. 157, n. 20) doubts the authenticity of this request, finding no support for it in the literature on the subject. My own checking of citations brings me to the same conclusion. Kirilov, Gmelin, and Waxell give no sources for their information, and the citations given by Belov are perplexing in their irrelevance to the episode.

It was not the foreigners we have mentioned, however, who first or alone brought this question to Peter's attention. Interest in it in Russia itself antedated Peter's discussions with the Dutch and French. As early as 1697, Andrei A. Vinius, head of the Siberian Department at Moscow, issued to the new voevoda, or commandant, at Iakutsk an instruction to have those cossacks under his command who were to sail down the Lena River to the Arctic Ocean use every means available to determine whether it was possible for boats to go by sea to the Pacific Ocean (Polevoi 1965b, p. 94). Fedor S. Saltykov, a naval expert and close associate of Peter who spent the years 1712 to 1715 in England purchasing ships for Peter's navy, addressed two proposals to him for Arctic exploration by Russians. In the first, in 1713, he proposed that a vessel be built at the mouth of the Enisei River in Siberia, whence it would be sailed to China and the coast en route would be placed under Peter's dominion. The second one, in the following year, proposed the building of ships on the Dvina, Ob, Enisei, and Lena rivers; each ship would sail eastward for the purpose of exploring portions of the route from Arkhangelsk to the Amur and China.[4]

Such proposals were not foreign to Peter's own interests. Even before Saltykov's proposals and Peter's second visit to Holland and Paris, Peter had evinced an interest in an Arctic route to the Pacific. The Englishman John Perry, who was engaged in Russian service as shipbuilder and engineer from 1698 to 1712,[5] wrote in 1716 that on several occasions he had heard Peter express a desire to learn whether or not a route through the Tartarian Sea, i.e., the Arctic Ocean, to China and Japan was practicable, but as long as Russia was at war with Sweden, Peter did not feel free to pursue this interest (1716, p. 61). When the fighting in the Great Northern War ended in 1719, Peter did take a first step by ordering two geodesists, or topographers, Ivan M. Evreinov and Fedor F. Luzhin, to go to Kamchatka and to survey there the local regions and to determine whether Kamchatka was joined with America. The results of this undertaking will be discussed in the next chapter. Peter also commissioned another expedition, if we can trust the authenticity of the information reported by M. de Campredon, the French ambassador at St. Petersburg (1719–26). In a memoir dated in December 1719, he reported that the tsar had sent to the mouth of the Ob River "men experienced in navigation, geography, and astronomy" to determine whether the Arctic Ocean was navigable at certain times of the year and

4. The second proposal is reproduced in Efimov 1949, pp. 104–5. See also Berg 1946, pp. 9–10; Andreev 1943a, p. 4 and 1965, pp. 14–15. This proposal was duplicated in its essentials in the instructions for the northern expeditions of the Second Kamchatka Expedition (Andreev 1943b, pp. 57–58).

5. *The Dictionary of National Biography*, 15:921–22; Efimov 1950, p. 23. Grekov (1960, p. 339, n. 5) incorrectly gives the year of Perry's departure from Russia as 1715.

whether harbors existed on the coast, in the hope that a route to Japan could be found which could be covered in much less time than the eighteen months required for the route used by the Dutch and English. The experienced men were Petr Chichagov, a geodesist, and Petr Meller, a man of Dutch ancestry, who was a geographer, merchant, and owner of iron foundries near Moscow and was well known in Russian learned circles. The expedition was unable, however, to leave the Ob Gulf, but did explore the shores of the Taz Gulf, an eastward extending arm of the former.[6]

II

In view of Peter's demonstrated interest in a northeast passage and the crucial question of the geographical relationship of Asia to America, it is not surprising that those who knew of Peter's dispatch of Bering to Kamchatka and the North Pacific concluded that Bering was being sent to determine whether Asia and America are joined or separate. This is the almost unanimous conclusion of those contemporaries of Peter and Bering who left a record of their opinions. One such person was Andrei K. Nartov, a protégé of Peter, a skilled mechanic and inventor, and a state councillor in rank, who soon after Peter's death set down in manuscript form a series of episodes or anecdotes about him (Nartov, pp. iv–v; Blackwell 1968, p. 36). In one of them he is quite explicit in stating Peter's reason for sending Bering to Kamchatka:

> In the beginning of January 1725, in the same month when the end of the life of Peter the Great was determined by the will of the Highest and when already His Majesty felt the illness in his body, his still indefatigable spirit labored for the benefit of glory of his fatherland, for he drafted and wrote with his own hand the instructions of the Kamchatka expedition, which was required to go and find out by a voyage if northeast Asia is not joined to America. He gave this instruction to General-Admiral Apraksin, himself naming for this undertaking Fleet Captain Vitus Bering, and Martin Spanberg and Aleksei Chirikov as his assistants.
>
> Being then continually with the tsar, I saw myself with my own eyes how His Majesty hastened to draft the directive of [this] so important undertaking, and as though he foresaw his imminent death, how calm and content he was when he had finished. Handing [it] over to the General-Admiral, who had been summoned to him, he said the following: "Bad health forces me to sit at home. I recall in these days a matter about which I have thought for a long time and which other matters prevented my undertaking, that is, about the route through the Arctic Ocean to China and India. On this marine map an open route called Anian is not shown for nothing. On my last journey I heard from learned men in conversation that such a discovery is possible. With the fatherland safeguarded from enemies, it

6. Imperatorskoe russkoe istoricheskoe obshchestvo 1884, pp. 422–23; Andreev 1946, pp. 190–95 [10–15] or 1965, pp. 18–26. No official Russian information about this undertaking has come to light. What little is known comes from indirect evidence (Belov 1973, p. 94; Novlianskaia 1966, p. 43, n. 14).

is necessary to find glory for the fatherland through the arts and sciences. Would we not be more fortunate in exploring such a route than the Dutch and English, who have often tried to explore the American shores? I have written out instructions regarding this. Because of my illness I entrust the arrangements to your care, Fedor Matveevich, so that whatever relates to these points should be carried out exactly" [Nartov 1891, pp. 98–99].

Although this anecdote did not appear in print until the nineteenth century and there is reason to question its accuracy or authenticity, surely it must reflect a belief common among Peter's associates after his death. A few years later, in 1733, another of Peter's associates, Ivan K. Kirilov, director of cartographic studies for the Administrative Senate, compiler of the first Russian atlas, a secretary of the senate from 1721 to 1727, and then senior secretary to 1734 (Novlianskaia 1964, pp. 11–16; Müller 1753, pp. 59–51; 1754, p. 4), wrote a long memorandum on the impending Second Kamchatka and Orenburg expeditions. In it he too appears to subscribe to the view that the solution of the geographical question was the objective of Bering's voyage.[7]

The understanding of the objective of Bering's first voyage expressed by these two men within the governing circle was also the official explanation stated publicly. On 16 March 1730, soon after Bering's return from Kamchatka, the first public notice about his voyage appeared in the *Sanktpeterburgskiia Vedomosti* (St. Petersburg Gazette). Since this journal was a government organ, the notice may be considered as official. Because no English translation of it has previously been printed, it is given here in its entirety.

St. Petersburg. 16 March. On 28 February past[8] Fleet Captain Bering arrived back here from Kamchatka. He was sent there on the personal [order] of the emperor Peter the Great and by a confirming [order] of the empress Catherine Alekseeva, under orders from the Admiralty College of 5 February 1725, with a large number of officers, geodesists, sailors, and soldiers. In the spring of 1727 he built the first vessel at Okhotsk on the distant Siberian frontier, on which he crossed the Penzhina Sea [Sea of Okhotsk] to Kamchatka, and there in the spring of 1728 on the Kamchatka River he built another vessel. Because he had been ordered in the personal [i.e., tsar's] ukaz to explore the northeastern limits of this land and to ascertain whether this land, as several think, is joined to the northern part of America, or whether there is some kind of an open water passage between them, he went that same year in the aforesaid vessels to the northeastern region. He reached the 67th parallel 19th minute of north latitude, whereupon he found that in this region there is in fact a northeast passage so that it should be possible, if the ice does not stand in the way in the northern area, to go by water from the Lena to Kamchatka, and farther to Japan, China, and the East

7. Andreev 1943a, p. 35; Efimov 1950, p. 289. Concerning the memorandum see chapter 6, section II at note 17; also, appendix 2.

8. Both Bering and Chirikov give 1 March as the date of their return to St. Petersburg (*EB*, pp. 65, 295; Golder 1922, p. 20).

Indies. He learned from the local inhabitants that fifty or sixty years ago a vessel arrived in Kamchatka from the Lena.

Moreover, he confirms the previous information about this land, that it is joined to the northern part of Siberia, and in addition to the map of his [land] journey, which extended from Tobolsk to Okhotsk, sent here in 1728, he drew still another original map, of Kamchatka and his ocean route, from which it can be seen that this land begins in the south at the 51st degree north latitude and extends to the 67th degree in the north. Regarding the geographical distance, he stated that 85 degrees of longitude are counted from the west coast [of Kamchatka] to Tobolsk, but from the northeastern limit to this same meridian 126, which if cut back to the common meridian of the Canary Islands [Ferro Island] will be 173 degrees from one side and 214 from the other. More details about these new discoveries will be given at the proper time. Captain Bering arrived again in Okhotsk in the last days of August 1729 and then returned [here] in the course of six months.[9]

The promise of "more details about these new discoveries" was not fulfilled, at least not in the kind of official statement in which it was made. Disclosure from authentic documents, however, did occur. Five years later, in 1735, the French Jesuit Jean B. Du Halde, usually credited with giving the first public notice of Bering's voyage, added to his description of China an account and map of Bering's voyage (1735, 4:452–58). His account is essentially Bering's "Short Account" rendered into French, an account which Bering wrote and presented to the Empress Anna soon after his return to St. Petersburg. Du Halde tells us that the account and map had been presented to the king of Poland, who in turn had made them available to him. A similar description of the voyage and the map, again from Bering's "Short Account," appeared in 1748 in the second volume of the revised edition of John Harris's *Navigantium atque itinerantium bibliotheca* (pp. 1018–22). The description was written by Dr. John Campbell, who revised and expanded Harris's original edition.[10] He specifies "a copy of Captain Behring's [sic] original journal" and a map as his sources,[11] though he does not say how he obtained access to them. Du Halde's and Campbell's accounts have the stamp of authenticity, though not any official Russian imprimatur (cf. Dall 1890, pp. 120, 122). In the statements of both writers the purpose of the voyage is affirmed to be the ascertaining of the northeastern limits of Asia and of the existence of a water passage there. The credentials for this view of the purpose of the voyage were becoming impressive.

The notice in *Sanktpeterburgskiia Vedomosti* did not, however, receive much attention outside St. Petersburg, whereas Du Halde's work did. It was widely read, went into a second edition, and was translated into English.[12]

9. Grekov 1956, pp. 108–9. This note was repeated later in 1730 in the Copenhagen journal *Nye Tidende* (Ibid.; Lauridsen 1889, pp. 35–36).

10. See appendix 1. For both editions see bibliographical entries.

11. For a third account and more about Du Halde's and Campbell's accounts see appendix 1.

12. For both editions see bibliographical entries.

Campbell's account gained a considerable readership also. Captain James
Cook studied it on his voyage into the North Pacific in 1778–79 (Cook 1967,
p. 433; Baer 1872, pp. 45–46). But neither Du Halde nor Campbell had any
connection with the Russian government. The firm establishment of the
view of the purpose of the voyage embodied in the three public notices
about the voyage was to come from a source close to the center of Russian
authority and to Bering himself. This source was Gerhard Friedrich Müller,
head of the academic section of the Second Kamchatka Expedition (1733–
43), of which Bering's second voyage was a part.

III

Müller was a young German scholar who in 1725 at the age of twenty had
left the University of Leipzig and come to Russia to work in the new Imperial
Academy of Sciences. There he rose rapidly, and in 1733 was appointed as
head of the academic section of the Second Kamchatka Expedition, after
Johann G. Gmelin, the German naturalist, and a member of the academy,
had stepped down for reasons of health. It was the task of the academic
section, which Gmelin later rejoined, to investigate the history, geography,
ethnography, and natural life and resources of Siberia. Müller spent ten
years in travel and research in Siberia, establishing thereby the foundations
of Siberian historiography, and he emerged from his experience as the
principal authority on Siberia, subsequently publishing several works on that
distant and not well-known part of the Russian empire. Later, Müller became permanent secretary of the academy.[13]

Müller first divulged information about Bering's voyage in an anonymous
pamphlet, *Lettre d'un officier de la marine russienne à un seigneur de la
cour*. . . , published in Berlin in 1753, and reprinted that same year in
Nouvelle bibliotheque germanique in Amsterdam;[14] it was translated into
English and published in London the next year (1754). The purpose of the
pamphlet was to correct mistakes on a map of the North Pacific and in the
memoir accompanying it, which had appeared in Paris in 1752; both were
prepared by Joseph N. Delisle, the noted French geographer and as-
tronomer who was one of the first foreigners to join the new Russian

13. Pekarskii 1870, 1:308–430; Mirzoev 1970, pp. 76ff; Müller 1937, pp. 147–49; Mazour 1958,
pp. 16–21.
14. Müller 1753, pp. 46–87. Citations will be to the journal. See also Breitfuss 1939, pp.
94–95; Andreev 1959, pp. 6–7; Pekarskii 1870, pp. 407–8. Golder (1922, p. 362 and 1925, p. 6,
n. 7, p. 265) erroneously attributes the pamphlet to Sven Waxell, Bering's second-in-command
on the *Sviatoi Petr* in the Second Kamchatka Expedition, but anyone reading carefully Waxell's
account of Bering's second voyage would readily conclude that a man of his predominantly
mariner's experience could not have known the information and circumstances revealed in the
"Lettre." Later in his *Nachrichten von Seereisen* (pp. 272–75) Müller virtually tells us that he
was its author.

Academy of Sciences and who had participated in the preparation for Bering's second voyage.[15] The "Lettre" contains a passage dealing with Bering's first voyage. In it Müller writes: "I do not say here what I have not heard said several times by Mr. Bering himself. . . ." He then states that among other things Bering was sent to see if the coasts of Siberia join America and that on the voyage Bering concluded from the information he obtained that the two continents are not joined and that having thus executed his commission, he returned to Kamchatka (1753, pp. 54–55; 1754, pp. 7–8).

Five years later Müller published an account of the Russian voyages in the Arctic and North Pacific oceans both in his original version in German and in a Russian translation, titled respectively *Nachrichten von Seereisen, und zur See gemachten Entdeckungen, die von Russland aus längst den Küsten des Eissmeeres und auf dem östlichen Weltmeere gegen Japon und Amerika geschehen sind,* and "Opisanie morskikh puteshestvii po ledovitomu i po vostochnomu moriu s rossiiskoi storony uchinennykh." An English and a French translation followed within a few years.[16] He begins by stating that the question of whether Asia and America are joined was a much debated and important one, to which western Europeans had been unable by their own explorations to find an answer and which the Russian emperor was well placed to do—a point made often to him during his visit to Holland in 1717. Because of the Great Northern War with Sweden, Peter was unable to devote his energies to a solution until shortly before his death, when he wrote out the instructions for finding a solution and entrusted their fulfillment to Admiral Fedor M. Apraksin, president of the Admiralty College (1758a, pp. 1–5; 1758b, 7:3–7). Further on in his account Müller quotes Peter's instructions and describes and narrates Bering's voyage (1758a, pp. 111–12; 1758b, 7:387–97). According to the Russian translation Bering is ordered, among other tasks, to "examine the northern coast, whether or not it is joined with America."[17] Müller's account was not as long or as detailed as some later ones; he was restricted as to what he could reveal (1890, pp. 252–53). His account became, however, the standard one to which subsequent accounts or discussions nearly always referred, and he, more than any one person, was responsible for establishing in the literature about the voyage settlement of the geographical question as its objective.

Others helped to reinforce this view of the purpose of the voyage. Delisle's memoir gained sufficient attention to warrant Müller's publishing his rejoinder to it. Though the memoir was concerned mainly with the results of

15. 1752. He had presented it as a paper two years before at a session of the Royal Academy in Paris.

16. For the four editions see bibliographical entries.

17. 1758b, 7:388. It is worded somewhat differently in the *Nachrichten* and in both versions of the letter. See chapter 4, note 38.

Bering's voyage, it did state that Peter sent Bering to explore the limits of Tartary (Siberia) to the northeast and to find out whether it was contiguous with America or very near it (1752, pp. 4–5). Contemporaneously with Delisle, Gmelin published an account of his travels in Siberia; and in his discussion of the reasons for Bering's voyage, he adduced much the same explanation as Müller (1751, pp. i–vii). Gmelin's considerable prestige gave added support to the geographical thesis.

IV

During the nineteenth century, the view that the purpose of Bering's voyage was scientific was continued and further entrenched by three Russian scholars in particular. Each dealt with the voyage in considerably more detail than had Müller and more than would others until the twentieth century. Two of the scholars made use of primary material that Müller had not drawn upon. The first was Vasilii N. Berkh, the historian of Russian voyages, geographical discoveries, and fur trade in the North Pacific,[18] who published in 1823 the first extended treatment of the voyage, using the journals of Chirikov and midshipman Petr A. Chaplin. Berkh's understanding of the purpose of the voyage was taken from Müller and is manifest in the title of his study: "The first Russian maritime voyage undertaken to decide the geographical question: Is Asia joined to America? . . ."[19] At midcentury Aleksandr S. Polonskii, who, like Berkh, became interested in Russian voyages in the Pacific and the Russian fur trade there, published the second detailed account of the voyage.[20] He drew upon Bering's "Short Account" and two other accounts authored by Bering (see app. 1), which Berkh

18. Berkh served as a midshipman on the *Neva* on its round-the-world voyage in 1803–6, which visited Kodiak and Sitka islands. Here he became interested in the activities of the Russian-American Company and for the rest of his life gathered materials and wrote about the Russians in the North Pacific (Makarova 1968, pp. 17–18; 1975, pp. 12–13).

19. 1823a. He states that Müller attributed Peter's action to the request of the French Royal Academy to send an expedition to Siberia to settle the question of a water passage between Asia and America. No mention of this appears in either the "Lettre" or *Nachrichten*.

20. "Pervaia kamchatskaia ekspeditsiia Beringa, 1725–1729 goda." This article appears in two versions. The longer one, the original one by Polonskii (only his initials "A. P." appear as the author's by-line), was published in *Otechestvennyia zapiski* in 1851 (q.v.). The second and considerably shorter one, but earlier in publication, appears in *Zapiski Gidrograficheskago departamenta* in 1850b (q.v.). This one carries no author's by-line. In the introductory paragraph the editors write: ". . . with great satisfaction we set down here new, very important details about [the expedition] gathered by A. S. Polonskii in local archives, details the more valuable in that they can not be found in the archives here [St. Petersburg]. In the account presented, with comments on its historical value . . . attention is given primarily to those features which have escaped other writers on this expedition; in the notes [not the same as those in the original version] the most important of those features and several corrections are pointed out" (pp. 536–37). Curiously enough, most Russian and Soviet scholars, as well as foreign scholars, notably Golder, cite the abridged version.

had not used, and upon local archives in Irkutsk and Kamchatka, thereby adding some new information about the voyage. Polonskii identified few of his sources, but his account was long the only place where certain information about the voyage could be found, and for one or two items of information of concern to us it still is today.[21] Its extent of treatment was not matched until Frank A. Golder's account of the voyage appeared early in this century. In his opening paragraph Polonskii writes that the "goal of the expedition [was] to learn whether or not Asia is joined with America in that place which is now called the Bering Strait." Vasilii V. Vakhtin put together the third account, published in 1890. It is not a narrative like the other two, but a collection of documents comprising Bering's "Short Account," extensive passages from the journals of Chirikov and Chaplin, and biographies of Bering and his officers. It repeated much of the material in Berkh's little book and some of that in Polonskii's article. Like Berkh, Vakhtin announces in the title of his collection his acceptance of what had become the traditional view of the objective of the voyage: "Russian toilers of the sea. Bering's maritime expedition to decide the question whether Asia is joined to America" (1890). It is to be noted that in none of the three accounts does the author or compiler give more than perfunctory attention to the purpose of the voyage. Each is content to quote Peter's instructions without comment or a detailed examination of the instructions for what they might tell us about Peter's intention; none of them noted that previous statements of Peter's instructions inaccurately paraphrased certain key passages in those instructions (see chap. 3, Sec. IV and chap. 4, beginning of Sec. VIII). It is Berkh, incidentally, who for the first time published the official version of the instructions.[22]

Oddly enough, though the contents of Bering's "Short Account" were well known through the French and English paraphrasings of it, the text of the Russian original did not become readily available until 1847, when it was published in an official journal of the Ministry of War, the *Zapiski Voenno-topograficheskago depo*, under the title "Donesenie flota kapitana Beringa ob ekspeditsii ego k vostochnym beregam Sibiri" (1847; see app. 1).

Nartov's story about Peter and his drafting of the instructions for the voyage appeared in print for the first time in the nineteenth century, per-

21. Polonskii served for twenty years in Petropavlovsk, Okhotsk, and Irkutsk. As a member of the Council of the Main Administration of Eastern Siberia at Irkutsk he had access to the local archives (Makarova 1968, p. 18; 1975, p. 14). Later the archives in Irkutsk and Kamchatka suffered losses of historical records from fire (Efimov 1950, p. 153). Andreev (ed., 1944b, p. 8; 1952, pp. 4–5) states that when he has identified Polonskii's sources he has found that Polonskii used them "accurately and correctly." Kushnarev (1976, p. 33), on the other hand, recently uncovered an instance in which he did not.

22. The first official publication of the instructions occurred in 1830 with the issuance of the *Polnoe sobranie zakonov*, in vol. 3, no. 4649, 413.

haps as early as 1819, very likely in 1842, and definitely in 1891.[23] No reference to the story by writers before 1891 appears, however, in the literature. After 1891 writers were to refer to or repeat Nartov's quotation of Peter's remarks as primary evidence that determination of the separation of Asia and America was the goal of Bering's first voyage.[24]

Meanwhile, other scholars, relying on Müller and Berkh, repeated this interpretation: Captain James Burney, who had served with Cook on his third voyage to the Pacific (1778–79) and was much interested in a northeast passage (1819, pp. 118–23); Karl E. von Baer, who was a well-known academician and one of the founders of the Imperial Russian Geographical Society, and who praised Peter's services in extending geographical knowledge (1849, pp. 236–37; 1872, p. 43); A. S. Sgibnev, historian of Kamchatka (1869a:42); the noted Russian historian, Sergei M. Solov'ev, who touched briefly on Bering's voyage in his monumental history of Russia (1894–96, 4:838–39, 1140); Nikolai N. Ogloblin, archivist and student of Siberian history and of Dezhnev and his voyage (1890, pp. 26–27); Adolf E. Nordenskiöld, geographer and Arctic explorer (1881, p. 180); Peter Lauridsen, member of the Royal Danish Geographical Society and apologist for Bering, whose biography of Bering was translated into English and published in 1889 (pp. 11–14); and William H. Dall, the American naturalist, student of Alaska, and several-time visitor to the Bering Sea, who first translated into English and published Bering's "Short Account" of the voyage together with a useful bibliographical discussion of works on the voyage and critique of Bering's actions (1890, pp. 111–66; see also app. 1).

V

For much of the present century the traditional view has retained its vitality. It was given renewed strength in western scholarly circles by Golder, the first non-Russian scholar after Hubert Howe Bancroft to interest himself in Russian eastward expansion (1886, chaps. 1–5), and the translator and editor of the first significant collection of documents relating to the Bering voyages (1922, 1925). In his *Russian Expansion on the Pacific*, Golder gave over a chapter each to Bering's two voyages, and in the first volume of his *Bering's Voyages* he published his own English translations of Peter's instructions and Bering's "Short Account." Golder unquestioningly accepted the traditional view of the objective of the voyage, citing (and translating) Nartov's story in support of it (1914, p. 147; 1922, chap. 2 and p. 328; 1925, p.

23. Nartov 1891, pp. III–IV. Seventy-two of Nartov's 162 anecdotes were published in 1819 in *Syn otechestva*, nos. 54–58. All but eleven, which were stricken out by the censor, were published in 1842 in *Moskvitin*, nos. 4, 6–8, 11. Our story, no. 149, is not among those listed as censored out. In the Russian literature it is always to Maikov's compilation that citation is made.

24. E.g., Andreev 1943a, p. 7; Berg 1946, p. 11; also Golder 1922, pp. 8–9, n. 10.

12, n. 12). Thereafter Golder was the authority usually cited by non-Russian authors who wrote derivative accounts of Bering's voyages.[25] Stuart R. Tompkins produced the next English-language account of Russian expansion to America based on Russian sources, and he too gave the standard version of the purpose (1945, pp. 23–24).

The acceptance in this century by western scholars of the standard version has been paralleled by scholars in the Soviet Union. The noted geographer and sometime historian of Russian exploration, Lev S. Berg, who has written one of the two book-length monographs on Bering's expeditions (1946), took the position that Peter, urged by Leibnitz and others, wanted to find the northeast route to the Pacific and so sent Bering to obtain the answer to the crucial question of the existence of an Arctic–Pacific passage (1942, p. 5; 1946, pp. 1, 7–12). Aleksandr I. Andreev, an eminent and highly respected student of Russian expansion in Siberia and the North Pacific and surveyor of archival material about Bering's expeditions, saw solution of the geographical question as the primary, though perhaps not the exclusive, objective of Bering's first voyage (1943a, pp. 3, 4, 6, 7; 1943e, pp. 35, 40; 1965, p. 32). Mikhail I. Belov, a leading historian of Russian Arctic exploration, sees the voyage as Peter's response to the French Royal Academy's request to send an expedition into Siberia to find out if America is separated from Asia by a strait (see n. 3 in this chap.). Several Soviet authors of derivative accounts, as might be expected, also share and perpetuate the traditional view.[26]

Over a period of two hundred years, this view became widely accepted and traditional, and remained unquestioned. Authors quoted or paraphrased Peter's instructions and without tarrying for critical analysis proceeded to an account of the voyage. At the end came a statement of the degree to which Bering had answered the geographical question, the presumed purpose of the voyage, often accompanied by criticism for Bering's failure to settle the question unequivocally by sailing west along the Arctic coast to the Kolyma River. At long last, however, this "mental set" has been called into question and seriously challenged.

VI

In the years shortly before World War II Soviet scholars began to manifest a growing interest in Russian geographical exploration. A few among them raised the question of the real purpose of Bering's first voyage. The pioneer in this new development was Aleksei A. Pokrovskii, who compiled and

25. E.g., Baker 1937, p. 157; Brooks 1953, pp. 138–40; Clark 1930, preface, p. 36; Hulley 1953, p. 40; Wroth 1944, p. 217.

26. Bodnarskii 1947, pp. 108–9, 122; Chukovskii 1961, pp. 5–11; Gnucheva, ed. 1940, p. 36; Ianikov 1949, pp. 7–10, 13; Makarova 1968, pp. 39–40; 1975, pp. 33–34; Riabchikov 1959, pp. 122–23; Znamenskii 1929, p. 77; Zubov 1954, p. 55; *Bol'shaia sovetskaia entsiklopediia*, 5:16–17.

edited the only other collection besides Golder's of documents relating to
Bering's two voyages, *Ekspeditsiia Beringa: Sbornik dokumentov*, published
in 1941. In his introduction to this collection Pokrovskii tentatively probes
the purpose of Bering's first voyage along two lines of inquiry: (1) a more
careful reading of Peter's instructions to Bering, by virtue of which he calls
attention to what had always been there, that they called for Bering to visit
America; and (2) an attempt to discern Peter's ultimate or large objective in
sending out the First Kamchatka Expedition, as the enterprise culminating
in Bering's first voyage is often called. The validity of his conclusions, especially about the purpose, will become evident in chapters 3 and 7.

Two decades later Vadim I. Grekov pushed Pokrovskii's first line of inquiry further in his chapter on the First Kamchatka Expedition in his superbly
researched study on the history of Russian exploration from 1725 to 1765,[27]
with striking though not conclusive results. He too noted that the instructions
called for Bering to visit America. Also he introduced a new element into the
inquiry, namely, Peter's concept of the geography of the North Pacific. In this
he was not wholly convincing if one accepts the results of further investigation
of the topic by Boris P. Polevoi. Polevoi, a student of seventeenth- and
eighteenth-century Russian exploration and cartography of Siberia, published
two articles, one in 1964, the other in 1967, which present the most plausible
commentary to date on Peter's geographical concept and remove the ambiguity found in Peter's instructions. His thesis will be discussed and both
elaborated and modified in chapters 3 and 4.

Pokrovskii's second line of inquiry was picked up after World War II by
Aleksei V. Efimov,[28] Dmitrii M. Lebedev,[29] and Vasilii A. Divin,[30] as well
as by Polevoi. They variously saw expansion of trade with eastern Asia,
extension of Russian dominion into and across the North Pacific, and concern
for the security of Russia's far eastern territory as the motivation behind not
only Bering's first voyage, but the Second Kamchatka Expedition as well.
These scholars thus moved discussion of Bering's first voyage, and his second
too, into the area of high policy and put it in a larger context, an approach
much neglected in previous treatments of the voyages and one that pretty
much submerges the scientific–geographical aspect of the purpose. Yet in
turn the challengers, specifically Pokrovskii, Grekov, and Efimov, have been
challenged by Evgenii G. Kushnarev, who in an article in 1964 and again in a
monograph in 1976 rejected their emphasis on America as the goal. He
stressed scientific goals and the exploration of the northeastern limits of
America for the state's purposes, for the opening of a northern sea route, as

27. 1960.
28. 1950:20–26.
29. 1950:3, 15–17 and 1951:94–95.
30. 1953:40–41.

the role of Bering's first voyage, thus making the search for a strait between Asia and America the focus of his interpretation as the traditionalists all along have done.[31]

We will examine Efimov's thesis, to which Lebedev's and Divin's views are similar, in chapter 7, as well as that of Polevoi, whose views differ from those of Pokrovskii and the other three, noting in the course of our examination the validity of some of Kushnarev's criticisms. In so doing, however, we must remember that this new approach has so far been largely a matter of speculation and opinion, dependent upon indirect evidence, particularly in regard to Bering's first voyage; about the purpose of the second we have some explicit evidence of intent. The judgments of purpose which the proponents of the new approach have rendered remain more as propositions to be investigated than as conclusions well supported by extensive and detailed research. The Soviet archives have yet to be mined for what they may or may not tell us on this subject. Nevertheless, these initial efforts to see the two Kamchatka expeditions in relation to other like developments, to explore their political and economic connotations are a welcome departure from the traditional approach of concentrating on the preparation for and the events of the two voyages, valuable though that scholarship has been. Meanwhile, it is hoped that by an examination here of such data as have been published and are known, a modicum of certainty will be added to the matter of purpose.

In the controversy over the question of purpose one fact remains incontrovertible: Bering did sail north through the Bering Strait and brought back persuasive, if not conclusive evidence that Asia and America are separate, the fact that has long been held both to have given rise to the traditional view and to have confirmed it. The question that has to be investigated first therefore is Why did Bering sail north through the strait? The first step toward an answer is the same one Pokrovskii took: an examination of Peter's instructions to Bering, to discover, if possible, Peter's intention in sending Bering to Kamchatka.

31. 1964:5–15.

3

The Intended Route and
Destination

To HELP US DETERMINE where Peter the Great intended Bering to go from Kamchatka, we have very little firsthand information. No documents from Peter's hand explaining why he ordered the voyage and what was his ultimate objective have been found,[1] nor has there been uncovered any similar kind of explanatory document written by Admiral Fedor M. Apraksin, the first president of the Admiralty College (1717–28), to whom Peter delegated the responsibility of seeing that the arrangements for the voyage were made and the voyage carried out. His instructions to Bering, dated 3 February 1725, deal only with the logistical arrangements of the expedition (*EB*, pp. 21, 373–74, n. 1). Three of the participants, Bering himself, Aleksei I. Chirikov, one of his two chief lieutenants, and midshipman Petr A. Chaplin, left accounts of the journey to Kamchatka and of the voyage itself, but as published they record almost nothing about the origins of or reasons for the voyage.[2] Andrei K. Nartov's report of Peter's remarks is the nearest thing to a statement of intent that we have on Peter's part. We do have, however, the instructions which Peter himself wrote for the commander of the expedition and an earlier document from the Admiralty College on which Peter wrote some brief comments, and these provide a basis for reaching an understanding of where Peter wanted Bering to go and what he was to do when he arrived there. But to confirm and solidify this understanding one has to turn

1. *EB*, p. 11. He also states (p. 21) that Peter usually gave an explanation of his instructions and probably did in this case; but if he left any written explanation, it has yet to be found.
2. Bering's accounts are noted in appendix 1. Excerpts from the journals of Chaplin and Chirikov are in Vakhtin 1890, pp. 4–73 and 74–85, respectively. The excerpts from Chaplin's journal begin with 24 January 1725 and end with 1 March 1730; those from Chirikov's begin with 23 May 1725 and end with 3 July 1727. Berkh's account (1823a) is largely a paraphrasing of these two journals. An English translation of Berkh's rendering of Chaplin's journal is in Dall 1891, pp. 761–70.

to other and indirect evidence, evidence that sometimes raises as many questions as it answers. But it is the best available. Our first step is to examine Peter's instructions to Bering.

I

¶ Peter's instructions to Bering were written on 23 December 1724 or 6 January 1725, a few weeks before Peter died.[3] They are, like so many of Peter's orders, written in his "usual hurried, careless, and laconic style" (Kliuchevskii 1961, p. 115), and without elaborative detail to guide Bering and those associated with the expedition.[4] Peter's ill health might also explain their brevity and ambiguity. Nartov writes that Peter "hurried to draft the directive for so important an undertaking as if he foresaw his death soon" (Nartov 1891, p. 98). Because previous translations of the instructions into English contain a significant error, our own literal translation is given here:

1. At Kamchatka or other place there you are to build one or two boats with decks.
2. [You are to sail] on these boats along the land which goes to the north, and according to expectations (because its end is not known) that land, it appears, is part of America.
3. You are to search for that [place] where it is joined with America, and to go to any city of European possession, or if you see any European vessel, to find out from it what the coast is called and to write it down, and to go ashore yourself and obtain first-hand information, and, placing it on a map, to return here.[5]

A careful reading of these instructions soon discloses that they do not confirm the traditional view of the reason for Bering's voyage. They say nothing about a strait or a search for one between the two continents that could serve as an Arctic–Pacific passage, leaving Nartov's statement without support. They say nothing about determining either the limits of northeastern Asia or the geographical relationship between Asia and America. Instead Peter says that the land which goes to the north seems to be part of America; and if the land Peter had in mind was the littoral north of Kamchatka, as has been commonly thought, then, as Grekov points out, one has to conclude that he rejected the idea of a strait.[6] Indeed, Peter's words indicate that he

3. Berkh (1823a, p. 2) gives the date as 23 December 1724; Polonskii (1851, p. 1) as 6 January 1725; and Vakhtin (1890, pp. 1, 86) both dates. Nartov states that Peter wrote them in early January 1725, whereas an Admiralty College report of 5 October 1738 gives the December date, as does a Senate report in 1743 (*EB*, pp. 85, 363). Andreev (1946, p. 200 [20], n. 4; 1965, p. 30, n. 67) prefers the later date as more likely the correct one. In *PSZ* (vol. 7, no. 4649, p. 413) they are dated 5 February 1725, the date of Bering's departure from St. Petersburg.
4. The instructions to Bering for his second voyage do not suffer from this insufficiency.
5. *PSZ*, vol. 7, no. 4649, p. 413; Polonskii 1851, p. 1; *EB*, p. 59; Grekov 1960, p. 20.
6. Baer believed that this statement in Peter's instructions reflected a general doubt about the separation of the continents (1849, p. 237 and 1872, p. 43). The editors of *PSZ* evidently interpreted Peter's instructions to mean that he thought Asia and America were joined. In the caption they provided the document they state: "About the junction of Asia with America" (vol. 7, no. 4649, p. 413).

took for granted a particular concept of the geography of the North Pacific and that he was not asking Bering either to confirm it or disprove it. Actually the real and final objective of the proposed voyage is expressed in paragraph 3, and that objective is not a strait, but America. Bering is to go to the place where "the land which goes to the north" joins America and from there proceed to a city of European possession, or until he encounters a European ship, and from either obtain information about the neighboring area. Since the only known cities of European possession on the west coast of North America were Spanish, Baja California or Mexico emerges as the most likely destination that Peter had in mind for Bering (Grekov 1960, pp. 20–22).

This conclusion that Peter intended Bering to reach America is supported in the other document dealing with the initiation of the voyage, the document from the Admiralty College. Late in 1724, before Bering was appointed to command the First Kamchatka Expedition, Peter drew up a directive to the Admiralty College for the selection of the personnel of the undertaking. On 23 December the Admiralty College responded with its recommendations and suggestions. On its reply Peter wrote this comment: "It is very necessary to have as navigator and assistant navigator men who have been in North America."[7] In the context of a search for the Strait of Anian this comment does not seem relevant. If Bering was to be sent along the Asiatic coast to the area of the alleged strait, why should Peter feel it necessary to have navigators who had been in North America? But if the expedition was to go to America, the desirability of such navigators is obvious. Thus, Peter's words, few though they are, force us to see America as the place to which Peter wanted Bering to go, presumably to obtain information about that part of America closest to his dominions.[8]

Peter's instructions are puzzling, however, in that they seem to direct Bering to take a northerly course, which in fact he did take. Such a course is hardly the direction one would have expected Bering to take if New Spain were his destination, unless Peter had in mind a coastal route all the way, which would have been a round-about and the long way of reaching New Spain indeed. Too, the fact remains that Bering did not reach America, but he did go far in settling the geographical question by virtue of his voyage through the Bering Strait.

All of this raises questions. Just what route did Peter want Bering to

7. Grekov 1960, p. 22. An English translation is in Golder 1922, p. 7.
8. The qualification which in the eyes of the admiralty officials particularly commended Bering for the command was that "Bering had been in the East Indies and knew the customs." His voyage there occurred before he entered the Russian service. Why this voyage was a point in his favor is not said. Maybe it was evidence that he had had experience sailing on the high seas, whereas the Russian officers' experience had been in the Baltic or on the Baltic–White Sea route. It also might have meant that Bering had had some experience in dealing with natives of a culture with which the Russians were not familiar.

follow? Were Peter's instructions a disguised means of sending Bering in search of a possible connection between Asia and America? Did Bering misunderstand Peter's instructions or reinterpret them? The uncertainty manifested in these questions arises from the ambiguity of paragraph 2 of the instructions, which is one of the bases of the traditional understanding of Peter's intent regarding Bering's first voyage. If the meaning of this paragraph can be established, we will have gone far in answering our questions. However, to establish its meaning or intent we need first to gain an understanding of the state of geographical knowledge of the North Pacific and its bordering lands in the late seventeenth and early eighteenth centuries, both in Russia and in the west, and particularly on the part of Peter himself. This understanding will also enable us better to comprehend other developments related to Bering's voyages.

II

In the late seventeenth and early eighteenth centuries knowledge of the North Pacific and adjoining lands, both in Russia and in the west, was uncertain, changing, and speculative, though it was expanding and becoming more accurate. It must be remembered that no western European had penetrated the North Pacific north of the latitudes of the island of Hokkaido, then sometimes called Jedso, or Esso, or Jeso. What little was known, or what was believed, about the geography of the region came from the Russians, and that related mostly to the Arctic and Pacific littoral of northeastern Siberia. The Russians had first reached the Pacific in 1639 at the Sea of Okhotsk by way of the Ul'ia River and had on two occasions in the 1640s sailed the Siberian waters of the Pacific. A party of cossacks from Iakutsk, led by Vasilii Poiarkov, sailed in 1643–44 from the mouth of the Amur northward along the coast of the Sea of Okhotsk to the Ul'ia River and from there traveled back to Iakutsk by river and portage (Golder 1914, pp. 255–56; Fisher 1943, p. 44). Semen Dezhnev and Fedot Alekseev five years later made their voyage from the mouth of the Kolyma River around the Chukotsk Peninsula to points somewhere south of the Anadyr River. Poiarkov's men presumably did not see Kamchatka, and such knowledge of Dezhnev's and Alekseev's voyage as survived and circulated in Siberia did so in a distorted version as a voyage from the Lena to Kamchatka, its participants not identified.[9] In Moscow and St. Petersburg, at least by Bering's time, this voyage was scarcely known.[10] To be sure, there is recently discovered evidence

9. The belief arose that Alekseev reached Kamchatka, and some scholars have accepted it as a fact, e.g., Ogryzko (1948, pp. 36–47; 1953, pp. 169–72); but Kuskov cogently disputes this conclusion (1966, pp. 94–100). His arguments are summarized in my 1973, pp. 17–18.

10. Even though this voyage does not appear to have been known then in European Russia, it is difficult not to believe that it was not known in Moscow in the later seventeenth century. In

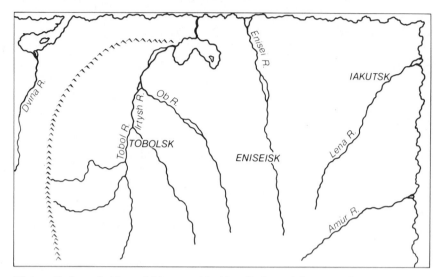

Fig. 1. Godunov's Map of Siberia, 1667 (detail), from *Atlas*, no. 28

pointing to the presence of parties of Russian cossacks in Kamchatka in the 1650s and 1660s, but the information that their activities generated was rather vague and misunderstood (Polevoi 1964c, pp. 232, 234 and *passim*; 1964b). Thus, at the end of the seventeenth century, the Russians still had little solidly established information about the northeastern part of their domain; westerners knew no more, for they derived their information about this part of the world directly or indirectly from the Russians.

The best source of information about the state of Russian knowledge of northeastern Siberia in the second half of the seventeenth century and early eighteenth century is the contemporary Russian cartography of Siberia. The Siberian maps of this time are manuscript sketch-maps or drawings (*chertezhi*), which lack scale and coordinates and are based on river systems rather than astronomically determined base points. Their data were derived from other sketch-maps and reports of cossacks and travelers in Siberia (Bagrow 1952, p. 83; 1954, pp. 114, 123). The best known is the Godunov map of 1667 (fig. 1), the first map to show all of Siberia.[11] Another like it is a map of Siberia prepared in 1684 and known to us from a copy of it made by the

1662–65 Dezhnev was in Moscow and presented to the Siberian Department a petition for payment of accrued salary in which he briefly described the voyage (Ogloblin 1890, pp. 46–54; Belov 1955, pp. 101–5, 112; Samoilov 1945, pp. 106–15). Witsen (1785, pp. 668, 676 [quoted by Vize 1949, pp. 83–84]) mentions reports from Moscow and Arkhangelsk of a voyage in which an attempt was made to round the Ice Cape, i.e., some promontory of the Chukotsk Peninsula, there being seven boats according to one report, eight according to another. Some of the details are wrong, but the fact of the voyage is stated.

11. *Atlas*, no. 28 and p. 18; Breitfuss 1939, p. 88 (simplified).

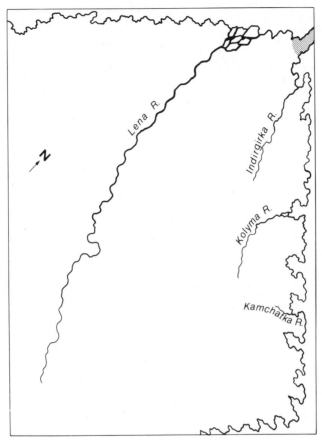

Fig. 2. Remezov's Map of Eastern Siberia, before 1696, from *Atlas*, no. 44

noted Siberian cartographer, Semen U. Remezov, as is a map of eastern Siberia made before 1696 (fig. 2), also by Remezov.[12] They are typical of

12. The 1684 map is in Bagrow 1947 after p. 70 (erroneously dated 1687) and in *Atlas*, no. 34 and p. 29; the map of eastern Siberia is in *Atlas*, no. 44 and p. 30. Other such rectangular maps are shown in *Atlas*, nos. 30 and 45; and Bagrow 1954 before p. 111.

Semen U. Remezov (ca. 1663–1713) was the son of Ul'ian M. Remezov, an exile in Tobolsk who helped prepare the Godunov map. The younger Remezov became the outstanding cartographer of Siberia during a lifetime spent mostly in Tobolsk where he had access to much official information about Siberia. Most of his many maps of Siberia are comprised in three holographic atlases: (1) *Khorograficheskaia Chertezhnaia Kniga* [Chorographic Book of Maps], (2) *Sluzhebnaia Chertezhnaia Kniga* [Service Book of Maps], and (3) *Chertezhnaia Kniga Sibiri* [Book of Maps of Siberia]. They are referred to in shortened form as *Khorograficheskaia Kniga*, *Sluzhebnaia Kniga*, and *Chertezhnaia Kniga*, respectively (Bagrow 1954, pp. 111–26; Fel' 1960). For a detailed discussion of Remezov and his work see Andreev 1960, pp. 96–148, and Gol'denberg 1965, especially chapters 2–3.

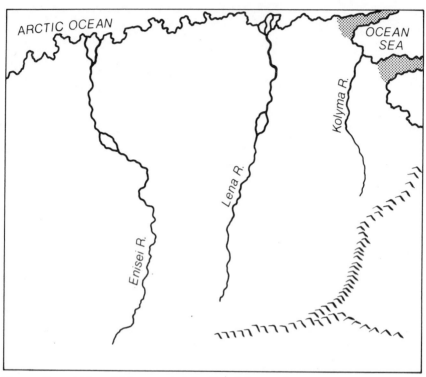

Fig. 3. Vinius' Map of Siberia, 1678–83 (detail) from *Atlas*, no. 46

seventeenth-century Siberian cartography in that they represent Siberia as rectangular in form, the northern and eastern coasts of Siberia from the Ural Mountains to the Amur River trending in more or less regular east-west, north-south lines to form a right angle at the northeastern corner of Asia— evidence that the true coastal configuration of Siberia was not yet really known (Keuning 1954, p. 102; Bagrow 1952, p. 86). The two great extensions of the continental mass, the Chukotsk and Kamchatka peninsulas, are not shown as such.[13] This primitive concept of the coastal outlines of northeast Asia is found on a Russian map of as late a date as 1718 (Atlas, no. 51).

Several of these maps, however, carry a feature of particular interest to us: a narrow neck of land, sometimes represented as mountainous, extended eastward or northeastward into the ocean until it is cut off by the frame of the map, as on the Remezov map of eastern Siberia (fig. 2) and the Spafarii map of 1678 (fig. 7), to be discussed shortly.[14] Three maps, one composed some-

13. Kamchatka does appear as a small peninsula, perhaps for the first time, on the ethnographic map of 1673.

14. Another and later map of eastern Siberia by Remezov (*Atlas*, no. 45) carries this feature.

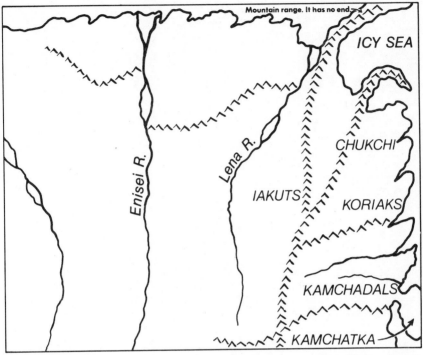

Fig. 4. Ethnographic Map of Siberia, 1673, from *Atlas*, no. 41; Baddeley 1919, I, between pp. cxxxviii and cxxxix

time between 1678 and 1683 by Andrei A. Vinius, the head of the Siberian Department (fig. 3), an ethnographic map made in 1673 (fig. 4), and another ethnographc map drafted by Remezov sometime before 1700 (fig. 5) show two such peninsulas.[15] So does the famous map of Russia, dated 1687 or 1691, by the Dutchman Nicolaas C. Witsen (fig. 6), though his two peninsulas are open-ended instead of cut off by the frame of the map.[16] The stereotyped form and truncation of these peninsulas reveal the mapmakers' uncertainty as to whether a peninsula or an isthmus was to be found there and where it ended. Witsen frankly admitted that he was guessing about the location and shape of these peninsulas (Keuning 1954, p. 102). Their existence does not, however, seem to have been doubted. The basis for the belief

15. *Atlas*, nos. 46, 41, and 42, and pp. 31, 26–27, respectively. The ethnographic map of 1673 is printed in color in Baddeley 1919, vol. 1, between pp. cxxxviii and cxxxix. Bagrow (1947, p. 69) dates the Vinius map between 1672 and 1689.

16. "Nieuwe landkarte van het noorder en ooster deel van Asia en Europa" (Amsterdam, 1687). The map was to accompany his work *Noord en oost Tartaryen*. Scheduled for publication in 1687, it was not actually issued until 1691 (Polevoi 1964c, p. 260). It appears in *Atlas*, no. 33 and p. 32; Keuning 1954, between pp. 98 and 99.

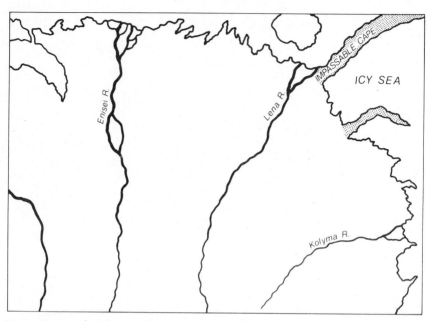

Fig. 5. Remezov's Ethnographic Map of Siberia, before 1700 (detail), from *Atlas*, no. 42

in their existence was reports of a "rocky barrier" (*kamennaia peregrada*) or "impassable cape" (*neobkhodimyi nos*) in the northeast (Titov 1890, pp. 49, 53–54; Polevoi 1964c, pp. 224–25, 239), of a "great rocky cape" by Dezhnev in 1655 (*DAI*, 4:21, col. 1; Belov, ed. 1964, p. 138), and of a "sacred cape" (*sviatoi nos*), i.e., a cape difficult or impossible to circumnavigate, situated on the arctic coast somewhere east of the mouth of the Lena River (Polevoi 1964c, p. 252; cf. Grekov 1960, p. 334, n. 5). Though there is persuasive evidence for concluding that the "rocky barrier" was in fact the Kamchatka Peninsula (Polevoi argues this in 1964c, pp. 225–36), it came to be identified as the peninsula which we now call Chukotsk; it was thought too to be the same as Dezhnev's "great rocky cape" (Polevoi 1964c, pp. 243–45; Berg 1946, pp. 39–41). Because those Russians who visited Kamchatka did not sail around it, the belief arose that it was "impassable"; but since other Russians knew only of one large peninsula, the Chukotsk Peninsula, it was this latter one that came to be thought of as the impassable "rocky barrier" (cf. Bagrow 1952, p. 88), a belief at variance, of course, with the report that Russians had reached Kamchatka all the way by sea. As for the "sacred cape," that was the present Cape Shelagskii, the corner at the eastern side of the entrance to Chaun Bay some 225 miles east of the mouth of the Kolyma.[17] Except for the cossack

17. Polevoi 1964c, p. 252. Dezhnev refers to it in his reports (Belov, ed. 1964, pp. 131, 138; *DAI*, 4:21, 26).

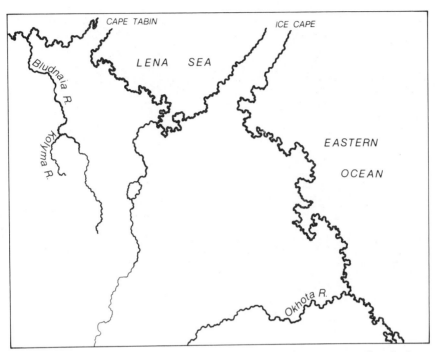

Fig. 6. Witsen's Map of North and East Asia and Europe, 1687–90 (detail), from
Atlas, no. 33; Keuning 1954, between pp. 98 and 99

leader Mikhail Stadukhin, who a year after Dezhnev's voyage attempted to
follow the latter's route to the Anadyr, but had to turn back because of a shortage of provisions (Belov 1973, pp. 109–10, 111–12), no one for a long time
thereafter succeeded in sailing around that cape as Dezhnev and Stadukhin
had. Meanwhile, there was some speculation that one of these peninsulas
might be connected with America (Polevoi 1964c, p. 248). Because these
peninsulas, the Chukotsk Peninsula, the so-called "sacred cape" west of it,
and the Kamchatka Peninsula to the south, enter our story sooner or later,
a discussion of each in more detail is in order.

In Europe particular attention was devoted to the Chukotsk Peninsula. It
was here, with the notion from classical times of the Tabin Cape and from the
sixteenth century of the Strait of Anian in mind,[18] that western geographers
most expected to find the union of Asia and America or their separation by a
strait—a notion reinforced by such information as found its way west from
Russia. Some of the Russian seventeenth-century maps, as we have just
noted, depict in northeastern Asia an elongated peninsula pointing toward

18. For the concept of the Strait of Anian and its origin see Berg 1946, pp. 15–24; Nunn 1929;
Sykes 1915.

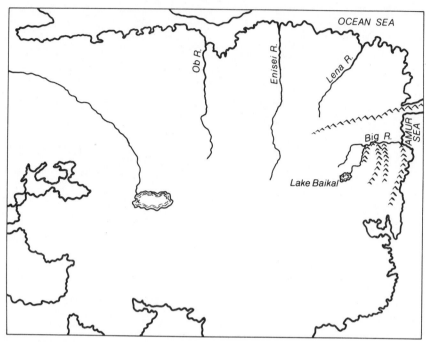

Fig. 7. Spafarii's Map of Siberia, 1678, from *Atlas*, no. 32; Andreev 1960, facing p.
56; Bagrow 1947, facing p. 69

America (figs. 2–6). Although copies of these maps did not circulate in western Europe, some of the information on them, including the suggestion of a connection between Asia and America, did become known there through certain foreigners, in particular: Nikolai Milescu, a Moldavian Greek better known to the Russians as Spafarii, who was sent by the tsar on a commercial mission to China in 1675–76; the French Jesuit fathers at Peking who assisted the Chinese in their negotiations with the Russians at Nerchinsk in 1689; and Witsen, the burgomeister of Amsterdam who earlier visited Moscow, in 1665, and thereafter maintained a correspondence with informed Russians from whom he obtained much geographical data.[19] The information that these three men relayed to the west gave rise to considerable speculation about this corner of Asia before and after the turn of the century.

During his mission to China in 1675–76, Spafarii made a map of Siberia and China, dated 1678 (fig. 7).[20] This map in turn, it is believed, became the

19. For some of his sources see Polevoi 1971, p. 20; Trisman 1951, pp. 15–19.

20. *Atlas*, no. 32 and pp. 20–21; Andreev 1960, facing p. 56; Bagrow 1947, facing p. 69 and 1975, p. 36. Bagrow uncovered this map, long thought lost, in Berlin and dated it 1682, but Belov (1955, p. 116) corrects the date to 1678. Polevoi discusses the map in 1964c, pp. 245–48 and in 1969.

basis of the map used by the Russian and Chinese negotiators at Nerchinsk in 1689. From this latter map and a second one carried by the Russian negotiators, as well as from conversations with the Russians, one of the Jesuit fathers, Jean F. Gerbillon, obtained information about eastern Siberia which he incorporated in his account of the negotiations leading to the Treaty of Nerchinsk and which his fellow Jesuit, Du Halde, published much later in his description of China. Gerbillon states:

> The Muscovites indicated that they had travelled along the coasts of the Icy and Eastern Seas and had found the sea everywhere, except in one place toward the northeast where there is a chain of mountains projecting far into the sea. They could not reach the end of these mountains, which are inaccessible.
>
> If our continent touches that of America, it can be only in that place; but whether it touches there or not, it is certain that it can hardly be far away, for if it is true that our continent extends from this side six or seven hundred leagues in that direction beyond the meridian of Peking, as those who have travelled over the region assure us and as the two maps which the Muscovite plenipotentiaries showed us testify; and further, if one reflects on the number of degrees there must be for as great an extent of territory along the parallels between 70 and 80 degrees of latitude as that of the corner of Tartary, one will have no difficulty in determining the short distance that there must be between the two continents in this direction.[21]

The Belgian Jesuit, Antoine Thomas, who also served in Peking and knew Spafarii, published a map of Tartary (Siberia) in 1690 (fig. 8) which likewise affirmed this theory. On it an open-ended peninsula, shaped like a bird's beak, extends into the sea at the northeastern corner, and near it appears this inscription in Latin: "Whether this hook touches North America or gives on to the Strait of Anian is still uncertain" (Florovsky 1951, pp. 104, 107; Bagrow 1952, pp. 85, 90). On the mainland from which the "hook" extends there is this legend: "The Muscovites have travelled this whole area but not all the way to the end."

It was at this time that Witsen published his famous map of Russia (fig. 6), a map which exerted considerable influence on other European cartographers (Keuning 1954, pp. 105, 107–9, map facing p. 98; *Atlas*, no. 33). One of the two open-ended peninsulas in the northeast he labels "Ice Cape" and by it places the inscription: "The end of this head is not known." Witsen, however, was not convinced of a connection between Asia and America. "Some indeed allege this," he writes in *Noord en Oost Tartaryen*, "but it is uncertain because it has been attempted neither by sea nor by land. The naviga-

---

21. Du Halde 1735, 4:57. Polevoi (1964c, pp. 245–48), using Spafarii's manuscript "Opisanie velikoi reki Amura" [Description of the Great River Amur], argues that Spafarii's truncated peninsula and his impassable mountain barrier combine features of both the Kamchatka and Chukotsk peninsulas. On his map the position suggests Kamchatka, but its direction corresponds with that of the Chukotsk Peninsula. Because what later is known as Kamchatka was, with one or two exceptions, not known in the west, Spafarii's peninsula was associated with the northeastern corner of Asia. The information giving rise to Spafarii's depiction of the peninsula was information about Kamchatka, not Chukotka.

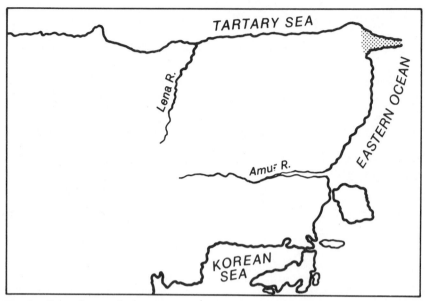

Fig. 8. Thomas' Map of Tartary (Siberia), 1690 (detail), from Florovsky 1951, p. 104;
     Bagrow 1952, p. 85

tion between both continents is, however, very difficult, if not impossible"
(Keuning 1954, p. 102 citing Witsen 1692 ed., 2:542; Witsen 1785, p. 667). He
mentions proposed or unsuccessful attempts to reach this strait, though
some, he asserts, were successful.[22] Later the English cartographer, John
Thornton appended to his *Atlas Maritimus Novus* (London, [1704?], vol. 3) a
map (fig. 9) showing the northeastern corner of Asia, at which appears a
short open-ended cape with this inscription: "It is not known whether this
joins to America or not" (Bagrow 1952, pp. 90–91, 92 [map]). Guillaume
Delisle, the "first royal geographer," published a "Carte de Tartarie" at
Paris in 1706 (fig. 10), which owed much to Witsen's map (Bagrow 1952,
89–90), and on it appears a mountainous open-ended peninsula next to which
is an inscription: "It is not known where this chain of mountains ends and
whether it does not join some other continent" (Bagrow 1952, p. 89 [map],
90, 91). This map was copied by the cartographer who made the map (fig. 11)

22. Witsen 1785, pp. 90–91, 668, 676, 728, 854; Vize 1949, pp. 83, 84, 87. In one passage
Witsen 1785, pp. 106–7) says more about the Ice Cape. He says that on one side of it is the
Mangazeia Sea, on the other the Amur Sea, i.e., the Arctic and Pacific oceans. It is not known
how far it extends into the sea. Some maps in his possession show it as a straight line running
northeast, others as a curved one. To travel via the Ice Cape one has to sail in the summer when
the small vessels can be portaged across it and supplies backpacked. Some say there is a barely
passable forest on the south side. The cape is variously described as high and low, wide and
narrow, wider than he depicts it on his map.

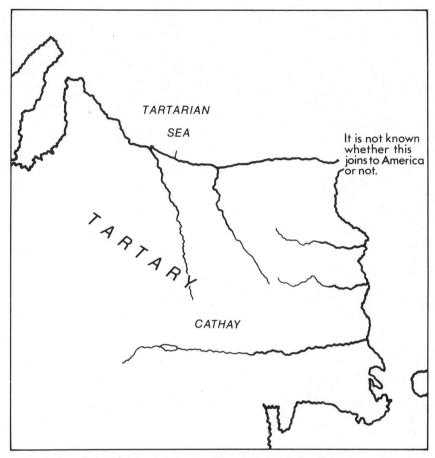

TARTARIAN

SEA

It is not known
whether this
joins to America
or not.

TARTARY

CATHAY

Fig. 9. Thornton's Worldmap, ca. 1700 (detail), from Florovsky 1952, p. 92

that appeared in 1725 or 1727 in the first volume of Friedrich C. Weber's
Nouveaux Memoires sur l'Etat Present de la Grande Russie, ou Moscovie.[23]
The legend next to the peninsula on this map goes so far as to state: "Moun-
tain chain which is joined to what is believed to be the continent of
America." Delisle's authority as the first royal geographer was such as to
throw strong doubt on the view that Asia and America are separated.

Clearly no one really knew whether Asia and America were separate or
joined, and if joined, where. Until the answer was obtained, no one could
know whether a northeast or a northwest passage from Europe to the Pacific
was possible. It is no wonder, given the great interest in this matter that

23. 1727 (?). This map faces p. 1 of vol. 1. The same map appears in the English translation.
The map of the German original was not available to me. See bibliographical entries.

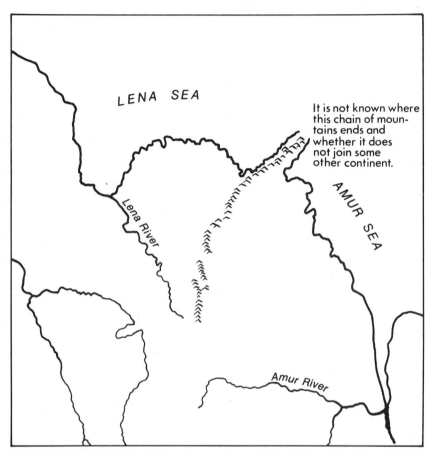

Fig. 10. G. Delisle's Map of Tartary (Siberia), 1706 (detail), from Bagrow 1952, p. 89

Leibnitz should have importuned Peter to have the eastern extremities of his dominions explored, that Dutchmen and others should have pressed him to find an answer, or that this question should affect what the western academicians, mostly Germans, who moved to St. Petersburg with the founding of the Russian Imperial Academy of Sciences in 1725, viewed the purpose and results of Bering's first voyage to be.

In the last years of the seventeenth and the first decade or so of the eighteenth century the Russians became better acquainted with the coastal areas of Siberia between the northeastern corner and the mouth of the Amur River. This was the result particularly of the conquest of Kamchatka, which began with the expedition of Luka Morozko (1695–96) and was made effective by the expedition of Vladimir Atlasov (1697–99). Both expeditions ap-

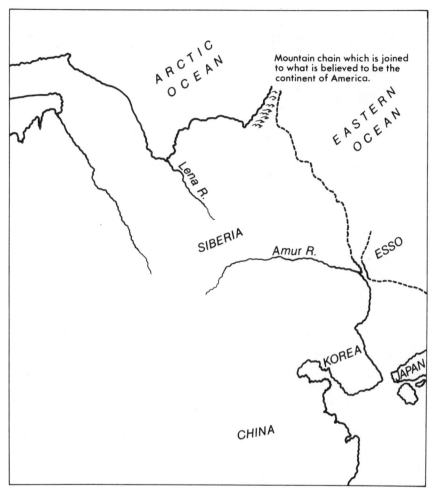

Fig. 11. General Map of Great Russia and the States of the Tsar, 1725 or 1727, from Weber 1727, facing p. 1

proached Kamchatka overland, as did others, by way of Anadyrsk, and thus not only was more learned about Kamchatka, but increased contact with the Chukchi yielded new information about their land, although the Russians were not able to confirm it by firsthand observation. We know this to be true in the case of Atlasov. In one of his reports he tells of learning from the Chukchi near Anadyrsk of an "impassable cape" between the Kolyma and Anadyr rivers, on the left side of which the sea had drift ice in the summer and was frozen in the winter and on the other side of which the sea had drift ice in the spring and was free of ice in the summer. Opposite the cape,

according to the natives, was an island whose inhabitants crossed the frozen
sea to the cape, bringing with them a poor quality of sable for trade (Sgibnev
1869b, Aprel', p. 72; Efimov 1950, p. 83; Ogloblin 1891, p. 12). A similar
report was made in 1711 by the cossack leader Petr Popov, who led a party
from Anadyrsk to the Chukchi in an unsuccessful attempt to induce them to
submit to Russian authority. The Chukchi told the Russians about islands
situated a one- or two-day journey by *baidary* east of their land and of a Big
Land (*bol'shaia zemlia*) another day's journey beyond the islands (*PSI*,
1:456–59). The Chukchi were referring presumably to the Big and Little
Diomede islands and to the Seward Peninsula or Cape Prince of Wales.
These reports point to the conclusion that the two continents are separate,
but there is no conclusive evidence that the Russians yet identified this Big
Land as part of America.

The Russians' increased knowledge about northeastern Siberia, about
Chukotka, the area inhabited by the Chukchi, and Kamchatka, manifested
itself in their sketch-maps made at the end of the seventeenth and in the
early eighteenth century. The elongated and truncated or open-ended
peninsula at the northeast corner disappeared, and in its place on three maps
in particular—the Remezov map of Kamchatka, 1712–14, the so-called
Kozyrevskii map, 1713,[24] and the so-called L'vov or Anadyrsk map (figs. 12,
13, and 17)—there appeared a blunt, somewhat squarish one whose configuration is recognizable as that of the Chukotsk Peninsula and which clearly is
washed by the ocean on three sides (*Atlas*, nos. 48, 50, and 55, and pp. 3,
34–36). On the Anadyrsk map, two islands are shown opposite the eastern
end of the peninsula. On the Remezov map of Kamchatka, 1712–14, and the
Anadyrsk map, and on a third, Fedor Beiton's Iakutsk map of 1710–11 (fig.
14) (*Atlas*, no. 54, and pp. 38–39; Berg in Krasheninnikov 1949, p. 779), a
new feature appears, a long, rather curved arm of land just east of the
peninsula and islands, cut off by the northern or eastern edge of the map, the
Big Land to the east. The makers of these maps, it seems, did not doubt that
the eastern part of Chukotka was a peninsula attached to Asia, but they did
show doubt about the Big Land. It is not shown as a section of a continent,
and thus could be an island or an appendage to a continent; in other words,
an unbroken connection with America is only intimated. It is at this stage,
too, that the Russians for the first time gave the Chukotsk Peninsula a name.

24. The map called here the Remezov map of Kamchatka, 1712–14, is called the Remezov-
Atlasov map of Kamchatka in *Atlas* (no. 48 and pp. 34–35) and dated about 1700. Polevoi (1965c,
pp. 95–96) presents convincing evidence that this map was made no earlier than 1713, not in
1700 or 1701, and thus is not the map for which Remezov first used information about Kamchatka provided by Atlasov's reports. Gol'denberg (1965, pp. 189, 193) likewise dates it in
1712–14. Polevoi (pp. 100–1) expresses doubt that the so-called Kozyrevskii map of 1713 is
properly attributed to him.

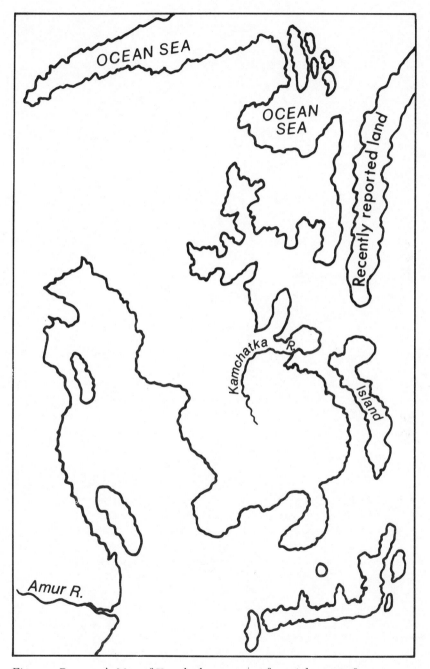

Fig. 12. Remezov's Map of Kamchatka, 1712–14, from *Atlas*, no. 48

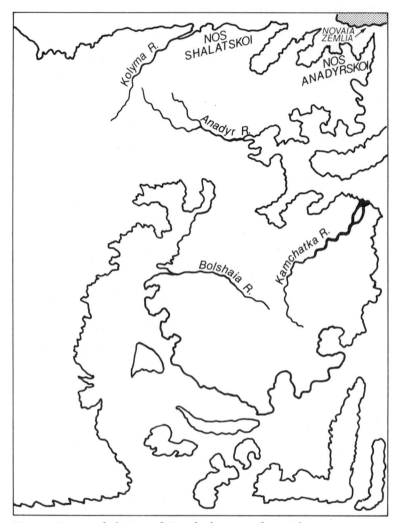

Fig. 13. Kozyrevskii's Map of Kamchatka, 1713, from *Atlas*, no. 50

On two of the maps (figs. 13 and 17) it is called Nos Anadyrskoi,[25] and on a third (fig. 14) it is called Nos Shalatskoi (*Atlas*, p. 38 [*nadpisi* A-2]). A fourth map (fig. 12) leaves the peninsula unnamed. There is a fifth map, it should be added, that also incorporates this changed configuration, though not the name Nos Anadyrskoi; this map is the so-called Homann map of 1725 pub-

___

25. *Atlas*, p. 35 (*nadpisi* A-2) and p. 39 (*nadpisi* A-2 [*sic*, should be B-3]). "Nos," meaning "nose," was the term most commonly used by the Russians in the seventeenth and early eighteenth centuries to designate a peninsula (Polevoi 1962b, p. 150).

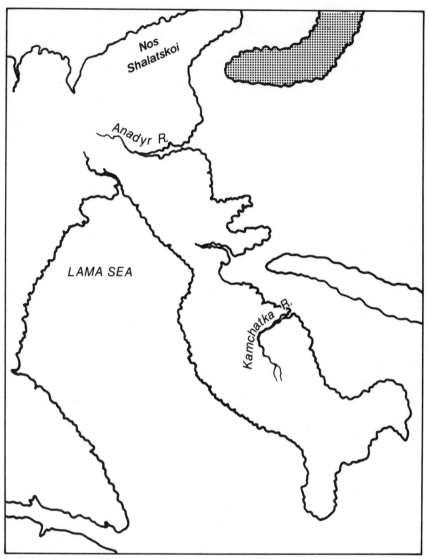

Fig. 14. Beiton's Iakutsk Map, 1710–11, from *Atlas*, no. 54

lished at Nürnberg (fig. 25). Until its publication the new information on the Russian sketch-maps was scarcely known outside Russia. We will have more to say about this map later. Meanwhile, on the basis of such information as the Russians had about Chukotka, one would have had then (ca. 1713) to conclude that no land connection between Asia and America existed, but this had not been proved scientifically.

The second peninsula to engage our attention is the so-called "sacred cape" between the Kolyma River and the Chukotsk Peninsula. This one drew the least attention of the three in Peter's time from either the Russians or western savants, and scholars dealing with Bering's voyages, except Müller, have given it scant notice since. This is perhaps not surprising in view of the fact that this peninsula was only one of several, including the Chukotsk Peninsula, on both the Arctic and Pacific coasts of Siberia to be called a "sacred cape."[26] Moreover, though the two elongated promontories near the northeastern corner of Siberia which appear on the Vinius map (fig. 3) and ethnographic maps of 1673 and before 1700 (figs. 4 and 5) might represent the Chukotsk Peninsula and the sacred cape west of it, we can not be sure; they could just as well represent the Chukotsk and Kamchatka peninsulas. But whatever their origin may have been, the fact is that two peninsulas appear in northeastern Siberia where only one should be, and though scholars say little or nothing about this extra cape, these and other maps of the time attest to the belief that a prominent headland existed between the Kolyma River and the eastern tip of Asia.

Belief in this particular sacred cape has seventeenth-century origins and is most likely based on Cape Shelagskii. In one of his reports Dezhnev remarks that the "great rocky cape" is "not the first sacred cape from the Kolyma," one which Mikhail Stadukhin probably saw on his eastward voyage in 1649 and which is Cape Shelagskii (DAI, 4:21; Belov, ed. 1964, p. 138). Later, Witsen placed an Arctic cape east of the Kolyma and west of the Ice Cape on his map, identifying it as Cape Tabin, a relic of classical geography and nomenclature. Its end is left open, and next to it Witsen inscribed this legend: "Since this and the Ice Cape have never been circumnavigated, it is not known how far they extend."[27]

This view of an apparently impassable promontory, or at least a major promontory, between the Kolyma River and the end of the Chukotsk Peninsula was destined to continue long into the eighteenth century, though the concept of its shape and size changed. On the Remezov map of Kamchatka of 1712–14 (fig. 12) a large promontory is shown northwest of the Nos Anadyrskoi, without name or inscription.[28] Another of Remezov's maps, one dated 1701 and based on data provided by Atlasov (fig. 15),[29] shows

26. Polevoi 1964c, p. 252; Belov 1956, p. 246. Atlas, p. 30, mentions a "sacred cape," and maps nos. 42 and 45 show such a cape east of the Lena River.

27. Witsen incorrectly designates the Kolyma River as the Bludnaia (now Omolon) and makes the Kolyma a western tributary of it. The Kolyma is the main stream, and the Bludnaia an eastern tributary. He also places the Indigirka River incorrectly, east instead of west of the Kolyma.

28. Efimov (Atlas, p. 31), Gol'denberg (1965, pp. 192–93), and Polevoi (1965c) all fail to explain this promontory.

29. This map appears in Atlas (no. 47 and p. 31) as one made from data provided by one Vladimir Kubasov. Polevoi (1965c, pp. 96, 98–99) finds no record of a Vladimir Kubasov at

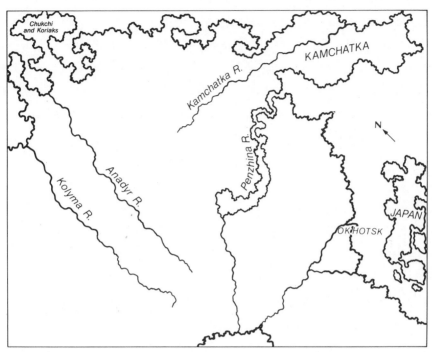

Fig. 15. Remezov's Map of Kamchatka, 1701 (based on Atlasov's data), from *Atlas*, no. 47

southeast of the Anadyr River a large peninsula on which Chukchi and Koriaks lived (presumably this is the Chukotsk Peninsula incorrectly placed) and northwest of it between the Anadyr and Kolyma rivers an unlabeled peninsula. The bay southeast of it carries the inscription "Ocean sea beyond the Ice Cape."[30] The later so-called Kozyrevskii map of 1713 (fig. 13) shows a large promontory east of the Kolyma River and labels it "Shalatskoi Nos" (*Atlas*, no. 50 and p. 45 [*nadpisi* B-1]). On still another of Remezov's maps, Siberia from the Enisei to Kamchatka, a map made sometime between 1706 and 1711 (fig. 16),[31] a pointed cape appears just east of the Kolyma River

Iakutsk or in Kamchatka and concludes that Remezov in acknowledging the name of his source wrote by a slip of the pen "Kubasov" instead of "Atlasov." From evidence on the map itself Polevoi is convinced that this is the map for which Remezov first used Atlasov's new information about Kamchatka. Gol'denberg (1965, pp. 188–91) agrees that Atlasov, not Kubasov, was the source of the information used for this map and dates the map in 1702, not in 1701.

30. *Atlas*, no. 47 and pp. 31–32 (*nadpisi* C-2). The map is badly oriented, north being difficult to establish.

31. *Atlas*, no. 49 and p. 34 (*nadpisi* B-1). Polevoi (1965c, p. 100) sets the date of composition between 1706 and 1711, Gol'denberg (1965, p. 192) in 1706–7 or 1708. Efimov places it between 1699 and 1715.

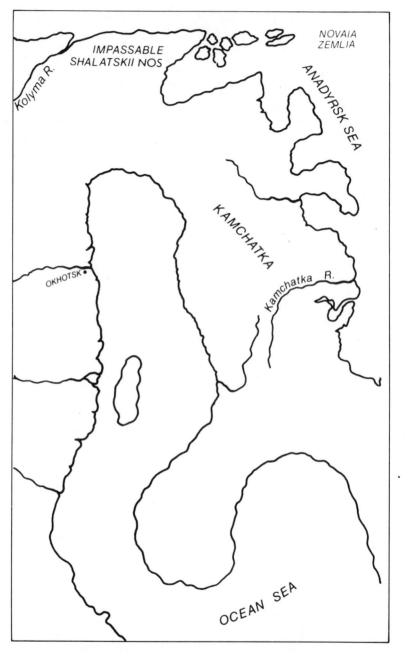

Fig. 16. Remezov's Map of Siberia from the Enisei to Kamchatka, 1706–11 (detail), from *Atlas*, no. 49

with this caption: "Impassable Shalatskii Cape. . . ." This could refer to the Chukotsk Peninsula under a different name, but the Soviet historian of cartography, Leonid A. Gol'denberg, sees it as Cape Shelagskii, the Chukotsk Peninsula not being represented on this map (1965, p. 192). More impressive, however, is the appearance of this promontory on the so-called L'vov, or as we prefer to call it, the Anadyrsk map (fig. 17).[32] On this Anadyrsk map appear the bluntly shaped Chukotsk Peninsula or Nos Anadyrskoi and two elongated islands east of it. West of it on the northern coast is shown a large promontory, broad at the base and tapering to the north where it is cut off by the edge of the map, larger than the Nos Anadyrskoi. Its eastern coast merges with the northern coast of the Nos Anadyrskoi. The sea washing its western coast is marked Kovyma, i.e., Kolyma, Sea. The promontory itself is labeled Shalatskii Nos and carries the note: "The Shelagi live here, a Chukchi tribe." To the east, extending two-thirds of the way down from the northern edge of the map is an arm of land marked *Zemlitsa Bol'shaia,* "a big piece of land."[33] The northeastern turn of the upper part of the Shalatskii promontory and the northwestern turn of the

32. In contemporary Soviet historical-geographical literature, it is usually called the L'vov map, though in a register of the old Ministry of Foreign Affairs it is listed under the designation "A map depicting the Anadyr ostrog and Anadyr Sea" (Efimov 1971, p. 161). It is believed to have been made between 1710 and 1711 or 1714 by one Ivan L'vov, commandant at one time at Anadyrsk. Müller (1758a, pp. 51–52; 1758b, 7:195) states that he received this map from its maker, Ivan L'vov, a retired service-man living in Iakutsk at the time of Müller's visit there in 1736–37. Müller does not explain how he knew that L'vov had made the map. Efimov uncovered this map in the Central State Archive in 1948, it never having been published and only rarely mentioned since Müller's time. He claims that the map was composed in Iakutsk in 1710–11 at the order of the governor of Siberia and the voevoda at Iakutsk and on the basis of reports of various service-men or cossacks. Efimov (1950, p. 102–3, 109–10, 113) states further that L'vov was commandant at Anadyrsk from 1710 to 1714, which accounts for the fact that Anadyrsk was put at the center of the map. Fel' (1960, p. 73–74), the Soviet historian of eighteenth century Russian cartography, finds Efimov's claims to be without foundation. Fel's examination of the documents reveals that L'vov was not commandant at Anadyrsk, but at Ustiansk and that he was not ordered by the Iakutsk voevoda to make a sketch-map of "the Anadyrsk fort and Anadyr Sea." During the time L'vov is alleged to have made the map, he was engaged in a search for islands near the mouth of the Iana River (Belov 1956, p. 245; *PSI,* 2:504). Fel' asserts that the map was made by an unknown person before 1700, it being listed in the catalog of the Central State Archive as anonymous and without a date. He states further that there were two copies of the sketch-map, one copied by an unknown person from the original of the unknown maker and sent to Moscow sometime before 1700. This is the copy in the archive. The second copy is the one Müller obtained from L'vov in 1736, which has since disappeared. Fel' presents mostly his conclusions and little of his evidence—none at all for his statement that the map was made before 1700. Its representation of the Chukotsk Peninsula and Kamchatka is quite unlike those of figs. 1–11 (1667–1706), but it does resemble in several respects Remezov's map of 1712–14 (fig. 12). Thus one suspects that if Fel' is right, the Anadyrsk map was made only shortly before 1700. On the other hand, the presence of two islands and land east of the Anadyrsk Cape point to a composition date after Popov's report of 1711. Meanwhile, as late as 1971, Efimov still held to his views on the date and authorship of the map, apparently ignoring Fel's criticism (1971, pp. 155–58, 161–62).

33. *Atlas,* no. 55 and p. 39 (*nadpisi* A-1 [*sic,* should be B-4], and B-1[*sic,* should be A-4]).

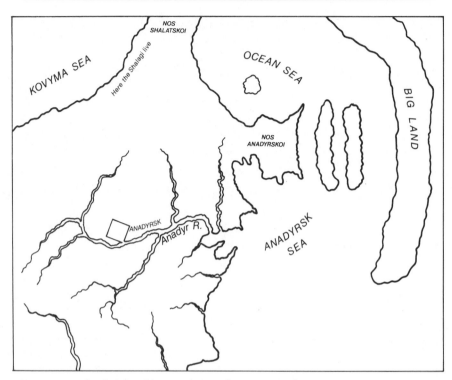

Fig. 17. Anadyrsk (L'vov's) Map, from *Atlas*, no. 55; Efimov 1950, p. 111; 1971, pp. 156–57

upper part of *Zemlitsa Bol'shaia* suggest that the two could be connected beyond the northern edge of the map. These features, unnamed, appear also on the Homann map (fig. 25), although there the Shalatskii promontory is closed and does not extend beyond the frame of the map (*Atlas*, no. 58). Uncovered fewer than three decades ago, the Anadyrsk map was not seen by scholars other than Müller until then (Efimov 1950, p. 110, n. 1). Its importance appears to be greater than has been appreciated.

Reports about the Shalatskii promontory spread from Anadyrsk to western Siberia. Philipp Johann Tabbert von Strahlenberg, the Swedish officer who as a prisoner of war lived in Tobolsk from 1711 to 1721 and traveled in western Siberia,[34] mentions in his description of Russia, published in 1730,

34. While in captivity at Tobolsk, Strahlenberg spent much time gathering data about Siberia. He talked with Lorenz Lange, the Russian resident at Peking, who was in Tobolsk on three occasions; with Vasilii N. Tatishchev, the father of Russian historiography; with the geodesist Petr Chichagov, who had been sent to the Ob Gulf by Peter and who surveyed parts of

that he heard of Atlasov's report of a cape between the Kolyma and Anadyr rivers. But the cape, in the version he reports, had become a "double cape" whose two parts were called Shalatskii Nos and Anadyrskoi Nos. No boat could sail around it because on the western side the sea was full of drift ice in the summer and was frozen in the winter (1730, p. 432; 1736, p. 456; 1970, p. 456). This information is expressed on the map (fig. 18) included in his book, a map that was carefully prepared, and that is one of the best of northern and eastern Russia for its time.[35] Just east of the Kolyma River appears an elongated *Noss Tszalatskoi* stretching into the ocean at right angles to the coast, and at the northeastern corner of Asia a somewhat pointed peninsula bends southeastward, its extreme point labeled *Noss Anadirskoi* (Novlianskaia 1966, pp. 99–100). Also on the map, close to the coast between the Lena and Kolyma rivers, Strahlenberg placed this inscription: "Here the Russians from the beginning have sailed to Kamchatka with much courage and mortal danger among the icebergs, which the northern wind drives to the shore and the southern winds to the sea." This peninsula was essentially a mythical peninsula, even though the belief in its existence was derived most likely from the real Cape Shelagskii, which is a cape, not a peninsula, and the ice surrounding it, which was to frustrate the efforts of Russians, after Dezhnev and Stadukhin to sail around it until the late nineteenth century. This mythical or imaginary peninsula, which we shall refer to hereafter as the Shalatskii promontory to distinguish it from Cape Shelagskii, was an exaggerated excrescence on the northern coast of Chukotka on the maps of northeastern Siberia, a distortion of that coast which in actuality has two major indentations, but no prominent outward extensions to interrupt its generally even contour. Though not "for real" as are the other two peninsulas, it nevertheless played a hitherto unsuspected role in Bering's first voyage, as we shall see in the next chapter.

Kamchatka appears to have been visited by Russians as early as the 1660s and again in the early 1690s before the expeditions of Morozko and Atlasov (Belov 1957, pp. 25–35; Polevoi 1964c, pp. 232–34), but it was not until its conquest by Atlasov at the very end of the century that it became widely known as Kamchatka and as the major peninsula that it is. Atlasov's reports were the first to gain a considerable audience, and the reports of the Russian leaders who followed him augmented the information about Kamchatka he

western Siberia; with Daniel G. Messerschmidt, who was commissioned by Peter to survey the human and natural resources of western Siberia and with whom Strahlenberg traveled in 1721–22; and with Semen Remezov, a copy of whose *Sluzhebnaia Chertezhnaia Kniga* Strahlenberg possessed. Strahlenberg made three, possibly four, maps of Siberia during his sojourn in Tobolsk (Novlianskaia 1966, pp. 29–33).

35. Bagrow 1975, p. 119 (reduced). A detail of the map is in *Atlas*, no. 74 and Novlianskaia 1966, facing p. 65. It is not included in the reprint edition (1970) of the English translation.

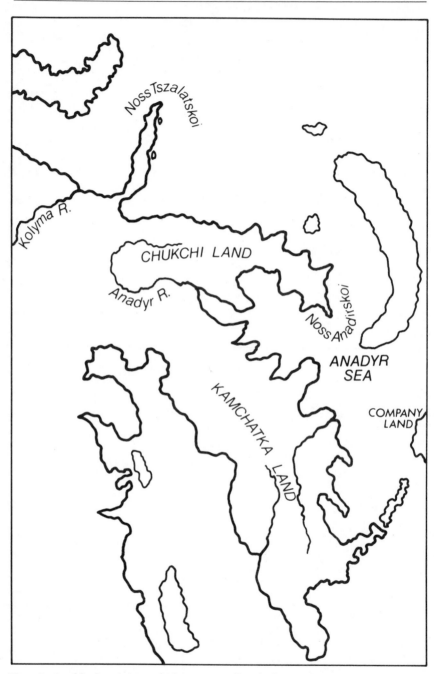

Fig. 18. Strahlenberg's Map of Siberia, 1730 (detail), from *Atlas*, no. 74; Novlianskaia 1966, facing p. 65

provided. Particularly important was the information furnished by Ivan Kozyrevskii, a Iakutsk cossack leader who lived in Kamchatka for nearly two decades and who visited the Kurile Islands two or three times in 1711–13 (Ogryzko 1953, pp. 175–88; Polevoi 1965c, p. 100, cf. Grekov 1960, p. 335, n. 1). Meanwhile, the Russians established two outposts on the Kamchatka River, which flows northeastward into the Pacific—at Nizhne–Kamchatsk near its mouth and at Verkhne–Kamchatsk in the mountains on its upper course—and one outpost at the mouth of the Bol'shaia River on the southwest coast where Bol'sheretsk was founded (Ogryzko 1953, p. 176, n. 7). After two decades of traveling to Kamchatka via the long roundabout route through Anadyrsk, the Russians opened up the sea route in 1716 from Okhotsk to the west coast of the peninsula.[36]

The news about Kamchatka did not, however, result immediately in full and certain knowledge of the geography of this land. Much remained to be learned about its configuration, about what lay east and south of it, about the possibility that it might be connected with land to the east. The Russian sketch-maps showing Kamchatka at this time reveal the uncertainty and conflict of views about this region. Remezov composed at least three maps dated 1700 or later which depict Kamchatka, and each differs in important details, a reflection of the divergent sources of information (Andreev 1948, p. 8). One of them is the Remezov map of Kamchatka, 1701 (fig. 15). The position of Kamchatka relative to other geographical features is reasonably accurate, but the peninsula narrows to a pinched-in waist more than halfway down, its southern end is double-tipped, and it points southeast instead of south by southwest. No offshore islands are shown. A second is the Remezov map of 1712–14 (fig. 12), and it shows Kamchatka likewise oriented to the southeast and double-tipped at the end, but this time with five islands to the south. A third is his map of Siberia from the Enisei River to Kamchatka (fig. 16), which depicts a massive Kamchatka peninsula just below the Chukotsk Peninsula, with two peninsulas at the southern end and a deep saddle in between. A fourth map, the so-called Kozyrevskii map (fig. 13), shows a southern-oriented Kamchatka, fat and circular in shape, with thirteen islands distributed around its southern end. A fifth map, Beiton's Iakutsk map of 1710–11 (fig. 14), shows the pinched-in waist of Kamchatka and two capes at the southern end.

Remezov's map of Siberia from the Enisei to Kamchatka (fig. 16) is of special interest to us, not for the eccentricity of its shape, but for the fact that the more eastern of the two capes in the south, the one that seems to point southeast, is incomplete, cut off by the frame of the map. This suggests that Kamchatka was thought to extend an uncertain distance to the southeast, to approach or to be connected with some other land there. This characteristic

36. Grekov 1960, p. 10; Müller 1758a, pp. 102–3; 1758b, 7:316–18; Efimov 1950, p. 150.

is found also on a sixth map, the Elchin map of Kamchatka made no later than 1718 (fig. 19) (*Atlas*, no. 56). It too has two promontories at the southern end of Kamchatka, but the southeastern one is massive, widening to mainland proportions as it approaches the corner of the map, which cuts it off. It was thought to be an isthmus rather than a peninsula, as the notation on it indicates: "According to the account of Kamchatka cossack Ivan Eniseiskii and his companions, there extended on the left side [of Kamchatka, facing down-peninsula] a large land and peoples between the Warm [Pacific] and Cold [Arctic] Seas. Many natives told them that they know of no strait through that land connecting those seas."[37] Still another sketch-map, Beiton's Iakutsk map of 1710–11 (fig. 14), we have noted, represents the southern end as double-headed, but neither head is cut off by the edge of the map. Instead the southeastern coast is shown without rivers or other geographical features, indicating that little was known of that part of Kamchatka, and midway off the eastern coast a long finger of land extends westward from the map's eastern edge. It is labeled a "piece of land" (*zemlitsa*), inhabited by non-tribute-paying natives and visited by one Ivan Golygin (*Atlas*, no. 54 and p. 39 [*nadpisi* B-2]). The Komandorskie Islands are probably the kernel of fact behind this hypothetical east-west piece of land close to Kamchatka.

These maps reflect the currency at this time of the theory that Kamchatka was connected with land to the east or that there was land not far eastward of Kamchatka. To be sure, the fact that Japanese sailors had been thrown ashore by storms at Avacha Bay (1708) and north of there (1710) (Sgibnev 1869a, p. 38; 1869b, April, p. 82) was evidence that there was no isthmus between Kamchatka and another land mass, but this fact does not seem to have been widely known or its implications understood. It is pertinent to note too that Bering felt not enough was known of the weather and waters east and north of the southern tip of Kamchatka to risk using this route to transport his men and supplies from Bol'sheretsk to Nizhne-Kamchatsk in preparation for his first voyage, preferring to follow the arduous four-hundred-mile route over the spine of the peninsula.[38] In short, the coast south of the Kamchatka River to Cape Lopatka, the southern tip of the peninsula, appears to have been the part least known to the Russians. In respect to the eastern coast of Kamchatka north of the mouth of the Kamchatka River, the Russians seem to have known more of it, two or three voyages having been made between that river and the Oliutora River farther north.[39] But of the land and waters north of Cape Oliutorskii the Russians knew little or nothing.

In contrast with their growing knowledge of northeastern Asia, the knowl-

37. *Atlas*, p. 40 (*nadpisi* A-2); Efimov 1950, pp. 121, 123 (map); Polevoi 1964c, p. 265.
38. Polonskii 1851, p. 15; Sgibnev 1869b, April, p. 113; Vakhtin 1890, pp. 54–55.
39. Sgibnev 1869b, April, pp. 82, 87, 98; Ogryzko 1953, p. 174; Golder 1914, p. 105.

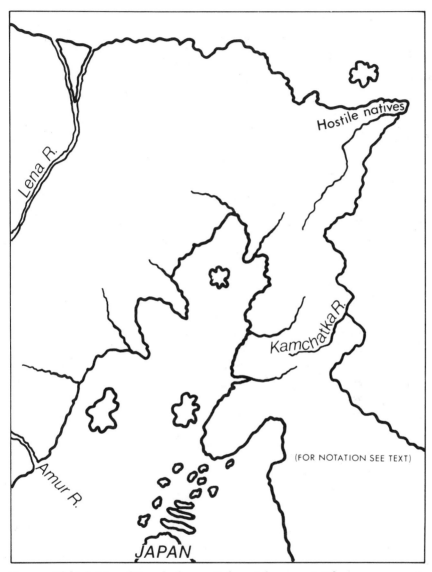

Fig. 19. Elchin's Map of Kamchatka, 1718, from *Atlas*, no. 56; Efimov 1950, p. 123; 1971, p. 197

edge of both Russians and Europeans of the waters of the North Pacific and of the coast of northwestern America remained sparse and almost wholly speculative. The Russians were aware that east of the Chukotsk Peninsula was some kind of land, as some of the maps indicate and as the Russians had been told by the Chukchi, but we can not be sure whether they thought the Big Land to be part of America or a large island in the North Pacific (Efimov 1950, p. 94). There is no explicit evidence either way. As early as the mid-seventeenth century and as late as the 1760s a belief did exist that there was a "rocky belt" of land in the Arctic Ocean which extended from the White Sea, from Novaia Zemlia, eastward past the mouths of the Taz, Enisei, Lena, Indigirka, and Kolyma rivers to the Pogycha or Anadyr River (this last river was first thought to empty into the Arctic).[40] In 1710 cossacks, when questioned at Iakutsk, testified about an island "which appeared across from the Kamchatka, Kolyma and Lena mouths" (Lebedev and Esakov 1971, pp. 173–74). This land was called *Novaia Zemlia*, the New Land, like its westernmost component. The basis of this concept was, of course, the offshore islands in the Arctic, which to Dezhnev's contemporaries, who were the Russians first to see them or hear about them, seemed a continuous belt of land. Only later did the insular composition of this belt become evident (*PSI*, 2:500, 504, 506; Orlova 1952, p. 222).

Among Peter's contemporaries there was an interest in the lands, insular or continental, north of northeastern Siberia. This interest found expression on two maps. On the so-called Kozyrevskii map of 1713 (fig. 13), there is lightly outlined in the northeastern corner a piece of land cut off on the north by the border of the map. It is labeled Novaia Zemlia. On the map of Siberia from the Enisei to Kamchatka (fig. 16) the words Novaia Zemlia also appear in the northeastern corner, but no land is outlined. On a later map, one belonging to Afanasii Shestakov (see chap. 7, sec. III), a large island, *Bol'shaia Zemlia*, is shown north of the mouth of the Kolyma River. Still later, in the instructions to the Second Kamchatka Expedition, investigation of this land was ordered (*EB*, p. 92, para. 4).

Inasmuch as the Russians did not see America north of the Aleutian Islands on either of Bering's voyages, and the reports of the voyage of Gvozdev and Fedorov to the Diomede Islands and the Seward Peninsula in 1732 were delayed and given little circulation, knowledge of the coast of the northwestern corner of America remained conjectural, and room was left for the continuation or re-emergence of the concept of the rocky belt or Novaia Zemlia,

40. Orlova, comp. 1951, p. 234; *DAI*, vol. 3, no. 24, pp. 99–100; Belov 1949, p. 467; 1952, pp. 59, 61, n. 2, 93–94. For a more recent identification see Polevoi 1970c. See also Belov 1973, pp. 90–94 *passim*. In 1972 he found a map in the marine ministry in Paris attributed to Petr Meller, who, with Chichagov, explored the Ob estuary and Taz Gulf in 1719. It shows a large elongated Novaia Zemlia extending from the mouth of the Lena River beyond the eastern end of the Chukotsk Peninsula (map faces p. 152 in ibid.).

as is indicated later by Daurkin's map of 1765 showing the Chukotsk Peninsula and northwestern Alaska (fig. 20). (*Atlas*, nos. 128–29). In September 1763 Nikolai Daurkin, a Chukchi cossack, returned to his native Chukotka and spent nearly a year there gathering information about the region and about the Diomede Islands and the Big Land. In 1765, after returning to Anadyrsk, he drafted a map of Chukotka and North America north of the Aleutian Islands (Alekseev 1961, pp. 18–29; Masterson and Brower, eds. 1948, pp. 65–66). Its unique feature is the depiction of the coast of North America north of the Seward Peninsula as bearing due north and then in the latitude approximately of Point Hope turning to the northwest and paralleling the northern coast of the Chukotsk Peninsula in its northwest-southeast direction until cut off by the top edge of the map.[41] To be sure, the northwest extension is not labeled Novaia Zemlia, but it is evidence of the idea that a large land, today identified as part of America, lay east and perhaps north of the Chukotsk Peninsula. This idea had not been dispelled by Bering's first voyage or Dmitrii Ia. Laptev's later voyages east of the Kolyma River as part of the Second Kamchatka Expedition. For us this idea is important in that it may have influenced Bering's selection of his course on the first voyage.

No more, or even less, was known about the American coast south of the Alaska Peninsula. The coast of California north of Cape Mendocino was thought by some to extend northwestward to a point somewhere south of the western most Aleutian Islands, as shown, for example, on Vasilii O. Kiprianov's "Description of America" and Homann's "Map of America" of 1725 (figs. 21 and 22). Mythical lands, Company Land and State Island, usually thought of as islands and presumably seen by seventeenth-century Dutch mariners, were sketched variously on maps of the time north of Japan and not far from Kamchatka.[42] A larger mythical land, situated east of Kamchatka, was Juan de Gama Land, along the southern coast of which a sixteenth-century Portuguese navigator was alleged to have sailed from China to New Spain. It was thought to be either a large island or part of America.[43] Its existence was taken seriously by the Russians, as we shall see when we discuss the selection of the route for Bering's second voyage.

41. According to Alekseev (1961, pp. 34–41) and Efimov (*Atlas*, no. 131 and p. 89) this map is not the one attributed to Colonel Fedor Kh. Plenisner in 1763, then commandant at Anadyrsk. In a later version of his map, drafted probably in 1774, Daurkin shows in the northeastern corner only a small section of the American coast across from the Chukotsk Peninsula. From this it is not clear whether or not he abandoned the concept that the American coast turned to the northwest (Alekseev 1961, pp. 58–60).

42. E.g., Strahlenberg's map (fig. 18) and Cornelis Dankerts' "Nieuw Aerdsch Pleyn" (ca. 1680), (Bagrow 1952, facing p. 136).

43. For an account of the origins and main features of the belief in the existence of these mythical lands see Wroth 1944, pp. 207–15. Golder (1914, chap. 5) and Wagner (1937, 1:138–39) give shorter accounts.

Fig. 20. Daurkin's Map of 1765: Chukotsk Peninsula and northwestern Alaska (detail), from *Atlas*, nos. 128 and 129

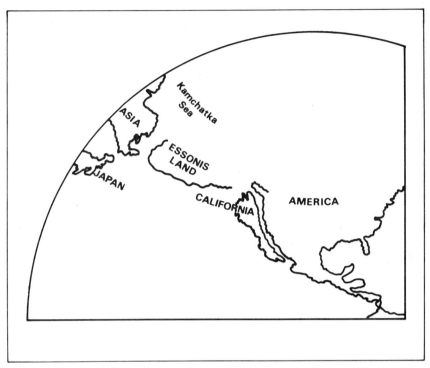

Fig. 21. Kiprianov's "Description of America," 1713 (detail), from Efimov 1950, p. 139

Sometimes it was called Essonis Land; at others, Terra Borealis (Polevoi 1967, p. 115). In 1713 Kiprianov, one of Russia's first map publishers, put out the map called Description of America (*Opisanie Ameriki*) (fig. 21) on which the southern coast of Essonis Land is shown just east of Kamchatka and extending close to America; no northern limits are shown (Fel' 1960, pp. 139–40; Efimov 1950, p. 139; 1971, pp. 187–88). In 1725 the famous German cartographer and map publisher in Nürnberg, Johann B. Homann, included in his *Grosser Atlas über die Gantze Welt*[44] a map of America (fig. 22) on which Juan de Gama Land is shown just east of Kamchatka and connected with California.[45] It was to be one of the main accomplishments of Bering's second voyage to bury the myth of de Gama Land and to make clear to the

44. It carried also a Latin title: *Atlas novus terrarum orbis imperia, regna et status exactis tabulis geographicé demonstrans.*

45. The map is titled "Totius Americae, septentrionalis et meridionalis." The copy used for figure 22 appears as no. 5 in *Atlas of the World*, a collection of eighteenth century maps (mostly from J. B. Homann) of various dates, bound together without a title page and kept in the Department of Special Collections of the University Research Library, University of California, Los Angeles. See the statement of Soimonov in chap. 7, sec. II in which the view is expressed that California may not be far from Kamchatka.

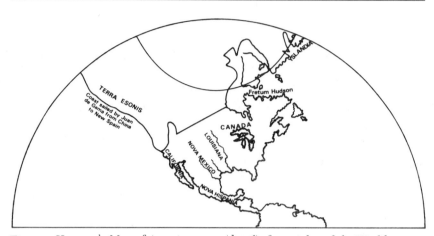

Fig. 22. Homann's Map of America, 1725 (detail), from *Atlas of the World*, no. 5

world that a large expanse of ocean separated Kamchatka from the American mainland.

It should be pointed out, before returning to the matter of paragraph 2 of Peter's instructions to Bering, that with the increased knowledge of northeastern Asia the European savants gave particular attention to one part of this section of the world and the Russians to another. In the west it was the Chukotsk Peninsula about which the greater interest was shown. If Asia and America were joined or approached each other closely—the question of major concern in the west—this was the most likely site of junction on the Asiatic side, as Gerbillon pointed out. The Russians, on the other hand, focused their interest on Kamchatka. Unlike Chukotka this was an area they were conquering; the natives were being brought under the payment of tribute in furs, and the state was gaining considerable income from it. Here exploration could be carried on as it could not in Chukotka. Equally important, the legendary Juan de Gama Land, which loomed large in the minds of some Russians in high places, was placed on western maps near Kamchatka and the Kurile Islands. Was it not possible that either or both of these latter places were close to America? In the west this different focus of Russian attention does not appear to have been appreciated. Though Russian cartographers produced several maps showing Kamchatka, these maps and the information on them, with an exception or two, did not find their way west as had some seventeenth-century sketch-maps. Thus, the western savants with their Chukotka orientation were disposed to take the explanations of Bering's first voyage at face value and not to probe its purpose more carefully. In the meantime it was the Russians' belief that America lay not far east of Kamchatka, which is the essential part of the explanation of the intent of Peter's instructions.

III

There are a couple of indications that Peter took seriously the idea that America was close to Kamchatka, or to the Kurile Islands.[46] One is an exchange between Peter and Fedor I. Soimonov, the naval officer who explored and mapped the Caspian Sea and who later was governor general of Siberia under Catherine the Great. During a conversation with Peter in the course of the naval expedition on the Caspian Sea against Persia in 1722, Soimonov had occasion to remark that Kamchatka might be found to be situated not far from America, from the "island of California." Peter's response was an emphatic assent (Andreev 1948, p. 198 [18]).[47] The other indication was the expedition of Ivan Evreinov and Fedor Luzhin.

In 1719, nine years before Bering's voyage, Peter sent these two geodesists to Kamchatka with these orders, dated 2 January of that year: "You are to go to Tobolsk, and taking guides you are to go to Kamchatka and farther, whither it is indicated to you (*kudy vam ukazano*, and you are to describe the local places [where *or* whether] America is joined with Asia, which must be done very carefully, not only in the south and north, but in the east and west, and to place everything correctly on a map. . . ."[48]

46. Polevoi (1975, p. 128) calls attention to the fact that Witsen, who dedicated his map and book *Noord en Oost Tartaryen* to Peter and with whom Peter talked while in Holland in 1697, develops in his book the idea that supposedly America approached the southern Kurile Islands.

47. The conversation is quoted at greater length in chapter 7, section III.

48. Andreev 1943a, p. 5, citing TsGADA, Kabinet Petra velikogo, *otd*. II, *kn*. 66, *l*. 40; *PSZ*, vol. 5, no. 3266, p. 607; Evteev 1950, p. 45; Grekov 1960, p. 11. At this point a textual matter arises. In the original document, which appears in a photocopy with transcriptions by Andreev (1943a, p. 5), the word "where" (*gde*) appears before the words "America is joined" and the word "Europe" in place of "Asia," and the clause "which must be . . . on a map" does not appear. Peter corrected and revised this passage in his own hand, deleting "where," replacing "Europe" with "Asia," and adding the clause that did not orginally appear. The addition of this clause argues that this was a matter he wanted thoroughly investigated. Meanwhile, as the corrected sentence stands, it is incomplete. Either the word "where" needs to be restored or, as did the editors of *PSZ*, the word "whether" (*l'*) should be supplied (they did so without indicating it). Baskin (1952, p. 363) and Evteev (1950, p. 45), include both words and thus make the meaning absurd. If the original "where" had been allowed to stand, the clause would then mean that Peter thought Asia and America to be joined at Kamchatka; but having struck it out, presumably he meant to replace it by "whether." In that case the connection between Asia and America was still an open question for him. In either case the focus of the question, where the union of the two continents might be, is Kamchatka.

The occasion for Peter's despatch of the two geodesists to Kamchatka is said by some scholars to have been a request submitted in 1716 to the Senate by two commercial houses in St. Petersburg to open trade with Japan and the East Indies by way of the Arctic Ocean to the Ob Gulf, thence by Siberia's rivers to the Amur River and down the Amur to the Pacific. The officials in St. Petersburg inquired of the governor of Siberia about the feasibility of such a route and about Japan, but neither he nor anyone else could provide the wanted information, so it was recommended to Peter by General Iakov V. Brius, one of his close associates, that a scientific description of the distant regions of Siberia and the water route to Japan be made by trained topographers (Sgibnev 1869a, p. 40; Andreev 1946, p. 186 [6]; 1965, pp. 16–18). The data are, however, too meager to be conclusive.

What led Peter to believe that America might be connected with Asia near Kamchatka cannot be said definitely, but certain Soviet scholars are of the opinion that the Elchin map (fig. 19) helped to shape his concept of the geography of Kamchatka at this particular time. This map was made at the request of Iakov A. Elchin, commandant (*voevoda*) at Iakutsk, and was based on information provided by Kozyrevskii and one Ivan Eniseiskii, who had also visited Kamchatka. In 1716 Elchin had been put at the head of the abortive Great Kamchatka Command, an expedition organized at Iakutsk on the orders of the governor-general of Siberia at Tobolsk to survey northeastern Siberia from the Kolyma River to the Amur. But Elchin quarreled with the authorities at Iakutsk and was ordered in 1718 to St. Petersburg. Prior to his arrival there he sent the map, accompanied by a memorandum, to Peter's Cabinet (his secretariat or chancery),[49] in whose files the map and memorandum were discovered after World War II (Grekov 1960, pp. 11, 12, 336, n. 16; Polevoi 1964c, pp. 256–66; Efimov 1950, pp. 120–21). We can assume that because of his great interest in the geography of his realm Peter was shown this map. Whether or not, however, he first saw this map before he considered sending the two geodesists to Kamchatka we do not know, for it is not known when the map and memorandum reached the Cabinet, and the decision to send Evreinov and Luzhin to Kamchatka was made at the end of May 1718, though the ukaz containing the order was not signed until 2 January 1719. Still, Peter could have seen them before that.[50] Be this as it may, this map and Remezov's Map of Siberia from the Enisei to Kamchatka (fig. 16) embody a view of Kamchatka that was then current. No one in St. Petersburg knew whether it was correct or not. Peter could best find out by sending specialists to see for themselves.

Evreinov and Luzhin went to Kamchatka, arriving at the Icha River near Bol'sheretsk in the fall of 1720. Taking their instruments with them, they made the difficult four-hundred-mile crossing of the peninsula via Verkhne-Kamchatsk to Nizhne-Kamchatsk near the mouth of the Kamchatka River. There they spent the winter.[51] Returning in the spring to Bol'sheretsk, they departed from there on 2 June 1721 in a small, inadequately outfitted vessel, the one used for the first voyage from Okhotsk to Kamchatka five years before. They explored the northern Kurile Islands to the fifth or

49. Monas 1961, p. 32; the Administrative Senate according to Grekov (1960, p. 11).

50. Evteev 1950, pp. 42–44; Andreev 1965, p. 16, n. 13, citing TsGADA, *f.* Senata, *no.* 1201, *l.* 185 *ob.*, and Kabinet Petra velikogo, 1, *no.* 56, *l.* 40. See also Andreev 1946, p. 186 [6]. Efimov argues for 1719 as the date of composition of the map, though he also specifies 1718 as the date (1950, pp. 121, 124; 1971, pp. 160, 174). The later date obviously is inconsistent with his claim that it was a factor in despatching the two geodesists to Kamchatka (see Grekov 1960, p. 337, n. 21).

51. Evteev 1950, p. 52; Baskin 1952, p. 371; Grekov 1960, p. 12. Sgibnev (1869a, p. 41) does not mention this wintering in Nizhne–Kamchatsk.

sixth island south of Kamchatka, but the deteriorated condition of the vessel, the loss of its anchor, and storms forced them prematurely to return to Bol'sheretsk at the end of the month (Grekov 1960, p. 11; Lensen 1959, pp. 36–38; Baskin 1952, pp. 373–75). Making an anchor of wood, the geodesists' party sailed to Okhotsk whence Evreinov headed west to report to Peter. He had an audience with the tsar in May 1722 at Kazan where Peter was pausing on his way to the Caspian campaign against Persia. There Peter "with much interest engaged [Evreinov] several times in conversation and examined with satisfaction the map of Kamchatka and the islands mentioned, made by him and his associate Luzhin, and the description of their entire voyage" (Grekov 1960, p. 12).

Later Müller and other scholars, knowing that Asia and America are close to each other in the high latitudes of the North Pacific, were puzzled by the fact that apparently the two geodesists made no effort, as Bering later did, to go by sea from Nizhne-Kamchatsk supposedly to determine whether Asia was joined with America. Instead of going north toward the Chukotsk Peninsula, they went south 'from Bol'sheretsk and explored the Kurile Islands. This has led scholars to hypothesize secret instructions to Evreinov and Luzhin—instructions not as yet uncovered—in which the real purpose of the expedition would be found to be a search for precious metals in the Kurile Islands and a search for the route to Japan. In other words Peter's instructions were a cover for this true purpose.[52] But Evreinov and Luzhin stated that "no other instructions were given" to them (Baskin 1952, p. 366). Moreover, one has to wonder why Peter sent two surveyors instead of assayers or mineralogists if the objective was to find ores rich in minerals and precious metals, as was done in the case of the Shestakov expedition in northeastern Siberia in 1727–32 and on Bering's second voyage (Grekov 1960, p. 46). Evreinov's report to Peter, long believed to have been lost, was discovered in 1945 in the files of Peter's Cabinet, and it reaffirms as Peter's objective the determination of whether Asia is joined to America. (Grekov 1960, pp. 14–15).

The theory of a secret objective is speculative and rests on tenuous evidence, evidence that is not documentary, but inferential (e.g., Sgibnev 1869a, pp. 40–41; Evteev 1950, pp. 44–45; Baskin 1952, p. 366). Scholars holding this view have overlooked the fact that Peter might have thought of America as being close to Kamchatka, not just to Chukotka (Grekov 1960, p. 12). Nor have they given attention to the wintering of the two geodesists at Nizhne-Kamchatsk. Why, if the Kuriles and Japan were there only objec-

52. Müller, 1758a, pp. 109–10; 1758b, 7:323–24; Sgibnev 1869a, pp. 40–41; Polonskii 1871, pp. 394; Baskin 1952, pp. 372, 374; Andreev 1943a, p. 4. Sgibnev (repeated by Andreev 1965, p. 17) states that Peter issued written instructions not yet uncovered, but does not explain how he knew Peter issued such instructions.

tives, should the two men have gone to the effort and expense of crossing and recrossing the mountainous peninsula, risking their valuable instruments, just to spend the winter on the east coast when it would have been simpler and safer to spend it on the west coast? Further, these scholars take that part of the instructions which say "whither it is indicated to you" as pointing to secret, probably oral, instructions. This interpretation is, of course, possible. Conceivably it could point to an unstated, and maybe the only, objective of the expedition, but such an interpretation becomes probable only in the absence of another or better explanation, and there is such an explanation: the clause could mean that the two geodesists might have to go beyond Kamchatka to determine where or whether America joined or approached Asia.

If Peter had thought Chukotka was the area of Asia most likely to be joined with Asia, one can justifiably wonder why Evreinov and Luzhin were not instructed explicitly to sail north rather than "to describe the local places. . . ." One can go further and ask why Peter did not send them to Anadyrsk, the outpost nearest Chukotka. But if Peter's instructions stemmed from the concept of Kamchatka exemplified by the Elchin map—that Kamchatka might be the part of Asia connected with America—then the actions of the two geodesists become consistent with Peter's order, and this consistency lends support to our interpretation.

The two men were to go to Kamchatka and farther and were to describe the local places. In the winter of 1720–21 they went north and east to Nizhne-Kamchatsk on the east coast of Kamchatka where any connection between it and America most likely would be found, their first item of business. Here, evidently, no shipping was available, but unlike Chukotka, Kamchatka was under Russian control, and if there were a land connection, there was no compulsion to conduct the search for it by sea; it could also be conducted by land. In fact, Peter's instructions, unlike those to Bering, say nothing about building a boat or going by sea. One can hardly believe that the two geodesists found at Nizhne-Kamchatsk any evidence of a connection such as portrayed on the Elchin map or on the Map of Siberia from the Enisei to Kamchatka. Returning to Bol'sheretsk, they went "farther" in the summer of 1721, for as long as the condition of their vessel permitted, exploring the Kurile Islands where a connection with America was thought possibly to exist (Grekov 1960, pp. 12–13; Polevoi 1975, p. 128). They went north and east in the winter, south in the summer, and they had come to Kamchatka and departed from it in the west.

Meanwhile, from O. A. Evteev (1950, p. 56) we learn that while at Nizhne-Kamchatsk, Evreinov and Luzhin inquired of the cossacks and natives about lands and islands, and about the rivers and lakes of Kamchatka. They placed this information on a map, and they recorded the statements of long-time residents about the distances to various places in Kamchatka and the islands off the east coast. From such inquiries there and elsewhere in Kamchatka they must have learned what Kozyrevskii, who had lived near Nizhne-Kamchatsk from 1717 to 1720 (Ogryzko 1953, p. 186), tells us on his Sketch-Map of Kamchatka of 1726, namely, that somewhat south of the mouth of the Kamchatka River, Japanese (*Nifontsy*) had on two occasions landed and been taken prisoner by the natives (Baskin 1949, pp. 228–30; Berg 1946, p. 167; Sgibnev 1869b, p. 82). The Russians knew that the Japanese came from islands to the south. This, of course, argued against an isthmus extending from southeast Kamchatka. Too, the information on this same map that in 1701 and 1715 Russians, including Kozyrevskii, visited the shores of Avacha Bay, still farther south on the east coast, and there collected tribute from the natives was further evidence probably available to Evreinov and Luzhin that no land connection to the east existed (Ogryzko 1953, pp. 201–2; *PSI*, 1:442; Sgibnev 1869b, p. 82). We can conclude that they neither saw nor heard anything to support the thesis of a land connection, for the map (fig. 23) that Evreinov later presented to Peter, the most accurate one of Kamchatka and the Kuriles to date, does not show any land connection to the east or the presence there of any other land that might be America.[53] Thus Peter's question had been answered in the negative: Kamchatka is not joined to America. And there is no evidence to indicate that Peter was dissatisfied with the work of Evreinov and Luzhin or that he disputed their findings.[54]

It is worth noting in passing that in his orders to Evreinov and Luzhin, Peter explicitly states that they are to seek an answer to the question of the connection of the two continents. Had this been his intent in sending Bering to Kamchatka, one could expect that he would have been equally explicit in his instructions to him. If the same objective had inspired both expeditions, why the specificity in the one case and not in the other? If any of Peter's actions was a direct response to the requests of Leibnitz and others to answer the question whether Asia and America are joined, it was his commissioning the expedition of Evreinov and Luzhin, not that of Bering (cf. Solov'ev 1894–96, 4:243).

Just what concept of the geography of Kamchatka in particular and of the North Pacific and its littoral in general Peter had in mind at a given time is a matter mostly of conjecture. We know that Peter saw some of the maps of that area, but we do not know if he saw all of them or which among those he saw he regarded as reliable. It is safest to assume that he suspended final

53. Map is in Grekov 1960, p. 15 (detail); Efimov 1948, p. 137 and 1950, p. 149 (entire); and *Atlas*, no. 61 (detail).

54. Baskin (1952, pp. 363–79) presents a narrative account of the expedition, based on the journals of Luzhin and two other members, but unfortunately it tells us almost nothing about the activity of the two geodesists in Nizhne–Kamchatsk and their efforts to answer the question assigned by Peter.

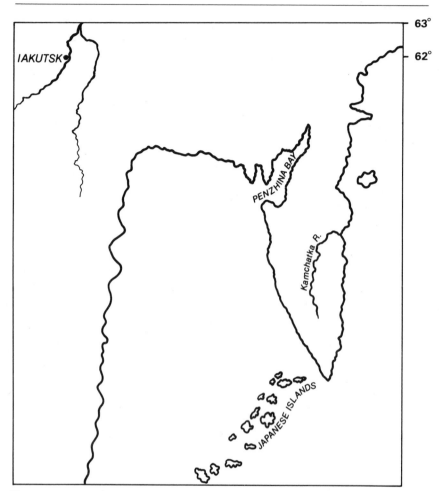

Fig. 23. Evreinov's Map, 1721 (1722?) (detail), from *Atlas*, no. 61 (detail); Grekov 1960, p. 15 (detail); Efimov 1948, p. 137 and 1950, p. 149 (entire)

judgment and changed his mind as he received new information about this part of the world. It is with this presumption in mind that we assume that Evreinov's map and his discussion of his findings convinced Peter that Kamchatka had no direct land connection with America. How seriously Peter took Evreinov's map is suggested by two incidents. In December 1724 he asked to have Evreinov found and brought to St. Petersburg, only to learn that Evreinov had died (Andreev 1965, p. 18; Grekov 1960, p. 21). At the same time, he had Evreinov's map made part of another map. Kirilov, senior secretary of the Administrative Senate, discloses in a long memorandum to

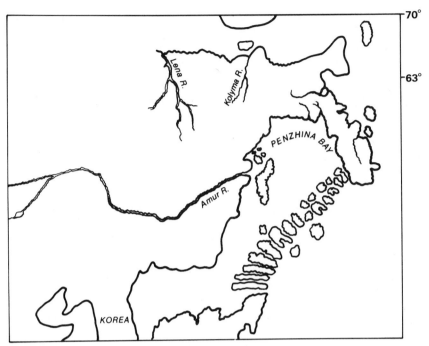

Fig. 24. Kirilov's Map of Northeast Asia, 1724, from Gnucheva 1946, no. 11; Bagrow 1955a, facing p. 131

the empress that in the course of a discussion of the Russo-Chinese boundary in the Senate in December 1724 Peter ordered him to combine Evreinov's map of Kamchatka and a Chinese map showing the area along the Amur River. This Kirilov did in one night and gave the resulting map to Peter, who in turn passed it on to General Iakov V. Brius for copying (Andreev 1943a, p. 35; Efimov 1950, p. 298).

With this manifestation of Peter's confidence in Kirilov's views on the geography of the Russian far east in mind it is pertinent to note Kirilov's conception of the area. It is revealed in a map of northeast Asia which he made in 1724 (fig. 24). His map extended northward to 70° north latitude, beyond the 63rd parallel, which is the northern limit of Evreinov's map, and thus included Chukotka. Like Evreinov's map it showed Kamchatka, as well as the rest of northeastern Asia, free of any connection or suggested connection with land to the east.[55] The evidence is impressive, accordingly, that the question whether Asia was joined to America had, on the eve of the First Kamchatka Expedition, been answered for Peter in the negative—an answer

55. Map is in Gnucheva 1946, no. 11, map pocket; Bagrow 1955a, facing p. 131; cf. Fel' 1960, p. 150.

incidentally which left open the possibility of an Arctic–Pacific passage and which argues that by "the land which goes to the north" Peter did not mean the coast north of Kamchatka since it did not join America.[56]

For Peter to have decided that America and Asia are not joined was not, however, for him to have rejected the idea that America was close to Kamchatka. One of the principal reasons for concluding that such was the case is the so-called Homann map of Kamchatka of 1725, the first printed map of Kamchatka (fig. 25).[57] This map, paired on the same page with one of the Caspian Sea, appeared in Homann's *Grosser Atlas*, previously mentioned.[58] The map shows Chukotka and Kamchatka as peninsulas and the Kuriles as islands. The unusual feature of the map is the presence of a large unnamed land area east of both the Chukotsk Peninsula and Kamchatka, extending westward from the eastern edge of the map so far as to be separated from Kamchatka only by a narrow strait. What else could this be than the Essonis or Juan de Gama Land shown on the map of America (fig. 22) in the same atlas?

What makes this map particularly important to us is that, although the names and captions are in Latin and German, it is Russian, not foreign in origin and was published at Peter's request. After his first visit to the Netherlands in 1697, Peter undertook to have Russian maps printed abroad (Bagrow 1952, p. 85). One of south Russia was in fact published in Holland in 1699; and an atlas of the Don River, a few years later (Varep 1959, p. 292; Bagrow 1954, p. 120; 1955b, pp. 152–54). In 1716, on Peter's order, General Brius corresponded with Homann regarding the publication of an atlas (Andreev 1943d, p. 3). The map of Kamchatka was sent in 1722 to Homann on the order of Brius, who in turn was carrying out Peter's order.[59] Peter wanted publicity given to Russian exploration in Kamchatka.

Who made the map and what sources were used are not known and so are questions subject to conjecture (Varep 1959, p. 291). Sergei E. Fel', the Soviet historian of eighteenth-century Russian cartography, suggests that Brius himself made the map. Brius was one of the best educated among Peter's close associates and maintained a life-long interest in cartography, geodesy, and geography, having made in 1699 a map of Russia between Moscow and Asia Minor. Too, he had been put in charge of the state's

56. Polevoi (1975, p. 130) states that as early as 1697 Peter had reached the conclusion that no isthmus connected the northeastern corner of Asia with America and while in Holland told Witsen so. Now he had evidence that Asia in the vicinity of Kamchatka likewise was not connected with America.

57. *Atlas*, no. 58; Efimov 1950, p. 112; 1971, p. 171; Varep 1959, p. 291.

58. Berg 1943, p. 5. Homann died in July 1724; publication of the atlas was carried through by his son and successor (Fel' 1960, p. 130, n. 3).

59. Andreev 1947, p. 301, n. 3, citing Brius' letter of 11 June 1722 (TsGADA, Kabinet Petra velikogo, *otd*. 1, *no*. 59, *l*. 138); Varep 1959, p. 294; Gnucheva 1946, pp. 155, 158; Fel' 1960, p. 150; Grekov 1960, p. 340, n. 15.

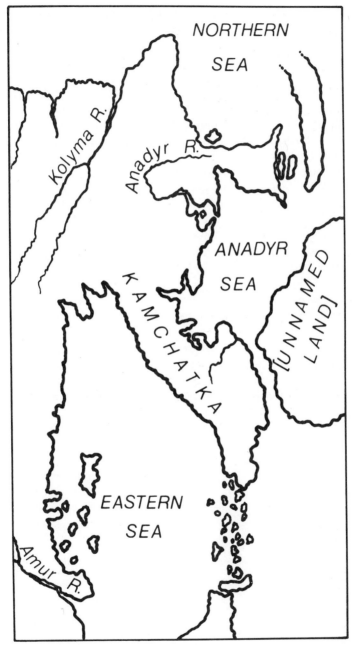

Fig. 25. Homann's Map of Kamchatka, 1725, from *Atlas*, no. 58; Efimov 1950, p. 112; 1971, p. 171; Varep 1959, p. 291

printing establishments and had maintained close connections with the
Navigation School. (Fel' 1960, pp. 133, 134, n. 2, 135, 150). There is no
reason to believe he did not have access to those maps now believed to have
been sources of the Homann map.

Fel' believes that the sources for the Homann map are the Anadyrsk map
(fig. 17), the Remezov map of Kamchatka of 1712–14 (fig. 12),[60] and
Kozyrevskii's map of 1713. From a comparison of the inscriptions on the
Homann map with the description of the first visit to the Shantarskie Islands
in 1713 by cossacks I. Bykov and S. Anbara and with the information about
the second expedition by P. Fil'keev in 1718, Fel' places the date of composition of the map in the period between the two dates.[61]

Mariia G. Novlianskaia and Polevoi, on the other hand, see Strahlenberg's
map of Siberia, or the eastern portion of it (fig. 18), as the source of the
Homann Map of Kamchatka. Between 1715 and 1718, while in captivity in
Tobolsk, Strahlenberg made three copies of his map. The first was stolen.
The second was confiscated by the governor, Prince Gagarin. The third he
was forced to sell. It found its way into the hands of the merchant of Dutch
ancestry in Moscow, Petr Meller, who in 1721 presented it to Peter the
Great (Novlianskaia 1966, pp. 23–32, 43–44, 64–65; Polevoi 1970a, p. 102;
Grekov 1960, p. 338, n. 27). Later, upon seeing the Homann map, Strahlen-
berg was prompted to write: "On first sight of the newly printed maps of
Kamchatka it is evident that they are copies of the map taken from me by
Prince Gagarin" (Novlianskaia 1966, p. 65). Particularly telling in equating
the Homann map with the eastern portion of Strahlenberg's map are the
inscription "*Terra Kamtzatka alias Jedso,*" which appears on Kamchatka in
Strahlenberg's map, and the inscription "*Kamtzadalia sinis Jedso,*" which
appears on Kamchatka in the Homann map.[62] The application of the name
"Jedso" to Kamchatka in these two instances is unusual, though not unique.
Strahlenberg explains his use of "Jedso" as an alternative name for Kamchatka on the ground that he learned at Tobolsk from a Japanese traveling
from Kamchatka to St. Petersburg (the castaway Sanima) that the Japanese
included Kamchatka in the area they called Jedso.[63] At the same time a
comparison of the two maps reveals other similarities: the shape of Kam-

60. Fel' (1960, pp. 122, 146, 150) identifies it as the map of Atlasov, 1700. Cf. *Atlas*, no. 48.

61. 1960, pp. 150–51; *PSI*, vol. 2, no. 15, pp. 47–50. Why between the two dates and not
after 1718 Fel' does not explain. Efimov (1950, p. 115) and at first Andreev (1947, p. 301, n. 3)
mistakenly identified Kirilov's map of northeast Asia of 1724 as the original of the Homann map.
Later, however, Andreev (1965, p. 37, n. 23) pointed out the similarity between the Strahlenberg and Homann maps.

62. Polevoi 1970a, pp. 100, 102–3; *Atlas*, no. 58. The cartouche on the latter map reads
"Kamtzadaliam seu Terram Jedso."

63. 1730–31, p. 438; 1738, p. 463; 1757, 2:190; Lensen 1959, p. 41; Polevoi 1970a, pp. 102–3.
Charlevoix made the same erroneous identification of Kamchatka with Jedso in the first edition
(1735) of his history of Japan (Charlevoix 1754, 6:78–79).

chatka, the islands to the south, and the fingerlike piece of land opposite the Chukotsk Peninsula. In respect to the land east of Kamchatka Strahlenberg shows a fragment of Company Land, whereas the Homann map shows a large unnamed land, a similarity of kind, though not of size.[64] On the other hand, the representation of the Chukotsk Peninsula and the mythical promontory to the north on the Homann map is much closer to that on the Anadyrsk map than to that on Strahlenberg's map. From all this evidence one is led to conclude that the Homann map was made in 1717 or shortly thereafter, and from information on Strahlenberg's map for the southern or Kamchatka portion, and from the Anadyrsk map, which does not show Kamchatka, and maybe from the other maps mentioned by Fel' for the northern or Chukotsk portion.[65] But whatever the sources of the Homann map, it was known to Peter (Polevoi 1970a, pp. 100–2): it was sponsored by him for publication, and it was made possibly by one of his trusted associates. Thus it must be considered as reflecting Peter's idea of the North Pacific and the relationship of Asia and America, and it makes evident the fact that the myth of Juan de Gama Land persisted in Russia. It is this belief that most satisfactorily dispels the ambiguity of paragraph 2 of Peter's instructions to Bering and clarifies Peter's intent.

IV

In paragraph 2 of his instructions Peter ordered Bering to sail "along the land which goes to the north, and according to expectations (because its end is not known) that land, it appears, is part of America." What land or area did he have in mind? He says that it is part of America and why he thinks so, but he does not say that it is also part of Asia. Yet, contemporaries of Bering and scholars thereafter answered this question by saying that it was the coast of Siberia north of Kamchatka. William H. Dall, Frank A. Golder, and Stuart R. Tompkins, the three who have translated the instructions into English, render the clause that in Russian reads literally "the land which goes to the north" as "the *coast* which extends northward," "the *shore* which bears northerly," and "the *coast* which extends to the north" respectively (emphasis added) (Dall 1890, p. 135; Golder 1922, p. 11; Tompkins 1945, p. 23; Lauridsen 1889, p. 13). Russian scholars, under no compulsion to use another wording, simply quote the instructions and make no comment on the wording, but their contextual remarks show that they understand Peter to have directed Bering to sail northward along the Siberian coast, as in fact he did. Even Grekov, who examined the instructions more closely than any

---

64. In the Russian version of the Homann map (*Atlas*, no. 58) the truncated islands is unnamed.

65. Efimov (1971, pp. 162, 164) arrived at the same or a similar conclusion. There is other evidence that puts the year of composition at 1721. See section IV of this chapter.

of his predecessors, is explicit that "the land which goes to the north" is the coast northward from Kamchatka (1960, p. 20). Unfortunately, most scholars have ignored the qualification or failed to see the implication of Peter's statement that the end or limits of this land were not known and for that reason it appeared to be part of America. In effect, unless they believed that somewhere north of Kamchatka the coast turned from northeast to east or southeast and joined America—which after Bering's first voyage they could not—the scholars detached this land from America and made it part of Asia.[66]

The most convincing answer to the question, and a refutation of the one traditionally given, is that of Polevoi, who, with Grekov, is the first, in 1964, to come to grips with the wording and implications of paragraph 2. However, in finding the most satisfactory answer yet to the question, he had to raise another question, as we shall see in chapter 4, to which his answer is less than convincing.

It is Polevoi's contention that Peter used the 1725 Homann map of Kamchatka in drafting his instructions to Bering, and that the large unnamed land mass east of Kamchatka on that map is the key to unlocking the ambiguity of paragraph 2. The longer dimension of this land runs north and south, and the land is cut off on the east by the frame of the map. Here is "the land which goes to the north, and . . . (because its end [i.e., to the east] is not known) that land, it appears, is part of America." Since it was not given any name on the map, Peter had to describe it somehow or other. To be sure, he might have been more explicit, but precision in written statement was not one of Peter's concerns. Peter, Polevoi points out, refers to "that" (ta) land, a particular land. The use of "that," he argues, is for the purpose of emphasis, and it points to a land apart from Asia; otherwise Peter, one would expect, would have written "along the coast" (1964a, pp. 89–90; 1967, p. 111), Peter uses the word "land," not "coast" or "shore," as do Dall, Golder, and Tompkins. In view of the fact that in paragraph 3 Peter specifies the Ameri-

66. The use of "coast" instead of "land" to translate the meaning here of the Russian word *zemlia* is common. Burney (1819, p. 118), Lauridsen (1889, p. 13), Dall (1891, p. 761), and Petersen (1947, p. 55) use the term. This practice can be traced to Müller, whose account and comments on the voyage (1758a, pp. 111–12; 1758b, 7:388; 1753, p. 54; 1754, p. 7) were the basis of other tellings of the voyage until Berkh's account in 1823. Given Müller's understanding of the instructions, which he derived from Bering (see chap. 4, sec. VIII, at n. 39), he quite reasonably took *zemlia* to refer to the coast of Siberia, not to "land" as a country or area. Thereafter, the set of mind among students of the voyage became so firm that when Berkh (1823a, p. 3) and later the editors of *PSZ* (vol. 7, no. 4649, p. 413) and Polonskii (1851, p. 1) published the instructions in their official form, few, if any, took the trouble, until recently, to make a careful examination of their wording. Indeed, in a report about the voyages of Bering and Chirikov submitted to the empress in 1743, the clause "the land which goes (*idet*) to the north" is made to say "the land which will be (*budet*) in the north." (*EB*, p. 363.) Meanwhile, the several derivative accounts of the voyage in English have depended upon Golder's treatment and have thus perpetuated the mistranslation.

can "shore" (*berega*) and again, the American "coast" (*kiust*), it must be presumed that he differentiated between "land" and "coast" and uses "land" in paragraph 2 wittingly and purposely. Thus it is not the Siberian coast north of Kamchatka to which Peter's description applies, but Juan de Gama Land or Essonis Land, which he believed lay just east of Kamchatka and the Kurile Islands, approaching close to or joining America, and which he took the unnamed land on the Homann map to be.[67] With this identification of what land it was along which Bering was to sail, it becomes evident that Peter intended that Bering should sail *east* along the southern coast of Juan de Gama Land (paragraph 2) and find where this land joined America (paragraph 3). Certainly, by sailing east the expedition would follow a more direct route than by sailing north to reach a city of European possession in America. With this explanation of paragraph 2, it and paragraph 3 become coherent, and our initial contention that America was Peter's goal for Bering is reaffirmed.[68]

Until recently the possibility that the Homann map might have had some bearing on the formulation of the instructions to Bering was ruled out by the common-sense consideration that Peter, who died on 28 January 1725, could hardly have seen the map, which was first published later in that year. But we have seen that it was at Peter's behest that the map was published in the first place; and in 1959 the Soviet scholar Endel F. Varep came up with the information that the sheets on which the map of Kamchatka appeared had been printed by Homann in 1723, and that Homann had sent one of the unbound sheets to his friend Johann A. Döderlein, rector of the college at Weissenberg and a member of the Prussian royal academy (1959, pp. 294, 296; Fel' 1960, p. 151). That some of the unbound sheets were also sent to St. Petersburg is indicated by Polevoi's discovery in 1964 of two such sheets in the Cartographic Division of the Library of the Academy of Sciences in Leningrad.[69] No explicit information has been uncovered to prove irrefutably that the Homann map was in fact the one which Peter had in mind when

67. Polevoi (1967, p. 115) argues that Peter did not give this land a name because on the maps of the time it carried more than one name, and on the Homann map it carried no name at all.

68. Kushnarev rejects this thesis, though he notes that the authors (more explicitly one of the authors, A. N. Kopylev) of a solid history of Siberia accept it. Kushnarev does not, however, deal with Polevoi's arguments head on. It is sufficient for him dismiss them on the ground that Bering made no attempt to go to America (1976, pp. 10–11). For my answer to that argument see chapter 7, note 26.

Polevoi states that Peter had to use the printed Homann map because, according to Kirilov (see app. 2), the chancery of the Senate had no Siberian map adequate to his needs (1967, p. 114). It should be noted, however, that the inadequacy of maps of Siberia which Kirilov mentioned to Peter applied to the Siberian-Chinese border, not Kamchatka.

69. Polevoi 1964a, p. 91. One of the sheets is complete with maps both of Kamchatka and of the Caspian Sea as they appear in the Homann atlas. The second one is a half-sheet with the map of Kamchatka alone.

drafting his instructions to Bering, but circumstantial evidence points to that conclusion. Not only was the map published on Peter's order—and would he have had a map published abroad in which he did not have confidence?—but there is reason to believe that this was the map that Admiral Apraksin handed to Bering, along with Peter's and his own instructions, when Bering left St. Petersburg on 5 February 1725 for Kamchatka. The map given to Bering is not described as one of Kamchatka, only as one made in 1721. The facts that no other map of Kamchatka had been published and that Bering had a German map of Kamchatka with him lead to the conclusion that the map he was given is the Homann map (at least the half of the sheet on which it appeared). The second fact we know because Bering sent a copy of the German map from Ust' Kut on the upper Lena River on 8 May 1726 to Sava Vladislavich, the Russian emissary to China, then wintering nearby at Ilimsk en route to Peking to negotiate the Treaty of Kiakhta. Vladislavich had requested from Bering "a map of Kamchatka to the Amur." He found the map that Bering sent him unsatisfactory in respect to the Amur River, and the Homann map in that respect is indeed unsatisfactory (Cahen 1912, p. 215, n. 3; 1911, p. 172). There being no other German map of Kamchatka beside the Homann map, it is safe to conclude that Bering's German map was the Homann map. It would be a cause for wonder for the Admiralty College to have given Bering a map other than the one on which his instructions were based. Meanwhile, the fact that no other contemporary map's representation of the North Pacific fits so well with Peter's instructions strengthens our belief that the Homann map must have been the one he used in drafting those instructions.[70]

Homann's map of Kamchatka supplies the missing pieces in the puzzle of the meaning of paragraph 2 of Peter's instructions. The meaning which we first gave to those instructions—that Peter was sending Bering to find the way to the western coast of America and there to gather information about it—is confirmed. When pains were taken to study the documents carefully

70. Grekov (1960, pp. 28, 30) considers the possibility that Bering may have had the Homann map with him in Siberia, in consequence of Cahen's conjecture (1911, p. 172) that the German map sent by Bering to Sava Vladislavich was the Homann map. But not knowing that the Homann map had been sent to Russia before publication in the atlas, Grekov was without evidence to know whether, or how, Bering came into possession of a copy of it. He does believe, however, that the map of Mikhail Zinoviev, a geodesist, made in 1726–27 (1960, pp. 29–30), contains evidence pointing to the Homann map as the one in Bering's possession. On the other hand, unaware of the availability of the Homann map to Peter, Grekov thinks that he probably used Evreinov's map (fig. 23). Not only did Peter ask in December 1724 to have Evreinov brought to him, but Evreinov's map shows the coast of Kamchatka going north and then turning east just above the 62nd parallel before it is cut off by the edge of the map. Thus its end was not known—or shown. If there were no Homann map, Evreinov's map might qualify as the one used by Peter, but too many other sketch-maps of the time do show the coast north of Kamchatka, and the existence of Chukotka was known to the Russians: the "end" of Kamchatka was known.

and to examine some of the ideas about the geography of the North Pacific in Peter's time, the traditionally accepted purpose and destination of the voyage were found to be wrong.[71] Nevertheless, the manner in which Bering carried out his assignment seems inconsistent with our analysis and furnishes support for the traditional interpretation. Explaining Bering's apparently contradictory execution of his assignment is the next step in our examination.

71. Of the prerevolutionary writers who have dealt with Bering's voyages only Georg W. Steller, the German naturalist who accompanied Bering on his second voyage, seems to have grasped and stated publicly that America was the goal of Bering's first voyage. In his journal of his voyage to America, Steller writes (Golder 1925, p. 10): "The great monarch Peter I, of glorious memory, was influenced by the discovery of Kamchatka as well as by the representations of the Paris Academy of Sciences, to cause an investigation to be made, by sending out the then Captain Bering in 1725, as to how far America is distant from Kamchatka, the extreme northeast corner of the Empire, or whether it [America] might not in the north be nearer to the extreme Chukchi headland, which the old map makers called Promontorium Tabin, or even be continuous with the latter."

4

The Evidence from the Voyage

PETER'S INSTRUCTIONS directed Bering to go to America and to do so by sailing along "the land which goes to the north" to where it joins America, that is, to sail east. But Bering sailed north—more accurately, northeast— along the coast of Asia. Whereupon two questions arise: (1) Why did he do so? and (2) Did he do so because the main purpose of his voyage became after all that of determining whether or not Asia and America are separated?

The information available for answering these two questions leaves much to be desired. Nevertheless, it does permit us to reach a firm answer to the second question and a highly probable answer to the first. The deficiency of information might be less if there were available to us the monthly reports to the Admiralty College, the administrative agency under whose immediate jurisdiction Bering came, which Admiral Apraksin's instructions to Bering of 5 February 1725 required him to make (*EB*, p. 374). We are told that they have survived in the state archives, but they have not been published (Andreev 1943c, p. 62; 1965, pp. 59–60). Meanwhile, in the official documents that have been published, in whole or in part, there is no elaboration of the purpose or destination of the voyage beyond Peter's terse instructions and the brief comment on the Admiralty College document quoted in the preceding chapter. We will have to make such information as we have do much work. Even so, we can extract from it more by way of conclusions than hitherto has been drawn.

I

A convenient point of departure for answering our two questions is Polevoi's answer to them, inasmuch as he has provided the most satisfactory explanation of Peter's instructions to Bering. He addresses himself primarily to our first question, why Bering sailed north instead of east, though he does give an answer also to our second.

The responsibility for the different direction taken by the voyage, according to Polevoi, was Bering's. He gave his own interpretation to the instructions, namely, that he must sail along the Asiatic coast. But, to a degree, it was Peter himself who led Bering into this error. Peter kept from Bering the real purpose of the expedition, which ultimately was the establishment of Russian dominion in North America. Any indication of Russian interest in North America, Peter feared, would provoke the European powers there into action against Russia to forestall her. He therefore circulated the story, preserved by Nartov, that Bering was being sent into the North Pacific for the purely scientific purpose of ascertaining whether an Arctic–Pacific passage between Asia and America exists, a question he knew to be of much concern in the west (cf. Efimov 1950, pp. 20, 25). This report reached Bering before he received Peter's instructions, which to preserve security of information were presented to him at the last possible moment, on the day of his departure from St. Petersburg, 5 February 1725.[1] The report set Bering's mind in a different direction from what Peter had intended. In the meantime, the authorities urged Bering to carry out Peter's orders scrupulously. Believing that Peter's concern was above all with the geographical question of a strait, Bering gave his own interpretation to the instructions. In so doing, he overlooked the fact that they say nothing about a passage between the Arctic and Pacific. He failed to understand that "the land which goes to the north" was the legendary unnamed land east of Kamchatka on the Homann map.

Polevoi elaborates this latter point. He notes that nothing on the Homann map indicates that the unnamed land might be "the land which goes to the north" in Peter's instructions. To understand this clearly, Bering needed the map of North America that also appears in the Homann atlas of 1725 (fig. 22), a map he did not have. Bering reached Iakutsk, the administrative center for all of northeastern Siberia from the Chinese border to the Arctic, and there the reports of those "who had been around" (*byvaltsy*) forced him to conclude that Asia might more likely be joined with America in the region of the Chukotsk Peninsula, which was still unexplored by the Russians. From this Bering concluded that the answer to the question whether Asia and America are joined could be obtained only by following the shores of Asia to the north. Thus the impression was created that the clause "the land which goes to the north" referred to the part of the Asiatic coast which lies north of Kamchatka. That the authorities at Iakutsk concurred in this understanding of Peter's orders is indicated by the fact that Grigorii G. Skorniakov-Pisarev, head of the port of Okhotsk at the time of the Second Kamchatka Expedition and one of Bering's detractors, who might be expected to have pointed out

1. An advance party departed nearly two weeks earlier, on 24 January.

any mistake on Bering's part, stated that Bering was to go north and "explore the coast beyond Kamchatka lying between north and east, the last cape of which is called [Chukchenskii Nos], whether that coast communicates with the west coast of the real America."[2] Thus, when Bering reached that point off the coast of the Chukotsk Peninsula where it turns west, he concluded that he had fulfilled the major part of Peter's instructions, proof of the separation of Asia and America.

Polevoi concludes his explanation of Bering's deviation from his instructions by noting again that it was Bering who gave the operative interpretation to them. Officials in the Admiralty College later complained that according to Peter's orders the expedition was to explore "where the Kamchatka land joined America," whereas Bering undertook something else and asserted that he was obliged to sail "by force of his instructions along the land from Kamchatka between north and east as far as 67° latitude." Thus, Bering, not any official in St. Petersburg, made the decision to sail north.[3]

Polevoi's answer to our first question, that Bering sailed north because he misunderstood Peter's instructions to mean that he was to find an answer to the age-old question about the relationship of Asia to America, answers our second question affirmatively: the purpose behind Bering's sailing north became the one publicly stated and traditionally accepted—the change being made, however, by Bering, not by Peter. We can agree with Polevoi's explanation and conclusion only in part. Indeed, Bering sailed north for some of the reasons Polevoi advances, but the search was not for a strait, but an isthmus. Had Polevoi examined the documents relating to the voyage itself as astutely as he did Peter's instructions, he would have had to come to a different conclusion than he did. But before presenting our own reading of the evidence it is in order to note in what particulars Polevoi's analysis holds up.

First, there is no hint in the evidence that the change in direction of the voyage was imposed on Bering by higher authority. Quite the contrary. The Admiralty College held to the view that Bering was to search for America near Kamchatka, as the passage quoted by Polevoi chiding Bering for his failure to do so indicates.

Second, there is little or nothing in the documents to enlighten us as to the extent, if at all, that Bering was briefed on his assignment. He could, of course, have been briefed orally, and probably was, but his subsequent actions do not suggest an extensive briefing. Peter's failing health precluded his discussing the prospective voyage with whoever was appointed commander, and he entrusted his written instructions to Admiral Apraksin with

2. *EB*, pp. 368, 408–9, n. 1. The "last cape," as we shall see, was undoubtedly the Shalatskii promontory.

3. Polevoi 1964a, p. 91; 1967, pp. 116–17; *EB*, p. 91; *PSZ*, vol. 8, no. 6291, p. 1004.

the request that Apraksin see to it that they were carried out.[4] Three weeks, at the most five, after writing them Peter was dead. His illness and death may well have diverted the attention of the officials in the Administrative Senate and Admiralty College from the voyage being planned to other matters more pressing. This, as well as the reasons of security advanced by Polevoi, could explain why Bering received no written explanation from Peter. On the other hand, the last-minute conveyance of the instructions and map to Bering does not necessarily mean that he had no prior knowledge of them. Unfortunately Admiral Apraksin's own instructions provide us with no background information. He recognized that the map given to Bering might not be accurate, for he authorized Bering to employ one or two of the geodesists stationed in Siberia to assist him if he thought it necessary (*EB*, pp. 373–74, para. 7; Kushnarev 1976, p. 22). Bering's own experience probably was no substitute for an extensive briefing. He had spent some time in Arkhangelsk no later than 1719, from which he had sailed to the Baltic and where he had talked with residents about navigation of the waters to the east, to the Ob River and beyond, but there is no reason to believe he had any certain knowledge of the North Pacific (Belov 1965, p. 48). He was going to have to get much of his information about it from others, and when he entered Siberia, he passed from the immediate influence of the authorities at St. Petersburg to that of the officials in Siberia, where the view of the North Pacific differed from that in St. Petersburg and where more was known about the eastern regions. It was in Iakutsk probably, as Polevoi contends, that Bering obtained the information that persuaded him to seek his objective by sailing north.

Third, Polevoi's point that Peter put into circulation the story of a search for the Strait of Anian as a red herring to throw foreigners off the scent of his true purpose becomes credible and probable when we learn that the commanders of the Russian vessels in the Second Kamchatka Expedition were instructed by the Administrative Senate to resort to the same subterfuge. In case they encountered any foreign vessel, they were to explain their presence in the Arctic or North Pacific as a second attempt to determine whether Asia and America are united, the first attempt, made at the request of the academies at St. Petersburg and Paris, having failed. The real objectives of their voyages were not to be disclosed.[5] Understood in this light, the conflict between the statements of purpose behind Bering's voyage as revealed in the Nartov story and Peter's instructions disappears. With these three points

4. Apraksin died before Bering returned to St. Petersburg and so was unavailable as a source of information in the controversy that arose after Bering's return as to whether he had fulfilled his assignment.

5. *PSZ*, vol. 8, no. 6291, p. 1010. These instructions are discussed further in chapter 6, beginning of section V. Polevoi does not use this datum to support his point.

of concurrence our agreement with Polevoi ends. Parting company with him, we proceed to our own answers to the two questions.

II

There is very little information from which we can discern what was Bering's understanding, after he left St. Petersburg, of the direction in which he was to sail in order to conform with Peter's instructions. There is one bit of information, however, that suggests what Bering's understanding at least should have been. In its report of 28 December 1732 (see chap. 6) the Admiralty College noted, as Polevoi points out, that "in accordance with the instructions of Peter the Great . . . given to Captain Commander Bering there was [to be] a search for where the Kamchatka land joined America; nevertheless (*tokmo*) . . . [Bering] sailed between north and east as far as 67° latitude" (ibid. at n. 39). From this statement, particularly from the use of the word "nevertheless," which points to a course different from that which had been understood, one can conclude that the Senate and Admiralty officials regarded America and Kamchatka as the focus of Peter's instructions and that they believed America was close to Kamchatka. That being the case, it is difficult to believe that at the time of his departure from St. Petersburg Bering had not been given this understanding by his superiors and had arrived at a different conclusion.

Bering reached Tobolsk in western Siberia in March 1725, and it was here no doubt that he first encountered the report of a Russian voyage from the Lena to Kamchatka "fifty or sixty years ago." During his captivity in this same city a decade earlier Strahlenberg had picked up the report, which he records in this passage:

> . . . in old times men crept in their boats along the shores of the ocean and other seas, from one place to another. In this way too Kamchatka . . . was first discovered by the Russians from the Lena River along the Arctic. . . . When the wind in the Arctic blew from the north and drove the ice to the shore, they retired in their small craft to the mouths of rivers, but when the wind came again from the south and the ice was driven from the shore, they moved out again and thus advanced farther eastward to . . . Kamchatka . . . [1730, pp. 99–100].

The voyage to Kamchatka mentioned here can be only that of Dezhnev and Alekseev to the Gulf of Anadyr, there being no record of any other such voyage prior to Bering's time, even though the initial and terminal points, as well as the lapse of time since the voyage, are incorrect and the names of the two men are not associated with it, and were not until Müller uncovered Dezhnev's reports in 1736. A variant version of this report was later brought to Bering's attention at Iakutsk, to which Dezhnev's reports had gone in the first place. In June 1726 Bering met with Kozyrevskii and was given a copy of the latter's map of Kamchatka. On it there is a note stating that Russians arrived there in two *kochi* from Iakutsk.[6]

Though we know that at the end of his expedition Bering gave great credence to this report, as its inclusion in the news item in *Sanktpeter-burgskiia Vedomosti* attests, we can only guess how reliable he thought the information to be at this early stage of the expedition. Yet it is difficult not to believe that it reinforced the idea that the northward-going land which appeared to be part of America was not a part of Chukotka, that Peter's instructions did not direct him to go north.

Another hint—and one cannot claim it to be much more than that—is given us by Daniel G. Messerschmidt, the German naturalist commissioned by Peter to survey western and central Siberia (see chap. 3, p. 68). He was in Eniseisk when Bering stopped there in July and August 1725. In his journal Messerschmidt tells us that he discussed certain maps with Bering, especially as they bore on his forthcoming voyage and that he loaned Bering Witsen's map of Tatary, "a new 'Mappa Sibiriae et Tattariae Magnae' published by Homann in Augsburg," one of Kamchatka, one of China, and one of Japan, which Bering returned before leaving, though presumably not before having them copied. Messerschmidt writes further that Bering "was pleased with this plan of the Eastern Ocean or Kamchatka coast, and he thought that it might be of use to him. The island Jesso was not Kamchatka itself, but a peninsula, by their conjecture, attached to America, which the English mariners have been so bold as to assure us in their recent maps" (1968, pp. 174, 176, 179; Polevoi 1975, p. 130). In light of this quotation one has to ask the question, "Did Bering at this point identify in his own mind the unnamed land on the Homann map, the northward-going land, as the 'island Jesso'?" He evidently rejected the identification of Jedso as Kamchatka found on the Homann map. Though the question suggests the answer, we cannot be sure; but one can read from this quotation the conclusion that Bering was still focusing his attention on the land and waters near Kamchatka.

We know of one other contact made by Bering while traveling eastward. This was with Petr I. Tatarinov at Ilimsk where Bering spent most of the winter of 1725–26. In 1713, and for several years thereafter, Tatarinov had served as commandant at Anadyrsk and in Kamchatka. From him Bering and Chirikov learned of the Big Land across from the Chukotsk Peninsula about which Tatarinov had been told by the Chukchi who visited Anadyrsk (Kushnarev 1976, pp. 30, 87). Chirikov later refers to this bit of information, but so briefly as to provide no basis for a conclusion as to what effect it had on their thinking at this stage.

6. Grekov 1956, p. 111; Baskin 1949, p. 227. Regarding the rejection of the notion that Alekseev reached Kamchatka see chapter 3, note 9.

From what little we have been able to glean from the meager evidence available as to Bering's understanding at this time of whither he was to sail, the most we can conclude is that it does not point to a northward course in search of a strait or land connection. This, however, was to change.

III

By the time Bering reached Nizhne-Kamchatka, he had decided that the unnamed land to the east did not exist and that Peter's instructions were to be carried out by sailing north. When he made this decision and on what grounds he made it are questions that cannot be answered with explicit evidence; one has to resort to conjecture. His change of mind occurred most likely at Iakutsk. We know that at a meeting on 6 June 1726 with Kozyrevskii, who wanted to go again to the Kurile Islands, Bering told him that he was not sailing south (Ogryzko 1953, p. 187; Baskin 1949, p. 227), which he would have had to do before he could sail east along the coast of the unnamed land as depicted on Homann's map (fig. 25). As to why Bering changed his mind, it is possible, as Polevoi argues, that he did not fully appreciate the significance of the land which appeared east of Kamchatka on the map since it is unnamed and he did not have the map of America which also appeared in Homann's atlas of 1725 and which would have clarified what Peter had in mind.

It is more likely, however, that when Bering reached Iakutsk, early in June 1726, he found that informants there such as Luzhin, who had re-mained at Iakutsk when Evreinov went to Kazan (Polonskii 1851, p. 10; Lauridsen 1889, pp. 19, 202, n. 3), Kozyrevskii, whom Bering himself sought out (Ogryzko 1953, p. 187; Baskin 1949, p. 227), and others who had been in Kamchatka knew of no land to the east that went north and might be joined with America. Juan de Gama Land, a notion that originated in the west, may well have been unknown to these men, and because the name did not appear on the Homann map and they did not have the companion map of America, they may well have wondered why this unnamed land appeared on the map in the first place. There was, on the other hand, a land elsewhere that was thought to go to the north and that might be joined with America since its end was not known. This land was the Shalatskii promontory. There is evidence from the voyage itself which leaves little doubt that Bering and his officers came to believe in this imaginary promontory and its connection with America, and that evidence will be presented in due course. Our interest for the moment is why Bering and the others accepted this belief.

Bering and his contemporaries, it must be kept in mind, knew nothing firsthand of the coast of Chukotka and the waters around it. It was *terra incognita* to the Russians. They had reports from the Chukchi of islands and another land across from the Chukotsk Peninsula, information indicating, of course, that to the east land ended and water began, but they had come to believe also in the existence of a large sacred or impassable cape, our Shalatskii promontory, extending north or northeast from the northern part of Chukotka. This belief, we saw in the preceding chapter, was reflected in the Witsen map with its two open-ended peninsulas, in the Remezov map of Kamchatka, the so-called Kozyrevskii map, Beiton's map of 1710–11, and Strahlenberg's map (figs. 6, 12–14, 18), as well as the Homann map. Bering could well have seen a copy of Strahlenberg's map in Tobolsk and copies of the other three in Iakutsk, or at least picked up there the information on which they were based. To be sure, the Homann map, which Bering carried with him, supported the view that no land connected the continents, for the northward extending promontory on it has an end, but the Anadyrsk or so-called L'vov map (fig. 17), as was pointed out in the preceding chapter, provided the basis for the idea of a large promontory stretching north, and with only hearsay to go on either view might be true. In short the cartographic evidence was ambiguous and left room for choice.

One is persuaded that it was the reports of an impassable cape in the north and the Anadyrsk and other maps which led Bering and his associates to reject the idea of a water passage from the Arctic to the Pacific and to accept the hypothesis of a land connection with America somewhere north of the Chukotsk Peninsula itself, and thus to decide that it was this connection to which Peter's instructions had to refer. On the Anadyrsk map the northern part of its massive promontory is cut off by the edge of the map and so directed as to suggest a connection beyond the map with the long arm which "hangs" farther east from that edge.[7] Was it not here that there would be found "the land which goes to the north, and . . . because its end is not known . . . [appears to be] part of America"? It is significant that when Müller left Iakutsk in 1737, he took a copy of this particular map with him and that in his account of Russian sea voyages and discoveries he pays it and its big promontory particular attention (1758a, pp. 51–52; 1758b, 7:195–96). He tells us elsewhere that he had discussed the voyage with Bering, who, we can believe, told him about the map. Further, if Bering also encountered at Iakutsk the notion of the "rocky belt," *Novaia Zemlia*, or the extension of North America westward north of Siberia as exemplified on Daurkin's map (fig. 20), it could well have reinforced the belief in the kind of land connection suggested by the Anadyrsk map.

The belief in an intercontinental land connection was still strong, and it was to survive Bering's voyages. The news item in the *Sanktpeterburgskiia*

7. The Remezov Map of Kamchatka, 1712–14, carries a similar implication north of the "Ocean Sea."

Vedomosti in March 1730 reporting Bering's first voyage comments that "several think" that the northeastern lands of the frontier are "joined with the northern part of America" (Grekov 1956, p. 109; cf. *PSZ*, vol. 8, no. 6291, p. 1004), and as late as 1818 the English sea captain, James Burney, advanced a theory of an overarching land bridge between Asia and America north of the Bering Strait on the basis of his observations while sailing with Cook in Arctic waters (1818, pt. 1, pp. 9–23). The northeastern corner of Asia and the northwestern part of America were still dimly perceived, and the idea of a land connection between the two could flourish even if the particulars about the American side were few and vague. In accepting the view of a land connection, Bering was, of course, rejecting the idea of an Arctic–Pacific passage, and in searching for the connection in the north he would also be providing information that would help to answer the longstanding geographical question, even though this was not what Peter had asked him to do.

IV

Whatever the reasons for Bering's conviction that he would find in the north "the land which goes to the north" and the place where it joined America, it is clear that he was so convinced. This we infer not only from his action of sailing north to Chukotka, but even more we conclude this from certain reports and statements made by Bering and his officers in the course of the outbound voyage, which culminated on 16 August 1728, as well as from the map of the expedition.[8] In these we find evidence not only of this conviction, but also that it was the mythical Shalatskii promontory that constituted the connection between the two continents. These reports and statements comprise much of the evidence from the voyage.

"On July 13," Bering wrote in his journal, "we cast off from the shore and sailed down the Kamchatka River. On the 14th we entered the sea . . . and . . . followed the stretch of land between north and east in accordance with the ukaz given in his own handwriting by H[is] I[mperial] M[ajesty]."[9] A week's sailing carried the *Sviatoi Gavriil* north of Cape Oliutorskii, and once past this cape Bering was navigating in waters no Russian was then known to have sailed. For the whole of the outward voyage Bering tried to stay within sight of land in keeping with Peter's orders. The Russians had no certain knowledge about the coast and the

8. Dating in the Russian navy was according to the nautical or astronomical day, which extends from noon to noon, whereas the civil day runs from midnight to midnight. Because the particular hours of the day when the events noted here took place are often not specified, it is better to adhere to the dates as given in the sources. In the case of Bering's turnaround the hour is known, three o'clock in the afternoon, so according to civil time the date is 15 August.

9. Polonskii 1851, p. 18. The statement in Bering's "Short Account" is more brief (Golder 1922, p. 18).

shape of northeastern Asia, and working their way along the coast would not only allow Bering to survey that coast, but would be the surest way of finding where "the land which goes to the north" joined America. Following the coast required Bering to circumnavigate the Gulf of Anadyr, though he failed in his efforts to find the mouth of the estuary into which the Anadyr River empties. He passed the gulf on 29 July (Berkh 1823a, p. 42).

On 1 August his vessel entered a bay, which Bering named Kresta Bay (Holy Cross Bay) and where he remained a couple of days in a vain search for fresh water (ibid., pp. 44–45). On the seventh the *Sviatoi Gavriil* was anchored offshore, probably near Providence Bay (Grekov 1960, p. 34), and a party was sent ashore to refill twenty-two barrels with fresh water, the supply having been reduced to one barrel (Berkh 1823a, p. 46). Water was found, and the vessel sailed the next day a short distance southeast and anchored in a small bay of the Chukotsk Peninsula in a latitude 64° 30′ north not far from where the coast turns north. There eight natives approached the vessel in their "skin boats," and one of them was bold enough to come aboard, while his companions remained in their boats alongside the *Sviatoi Gavriil*, enabling the Russians to question them, with some difficulty, through the two Koriak interpreters brought along for that purpose (ibid., pp. 47–48). This was the first of two occasions on which the Russians were able to talk with the natives; on the second occasion (20 August) the natives mainly confirmed what the Russians had earlier been told and added little that was new (ibid., p. 61). The Russians sought geographical information about the area to which they were sailing. Their questions and the native spokesman's answers were summarized in a memorandum signed by Bering and his two lieutenants, Chirikov and Martin Spanberg. We quote the entire memorandum to provide the context for certain questions of interest to us:

1. What is the name of the people? *Answer*: Chukchi.

2. Where is the Anadyr River and how far back from here is it? *Answer*: You passed the Anadyr a long way back. How did you come so far to this place? No vessels have come here before.

3. Do you know of the Kolyma River? *Answer*: We do not know the Kolyma River, but we hear from the reindeer Chukchi that they go by land to a river, and they say that Russians live on that river, but we do not know whether that river is the Kolyma or another one.

4. Do you have forests? Do any large rivers empty from the land into the sea? Does your land go far? *Answers*: We have no forests of any kind, and in all our land no large rivers empty into the sea. Such rivers as do are small. Our land very near here turns to the left and goes far from there. All our Chukchi live on it.

5. Does any kind of promontory (*nos*) extend from your land into the sea? *Answer*: No promontory of any kind extends from our land into the sea. All our land is even (*rovnaia*).

6. Are there not some islands or a land in the sea? *Answer*: There is an island not

far from the land, and if there were no fog, it could be seen. There are people on that island, and as for any more land there is only our whole Chukotsk land.[10]

In his "Report" of 10 March 1730 to the Admiralty College, Bering reported this conversation more briefly, but with some added details and a discrepancy. The native's response to the fourth question is reported in these words: "Their land forms two bays and turns toward the mouth of the Kolyma River, and the sea adjoins it everywhere, and there are large sandbanks. There is ice everywhere in the sea into which the Kolyma empties. . . . We do not go to the mouth of the Kolyma by sea. . . ."[11] It is to be noted here that the Chukchi of the memorandum did not know the Kolyma River. In this report they do.[12] In his "Report," Bering refers to the land about which the sixth question in the memorandum inquires as a "big land."

During the next few days the *Sviatoi Gavriil* worked its way around the Chukotsk cape or "corner" at the southeastern corner of the Chukotsk Peninsula.[13] In the afternoon of 11 August (10 August civil time) it passed to the west of the island mentioned by the Chukchi, to which Bering gave the name St. Lawrence. Early in the afternoon of 13 August (24 August N.S.), having reached 65° 35′ north latitude, the vessel passed out of sight of land.[14]

10. Grekov, 1960:33, citing TsGA VMF, *f.* 216, *d.* 87, *l.* 227 i *ob*,; Divin 1971, p. 54.

11. Grekov 1960, p. 341, n. 21; Polonskii 1851, p. 19. This passage is also translated by ·Golder in 1914, p. 143.

12. When writing his report, did Bering combine the information received in the second meeting with Chukchi, on 20 August, with the information obtained in the first meeting? The meeting of 20 August is reported in a document prepared in the Admiralty College and dated 5 October 1738. It reproduces part of Bering's "Report" of 10 March 1730 as follows:

> After they turned back on the 16th they saw an island between SE and ESE. When they reached latitude 64° 30′ [approximately forty] Chukchi came to them from the shore in four skin boats, among them a toyon. They brought a small number of local goods for sale. [The Russians] talked with them about what was needed for corroborative information. They asked the toyon specifically: (1) Where is the Anadyr River and how far is it? (2) Does he know the Kolyma River and is there a passage by sea from here to the Kolyma? (3) Are there any islands or lands in the sea opposite their Chukotsk land? To these he answered: (1) The Anadyr River is to the south and not close to here; he had been in the Anadyrsk ostrog to sell walrus tusks, and he has known the Russians for a long time. (2) He knows the Kolyma River and has gone there overland by reindeer. The sea opposite the mouth of the Kolyma is shallow, and ice is everywhere in the sea there, but he has not gone by sea to the mouth of the Kolyma. The people of their nation live along the coast from here to the Kolyma. (3) He said what the previous Chukchi had said [*EB*, pp. 86–87].

Berkh (1823a, p. 61) summarizes this passage; Polonskii (1851, p. 21) quotes the first four sentences only. This document adds the one detail about the shallowness of the water at the mouth of the Kolyma, but says nothing about the two bays, the sandbank, and the turning of the coast to the west toward the Kolyma. Altogether the three documents leave one somewhat uncertain as to which items of information were learned from the Chukchi on each occasion and therefore how much the Russians had learned from them about the route to the Kolyma before turning back on 16 August.

13. This may be a reference to present-day Cape Chukotsk, but more likely it is to Cape Chaplin, a short distance east and the more prominent of the two (Grekov 1960, p. 34).

14. At this latitude the *Sviatoi Gavriil* had still to sail more than fifty miles before it passed through the throat of the Bering Strait and before the coast of Asia turned west. Whether the

This fact, together with the information from the Chukchi that their land turned left to the west, prompted Bering to hold a sea-council with his two lieutenants as to what their course next should be: should they continue the voyage, or turn around and go back?[15] He asked each man to present his opinion in writing. Chirikov complied with the request the same day; Spanberg, the next. From Spanberg's reply we learn the principal questions Bering asked:

> In your oral request of the 13th of the present month your excellency deigned to ask: Because we have reached 65° 30′ of the northern region and according to our opinion and the Chukchi's report we have arrived opposite the extreme end and have passed east of the land, what more needs to be done? Do we go farther north and how far, and when do we look for harbors, where does it appear best [to spend] the long winter, for the interests of the state [and] the preservation of ship and men?

Spanberg's view was that they should continue northward along their route until the 16th or if they could not reach 66° north latitude, they should return to a winter haven on the Kamchatka River (Polonskii 1851, p. 20; Kushnarev 1976, p. 83).

Chirikov's reply is much the more important one for our purpose, perhaps the most important document for this chapter:

> On this date [13 August] your excellency deigned to summon us and stated your understanding of the land of the Chukotskii Nos in light of the reports of the Chukchi and in light of the extension (*prostertie*) of land from the aforesaid nos between N and NW and also because we now find ourselves at 65° 00′ [*sic*] north latitude. That land of the aforesaid nos, about which the opinion has been that it is joined with America, is separated by the sea. We are to present in writing our opinion as to how the present expedition should proceed.
>
> Complying with this command, I submit my humble opinion: Since we have no information as to what degree of latitude in the Northern Sea along the eastern coast of Asia Europeans of known nations have been, we can not accordingly know with certainty about the separation[16] of Asia and America if we do not go to the mouth of the Kolyma River, or as far as the ice, since it is known that ice exists there at all times.
>
> Because of this it is necessary for us without fail, by force of the ukaz given your excellency by His Imperial Majesty, to proceed along the land (if the ice does not

land could not be seen because of the fog or because the ship had moved too far from the shore is not known.

15. Grekov 1960, p. 33. It was a common practice in the Russian navy for the commander to hold a conference or sea-council with his officers when having to make a major decision. This sea-council can be placed in the early afternoon of 12 August civil time, not in the morning of 13 August either time. According to Chaplin's journal, the vessel was at 64° 59′ north latitude at noon beginning 13 August. During that nautical day it sailed ninety-four miles, advancing to 66° 17′ by noon beginning 14 August. The conference took place soon after passing latitude 65° 30′.

16. Here Grekov (1960, p. 34), quoting this same passage and citing TsGA VMF, *f.* 216, *d.* 87, *l.* 227 *ob.*, adds the words "by sea" (*morem*).

interfere or if the coast does not lead away to the west toward the mouth of the Kolyma River) to those places indicated in the aforesaid [ukaz] of His Imperial Majesty. If the land again turns N, then by the 25th of this month it will be necessary to look for a place hereabout where it will be possible to spend the winter, particularly across from the Chukotskii Nos, on land where according to the account obtained from the Chukchi through Petr Tatarinov there is a forest. If contrary winds occur before that date, a winter haven should then be sought [Polonskii 1851, pp. 19–20; Kushnarev 1976, p. 84].

V

To determine what persuaded Bering to sail north and what he expected to find there, we need to ascertain from these statements what they reveal about the concept Bering and his senior officers held of the geography of the northeastern corner of Asia and the adjacent regions. We look first at the questions which they asked the Chukchi. "Does any kind of a nos extend from your land into the sea?" From this question it appears that the Russians differentiated between "your land" and a nos, though in his statement of 13 August Chirikov refers to the Chukotskii Nos, i.e., to the Chukotsk Peninsula, indicating that the Russians viewed the Chukchi's land also as a nos. From this we may conclude that they conceptualized a second cape or peninsula, or an isthmus, which extended from the Chukotsk Peninsula. Another of the Russians' questions was "Are there not some islands or a land in the sea?" while at the end of his statement Chirikov mentions the land "across from the Chukotsk Nos" as well as Tatarinov, who learned about it from the Chukchi.[17] Together these two questions and Chirikov's remark are reminiscent of what the Russians in Eastern Siberia knew or believed about the geography of the northeastern corner of Asia as reflected in the Anadyrsk and Homann maps, as well as the Remezov Map of Kamchatka, 1712–14: namely, islands and another land opposite the Chukotskii Nos and another promontory or an isthmus that projected from the nos.

Where Bering and the others believed the promontory or isthmus to be located can be established from what Chirikov writes in the first paragraph. First, he refers to Bering's "understanding of the land of the Chukotskii Nos in light of the reports of the Chukchi [8 August] and in light of the extension (*prostertie*) of land from the aforesaid nos between N and NW. . . ." This reaffirmation of the belief in a promontory or isthmus, first expressed in the fifth question to the Chukchi spokesman on 8 August, goes further and

17. Berg (1946, p. 88), Lebedev (1950, p. 97), and Divin (1953, pp. 57–58), who follows Lebedev, express the opinion that Chirikov confused Tatarinov with Popov as the transmitter of the information from the Chukchi, but Grekov (1960, p. 340, n. 13) and Kushnarev (1976, p. 158, n. 60) reaffirm what Müller says in his statement that accompanied Bering's despatch of 27 April 1737 to the Admiralty College (Efimov 1950, p. 261; see this chap., n. 36) that Tatarinov, while commandant at Anadyrsk, gained his information from Chukchi visiting Anadyrsk in 1718.

places the location between north and northwest of the line of the vessel's northward course. The extension of land is seen as going north, not east from the Chukotsk Peninsula. Chirikov seems to have had this in mind also when he wrote in the second paragraph ". . . we have no information as to what degree of latitude in the Northern Sea [Pacific Ocean] along the eastern coast of Asia Europeans . . . have been. . . ." In other words, Bering and his officers had the imaginary Shalatskii promontory in mind, an interpretation borne out by what Chirikov says in his next sentence—though, admittedly, his wording is open to an alternate interpretation that, if accepted, confuses the picture. Chirikov says: "That land of the aforesaid nos, about which the opinion has been that it is joined with America. . . ." Did Chirikov mean by the words "that land" the Chukotsk Peninsula itself, as on quick reading they appear to mean and so introduce an element of confusion, or did he mean the *extension* of land from the nos, the meaning consistent with the rest of our evidence? The latter interpretation is supported by the use of "that" in "that land," which is denotative and which refers back to "land" in the phrase "extension of land from the aforesaid nos," not to the nos itself.

This interpretation becomes more likely also when one notes that in the original Russian the relative clause beginning "about which" not only immediately follows the words "that land"—not the phrase "of the aforesaid nos"—but the feminine ending of "which" (*kotoroi*) shows that this relative pronoun refers to "land," which in Russian is feminine, not to "nos," which is masculine. Chirikov evidently shortened "extension of land" to "that land." If one takes "that land" to refer to the nos or Chukotsk Peninsula proper, as at one point Grekov does,[18] then the idea that the Chukotsk Peninsula itself was not a peninsula, but an isthmus connected with America runs counter to all the evidence that the Russians believed that islands and a big land were to be found opposite the Chukotskii Nos. Further support of our interpretation of this sentence and of our thesis that the leaders of the expedition believed in the existence of the Shalatskii promontory will be found in the third paragraph of Chirikov's statement, which will be examined in the next section of this chapter. Before moving to it, however, let us jump ahead a bit in time and examine the depiction of the northeastern part of Asia on the map prepared by the expedition in 1729, a map that helped perpetuate the myth of the Shalatskii promontory.

Upon their return from the voyage, the members of the expedition pre-

18. Grekov (1960, p. 21) quotes this passage as evidence of the belief of the vessel's command that the shores along which they had been sailing, i.e., the nos, was joined with America. But he omits the phrase "of the aforesaid nos" after "that land," thus dissociating the passage from "the extension of land" and associating it with the coast along which the vessel had been sailing. Consequently his quotation reads: "That land [i.e., the coast] about which the opinion has been that it is joined with America." He does not repeat the excision when he repeats the passage later (pp. 34–35) in quoting the whole paragraph in which it appears.

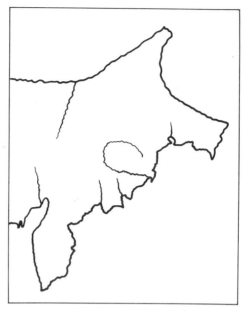

Fig. 26. Map of the First Kamchatka Expedition, 1729 (detail), from *Atlas*, no. 63;
   Berg 1946, facing p. 88

pared a map of the areas through which they passed en route from European
Russia to Kamchatka and of the coast along which the expedition sailed in the
North Pacific. The eastern third of the map depicts northeastern Siberia
from the Lena and Kolyma rivers to the Pacific Ocean and from the Sea of
Okhotsk and Kamchatka to the Arctic Ocean.[19] The basic map (fig. 26) and
others copied from it uniformly show the northeast corner of Asia as a large
double-headed peninsula: a broad Chukotsk Peninsula whose northern coast
at the eastern end starts westward and then turns in an arc sweeping from a
northwesterly bearing around to a northeasterly bearing to form the eastern
coast of a narrower Shalatskii promontory, which points northeast in the
general direction of America, and is shaped, in Baer's words, like a "bull's
horn" (1872, p. 138). On the version that first appeared publicly (fig. 27), in
Du Halde's description of China, it is labeled "Cap de Scheleginski."[20]
Much the same outline of the two headlands and the coast in between is seen
on a sketch (fig. 28) made by Joseph Delisle illustrating Bering's first voyage.

19. The original of this map (whether or not it was made by Bering himself is not clear)
appears to have been lost. The copy most often reproduced was made by Midshipman Chaplin
(Navrot 1971, p. 174). It is in *Atlas*, no. 63; also in Efimov 1950, facing p. 168; Andreev 1948,
pp. 17–18; and Grekov 1960, p. 41.

20. 1735, vol. 4, facing p. 452; Grekov 1960, between pp. 42 and 43.

Fig. 27. Du Halde's Map of the First Kamchatka Expedition, 1735 (detail), from Du Halde 1735, IV, facing p. 452

Fig. 28. J. N. Delisle's Map of the First Kamchatka Expedition, from Golder 1914,
    frontispiece

This sketch is based on his conversation with Bering. The Chukotsk Peninsula is marked "C," the Shalatskii promontory "E," the coast between them
"D," and the coast west of the former "F." Delisle makes this comment: "He
[Bering] subsequently learned from the inhabitants that the land turns [from
C] toward D and that it extends then to a point toward E, opposite which
there has been ice which frequently prevented doubling it. After that the
land turns toward F where the rivers Kolyma and Lena empty" (Golder
1914, frontispiece). On a fourth map (fig. 29), the expedition's map with
ethnographic data added, there is the notation on the Shalatskii promontory:
"Shelagi nomadize [here]."[21] Along the western and eastern coasts of the

    21. This statement recalls the statement "Here the Shelagi live" found on the Shalatskii Nos
on the Anadyrsk map (fig. 17), a similarity pointing again to the latter map as one taken seriously
by Bering and the others.

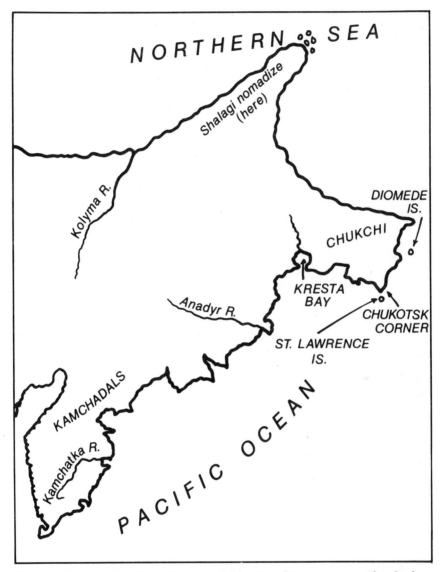

Fig. 29. Ethnographic Map, First Kamchatka Expedition, 1729–30 (detail), from *Atlas*, no. 65

promontory and along the northern coast of the Chukotsk Peninsula is written: "This part of the Shelaginsk and Chukotsk land is located from previous
maps and according to new information," from the Chukchi one would assume (*Atlas*, no. 65 and p. 46).

Only an outright statement from Bering that he believed in such a promontory would be more explicit than the expedition's map as evidence of his
continuing belief in the existence of this promontory. But that this extension
of land was an isthmus connected with America obviously was no longer
believed. Though Bering and the others rejected the Chukchi testimony
about an extension of land, they did not reject the testimony that the Chukchi land was washed by the sea all the way to the Kolyma. A large Shalatskii
promontory, or Shelaginskii Nos, was not necessarily incompatible with a sea
route between the Kolyma and the Pacific, as Müller later was to show; it
meant only that the northernmost point of the route was placed at about 71°
north latitude.[22] It is, incidentally, this depiction of the northern coast of
Chukotka on the basis of maps and hearsay that officials in the Admiralty
College criticized in the report to the empress of 28 December 1732 (*PSZ*,
vol. 8, no. 6291, p. 1004; Grekov 1956, p. 110).

Having established that Bering adopted the belief in the existence of a
northern promontory or isthmus, we can answer the first question posed at
the beginning of this chapter: Bering sailed north because he became convinced that he would find in the north rather than in the east the land which
went north, the end of which, because it was not known, was thought to be
part of America. Now we turn to the second question: Does Bering's change
in the direction of the voyage from east to north mean that he also changed
its objective to answering the geographical question? Our answer, it may be
noted, will demonstrate further the belief in the Shalatskii promontory.

VI

The answer to the second question is found in Chirikov's statement of 13
August and in certain of Bering's actions then and in the following summer.
We begin with the events of 13–16 August.

When the *Sviatoi Gavriil* passed out of sight of land, Bering, according to
Spanberg, asked: "Do we go farther north and how far, and when do we look
for harbors, and where does it appear best [to spend] the long winter, for the
interests of the state [and] the preservation of ship and men?" The expedition had been sailing along land which went north, but now that land ceased
going north. If Bering's task had been to demonstrate conclusively the existence or nonexistence of a strait, would he not have asked "Do we turn west?"
instead of "Do we go farther north?" The proper step for him to have taken

---

22. In 1733 Chirikov specified the latitude as 73° (*EB*, p. 205).

was clearly to have gone back to the coast and follow its course toward the Kolyma River, either to the river itself, to an impassable ice pack, or to land bearing north or northeast—the step which Chirikov specifies in the second paragraph of his statement as necessary to prove the separation of Chukotka from America, and which Bering has ever since been criticized for failing to take. The failure to do so, however, indicates that he was looking for an isthmus leading to America, not a water route leading to the Kolyma. It was this objective that disposed him not to turn west, though, for reasons which Chirikov sets forth in his next paragraph, Bering should have.

In the past scholars, believing settlement of the geographical question to have been Bering's mission and therefore critical of his failure conclusively to settle the question, have focused their attention on the second paragraph of Chirikov's statement, which they have interpreted as constituting his recommendation to Bering, to turn west to the Kolyma. But they have overlooked or not carefully read what Chirikov says in his third paragraph. It bears repeating:

> Because of this it is necessary for us without fail, by force of the ukaz given your excellency by His Imperial Majesty to proceed along the land (if the ice does not interfere or *if the coast does not lead away to the west* toward the mouth of the Kolyma River) to those places indicated in the aforesaid [ukaz] of His Imperial Majesty. If *the land again turns N*, then by the 25th of this month it will be necessary to look for a place hereabout where it will be possible to spend the winter, particularly across from the Chukotskii Nos, on land where according to the account obtained from the Chukchi through Petr Tatarinov there is a forest. . . [emphasis added].

Chirikov was right, of course, when he stated in the second paragraph that the only way to be sure Asia was not connected with America was to sail along the Arctic coast until they came to the mouth of the Kolyma River, a place known to the Russians. But sailing to the Kolyma is not what he recommends in the third paragraph. To be sure, he recommends that the expedition return to the coast along which it had been sailing and follow it until further progress was blocked by ice or *until it became apparent that the coast went continuously westward to the Kolyma*. If either proved to be the case, *they should sail no farther*. On the other hand, if the coast resumed its *northward* direction, the expedition should continue in *that* direction and look for the places indicated in Peter's ukaz. There obviously was no point in going to the Kolyma River in search of a city of European possession. When Chirikov mentioned the possibility that the land might "again turn to the N," he had in mind "the extension of land from the aforesaid nos between N and NW," the mythical Shalatskii promontory, shown on the expedition's maps as turning north and northeast. If this northward turn of the land were encountered, then, Chirikov advised, the expedition should continue along it until 25 August when it would become necessary to look for a winter haven in the land across from the Chukotskii Nos, the expectation being that the expedition would resume its search for America in the next navigation season. Put more succinctly, Chirikov's words say: We cannot be sure that the connection with America does not exist unless we go to the Kolyma River, but our order is to go to where the land joins America and thence to a city of European possession, so let us go back to where the land was last seen and see if the coast turns north again. If it does, let us continue until the 25th and then look for a winter haven. Implied in this recommendation are a turn-around and return if the coast was found not to continue northward. His concern was whether the coast went north, not whether it went west. In other words, the import of Chirikov's recommendation is the search for an isthmus.[23]

This interpretation of Chirikov's recommendation, it is obvious, runs counter to the usual meaning given to it by Russian and Soviet scholars, by Golder and those western scholars who have depended on him for their information about the voyage.[24] If one holds the view that settlement of the geographical question was Bering's task, then one is predisposed to read Chirikov's statement as it has customarily been read; and it must be conceded that in its published Russian text it does lend itself to this misinterpretation. But the statement should be read closely, particularly the passage "to proceed along the land (if the ice does not interfere or if the coast does not lead away to the west toward the mouth of the Kolyma River) to those places indicated in the aforesaid ukaz of His Imperial Majesty." Within this passage the crucial question is which verb, "proceed" or "lead away," governs the phrase "toward the mouth of the Kolyma River"? Polonskii, who first quoted the statement, and Grekov and Kushnarev, who quote it from a document in the Soviet archives, by their use of parentheses (which may or may not be in the original) clearly indicate that it is the verb "leads away" that governs the phrase, as do Andreev and Berg.[25] It is this form of punctuation that has been adopted here as the only one that makes sense of the statement. Other scholars, like Belov and Lebedev, use commas in place of parentheses to set off the phrase so that it may be governed by either verb; and they have chosen to read it as governed by "proceed" (Belov 1956, p. 255; Lebedev 1950, pp. 96–97). Golder unequivocally translates the passage to read "to

23. It seems to me that Chirikov's concern over proof of separation of Asia and America, as expressed in his second paragraph, stems not from the need to answer that question as the primary question, but to know whether there was northward-going land joined to America, whether the commanders' assumption about the existence of such a land was true or not.

24. E.g., Sokolov 1851b, p. 213, n. 1; Andreev 1943a, p. 40; Belov 1956, p. 255; Berg 1946, pp. 88–89; Dall 1890, p. 163; Divin 1971, pp. 55–57; Golder 1914, pp. 148–49; Lebedev 1950, pp. 96–97; 1951, p. 19.

25. Polonskii 1851, p. 19; Grekov 1960, p. 34; Kushnarev 1976, p. 84; Andreev 1943a, p. 10; Berg 1946, p. 88.

sail . . . to the mouth of the Koluima" (1914, p. 144; 1922, p. 19, n. 37).
This is incorrect, for reasons of word meaning and logic. The Russian preposition preceding the phrase "the mouth of the Kolyma River" is *k*, which
means "toward" or "in the direction of," not "up to" or "to the point of." Had
Chirikov meant that the expedition should sail to the mouth of the river
itself, would he not have used the preposition *do*, which does mean "up to"
or "all the way to" and which he does use in the second paragraph of his
statement when he notes that they would have to "go to (*do*) the mouth of the
Kolyma River" if they were to be sure Asia and America are separated?
Instead, in the clause in question he uses *k*, "toward." He does say that they
should go "up to" (*do*) those places indicated in the ukaz, that is, the place
where the northward-going land joins America and a city of European possession, located northward, presumably, and eastward, not westward of the
position of the *Sviatoi Gavriil*. If however, one takes the passage to mean
"proceed to the mouth of the Kolyma River, unless . . . the coast leads
away to the west," one in effect is saying, in order to prove the absence of a
land connection with America do not go there if the way is open; but if the
coast turns north, that is, if the land promises to bar the way, then keep
going to the Kolyma!

Read as we have read it, Chirikov's statement is quite explicit that the
expedition had not abandoned the goal of finding the route to America, but it
must be recognized that when Bering decided that "the land which goes to
the north" was a part of Asia and was to be found in the north, as would also
the juncture of that part with America, the task of finding that part and
where it joined America had become also a question of whether or not Asia
and America are connected. Even so, Bering's questions laid before his
lieutenants do not address themselves to that matter, and Chirikov's reply
shows that answering the geographical question was secondary to and derived from the main objective of the expedition. Their concern was what it
had always been, to follow Peter's instruction to find where the land which
went north joined America so that from there it could undertake a search for
a city of European possession. Thus we have answered our second question:
contrary to Polevoi's contention, when Bering changed the direction of the
voyage from southeast and east to north and northeast, he did not abandon
the final objective of the expedition, but the route he followed in pursuit of
that objective forced him to involve the expedition in answering the geographical question.

VII

Thus far our evidence points to the belief of the members of Bering's
command in the existence of the Shalatskii promontory and the likelihood of
its being connected with America. There is other evidence, however, from

Bering himself—his behavior in the climactic days of the voyage and his statements of his reasons for turning back—that does not so readily or obviously square with our interpretation. By itself, this evidence neither confirms nor denies our interpretation, but it does call for explanation.

Bering turned back on 16 August at three o'clock in the afternoon having reached 67° 18′ north latitude.[26] In his journal under that date he wrote:[27] ". . . when at sea (67° 18′) I consulted with the senior officers about returning because the time was growing late, and we decided that according to everything seen and the order given there had been fulfillment because the land no longer extended to the north, and no other land of any kind approached that end (the Chukotsk or eastern corner), and I turned back."[28] He then went on to say that the danger of adverse winds, the absence of forests, and the hostility of the natives decided him against seeking a winter haven in the area, and for returning to Kamchatka. In his "Report" to the Admiralty College of 10 March 1730 Bering gave additional reasons for concluding that he had fulfilled Peter's instructions: ". . . and on the right side of our course from the island [St. Lawrence] I saw no land and [the land] did not extend farther to the north and it turned west; accordingly I decided I had carried out the order given to me and turned back" (Andreev 1943a, pp. 9–10; EB, p. 86). Later, in April, in his "Short Account" he stated it essentially as he had in his journal: "On August 15 [civil time] we arrived at 67° 18′ north latitude. I judged that according to everything that had been seen and to the instructions given by His Imperial Majesty . . . there had been fulfillment because the land no longer extended to the north and no land of any kind approached the Chukotsk or eastern corner, and I turned back." Here too he expressed his concern for the safety of ship and crew.[29]

Bering, we see, justified his decision to turn back on the grounds that the land no longer went north, that it turned west, and that no other land approached "the Chukotsk or eastern corner," i.e., from the east, in the direction of America. He had sailed along the land that went north seeking the place where it joined America, but now it was evident that that land did not join America. He had done as much as he could, and in that sense he had carried out Peter's order, though he had not, obviously, carried out that part of the assignment contained in the third paragraph of the instructions—to reach a European city in America.

26. In the journal kept by Chaplin the latitude is more precisely put at 67° 18′ 48″ (Grekov 1960, p. 341, n. 22). The *Sviatoi Gavriil* reached the mouth of the Kamchatka River 2 September and anchored at Nizhne-Kamchatsk 7 September.

27. See the discussion of Bering's accounts of his voyage in appendix 1.

28. Polonskii 1851, p. 21. The article in *Zapiski po gidrograficheskago departamenta* (p. 553) based on Polonskii quotes instead from the "Short Account."

29. 1847, p. 74; EB, p. 64. In an opinion that Bering wrote the day before turning back, he elaborated a bit on the weather hazards and mentioned minor damage to the vessel (Polonskii 1851, p. 20; Andreev 1943a, p. 10).

In what respects do Bering's reasons for his conclusion about the fulfill-ment of Peter's orders fit in with the picture of the northern extension of land that joined or approached America? The land no longer went north; it turned west; no land was seen to the east. Presumably these facts convinced Bering there was no isthmus. But how could he be sure if he did not do as Chirikov recommended and go back to the coast to see if the land along which the vessel had been sailing bore again to the north after turning west? Bering does not say. Instead he continued northward for three days more before deciding to turn back. Maybe by the 16th he had abandoned the idea of a promontory or isthmus, but if so, why does the "bull's horn" promontory appear on the expedition's map? Further, Bering writes that no land of any kind approached the Chukotsk or eastern corner. That corner is identified in the memorandum of conversation with the Chukchi on 8 August: the inter-rogation occurred "close to the Chukotsk corner in latitude N. 64° 30′," that is, near the southeastern corner of the Chukotsk Peninsula, the identification given on the expedition's map. This could be either present-day Cape Chukotsk or Cape Chaplin. But in his journal Bering says it a bit differently: ". . . no other land . . . approached that end (the Chukotsk or eastern corner)." This second identification could apply to the eastern end or face of the Chukotsk Peninsula, that end being represented by the southeastern part of it, the part encountered first by the expedition.[30] In the "Short Account" Bering says that "no land of any kind" approached the corner, but since the corner was part of the Chukotskii Nos, land did approach it from the north and west. Therefore, he must have meant "no other land," as he wrote in his journal. In that case did he have in mind land that approached Asia from the east, southeast, or northeast? This possible interpretation is reinforced by his statement that he had seen no land on the right side of the ship's course after passing St. Lawrence Island. The finger-shaped piece of land shown in the northeastern corner of the Anadyrsk, Homann, and other maps could have given rise to such a concept. Some of them are shown as extending north without end. In short, Bering's statements leave us with a confusing picture of what he expected to find in these northern waters.

Of course, if one accepts the traditional view of the objective of the voy-age, there is not much of a problem in understanding the meaning of Ber-ing's statements and behavior. The land no longer went north; it turned west; and no land could be seen to the east except St. Lawrence Island. Therefore, he concluded there was an Arctic–Pacific passage. But what is disturbing about this explanation is Bering's failure to turn west, which every

30. Cf. Grekov 1960, p. 33. Elsewhere (*EB*, pp. 65, 66) Bering uses the term "corner" (*ugol*), but not "end" to refer to capes or like headlands. Thus, one is disposed to take "that end" to refer to the whole eastern face of the Chukotsk Peninsula. Later Müller refers to the eastern face as "the land's end" (cited in this chap., sec. VIII, at n. 41).

one of his critics says he should have done, as indeed he should have if demonstration of the existence of a water passage had been his objective. His refusal to turn west and his reiteration that the land no longer went north suggest that he was looking for something else, an isthmus, as we have been contending. Too, the traditional explanation overlooks the destination specified for the voyage, America, as well as the question to the Chukchi and Chirikov's statement about the extension of land. It also disregards his comment about "the land" that was believed to be joined to America. These are the facts with which we must try to reconcile Bering's statements.

It is difficult to believe that Bering had thought the southern coast along which the *Sviatoi Gavriil* had sailed from 1 August to 8 August continued eastward to merge with the coast of America, as his statements might be interpreted to mean. The Homann map that he carried and others that he may have seen do not posit such a conception, nor do the reports of islands and a land opposite the Chukotskii Nos. Had he thought this, his statement that the coast no longer went north would have to apply to the coast southwest of Kresta Bay, and his other remark that the coast turned west would be extraneous. That Bering had thought of an American promontory or land that came close to the Asiatic coast is more of a possibility. But this supposition does not take into account the extension of land joined to America that Chirikov mentions; it does not explain Bering's observation in all three documents that the land ceased going north; and it is opposed by the fact that in mentioning a land across from the Chukotskii Nos, i.e., the Big Land, as a place for winter refuge, Chirikov gives no hint that the members of the expedition thought of this as part of America.

We are brought back then to the northern promontory. What Bering could have had in mind is the location of the promontory at the northeastern corner of what he discovered to be a peninsula. This concept posits the extension of the eastern face of the Chukotsk Peninsula northward and eastward and could have been derived from the notion that America extended to the west north of the Chukotsk Peninsula. The end of the northward-bearing land, its westward turn, and the absence of land to the east would all be relevant evidence that such a connection did not exist. That a northern promontory later appeared on the expedition's map farther to the west proves only that Bering and the others still believed in its existence, but it leaves open the question where, before they reached the northern waters, they thought the promontory was situated. Not finding it at the eastern end, they could have moved it on the map to the west, in effect keeping the imaginary promontory and giving up any notion of the westward extension of America. The one flaw in this conjecture is that it places the promontory originally between north and northeast, whereas Chirikov locates it between north and northwest.

We are also brought back to the matter of Bering's unwillingness to follow Chirikov's advice to go back to the coast to see where it led. There are two possible explanations for his failure to do so. Bering may have thought, because of his concern over the safety of his ship and crew, to save time by taking a shortcut. Instead of taking a day or two, or longer if fog interfered, to go back to where land was last seen, he decided to continue his northerly course in the expectation that if the promontory did in fact bear north again and then east, then by following the chord of the arc that it formed his course would intersect the promontory, and he could proceed eastward from there. But after sailing for three days in this manner his concern lest he be trapped by adverse winds increased and led him to conclude that he had gone far enough to demonstrate that the promontory, if it existed, did not bear far enough north or east to join America, and so he had done as much as he could with the time available and the limited resources of his vessel.[31]

Furthermore, Bering's conclusion, after three days of sailing farther north without sight of land, that he had carried out Peter's order may well have been clinched in his mind by the several maps showing a water passage from the mouth of the Kolyma to the point of his turnaround and also by the report of the voyage "fifty or sixty years ago," information in both instances confirmed by what he had heard from the Chukchi. If the report of the earlier voyage had not entered into his decision, why was it mentioned as it was in the news item in the *Sanktpeterburgskiia Vedomosti*?[32] Too, his dependence on "previous maps" in depicting the entire coast east from the Kolyma as washed by the Arctic Ocean was later affirmed, as we know, by the Admiralty College. The information from these three sources certainly was evidence that supported Bering's conclusion that the land which went north did not join America.[33] It now appeared to Bering that of the two contradictory theories of an Asian–American land connection and a water passage around the northeastern portion of Asia, the latter was the correct one after all. This latter explanation of Bering's behavior in mid–August 1728 seems to be the most likely one.

31. One consideration that may have entered into Bering's decision to turn back, one that I have not seen mentioned in the literature, is his supply of fresh water. Between 13 July and 7 August, a period of three and a half weeks, 22 of 23 barrels of water were consumed.

32. Delisle (1752, p. 5) mentions the voyage as a factor in Bering's conclusion that he had carried out his instructions.

33. Cf. Baer 1849, p. 237; 1872, p. 44; Lauridsen 1889, p. 35. After Müller found Dezhnev's reports in 1736, Bering, then still in Iakutsk, passed this information on to the admiralty College in a despatch dated 27 April 1737, accompanied by a statement from Müller which for the first time related the Russian seventeenth-century maritime activity east of the Kolyma (*Materialy dlia istorii russkago flota*, 8:386; Efimov 1950, pp. 258–64; Müller 1761, p. 64; 1758a, pp. 155–56; 1758b, 8:24–25).

VIII

At the risk of belaboring our thesis that the northern promontory played a role in the thinking of Bering and the others, we may turn to Müller for further evidence. This will help also to explain the persistence of the belief for a half century more in the existence of this promontory.

Müller tells us both in his anonymous letter of a Russian naval officer and in his account of Russian voyages in the Arctic and Pacific that much of what he wrote about the voyage he learned from Bering. He asserts in the "Lettre:" "I say nothing here that I have not heard several times from Mr. Bering himself; I have also seen his instructions. . . ." (1753, p. 54; 1754, p. 7). Indeed, it must have been what Müller learned from Bering that led to his search for and uncovering in the Iakutsk archives in 1736 of Dezhnev's reports of his voyage in 1648 and Popov's and Tatarinov's reports of information obtained from the Chukchi. It must explain also his taking the so-called L'vov or Anadyrsk map with him back to St. Petersburg (1758a, pp. 51–53; 1758b, 7:195–96). It is doubtful that his discovery of Dezhnev's reports was accidental or fortuitous (Lauridsen 1889, p. 202, n. 3). We may assume accordingly that what he has to say about Bering's voyage, especially about the nature of the assignment and Bering's concept of the geography of the dimly discerned region into which the expedition sailed, was a reflection of the views of Bering and his associates.

The first bit of corroborating evidence is found in Müller's version of Peter's instructions to Bering.[34] This version, translated from the original German, reads thus:

> 1. At Kamchatka or another suitable place one or two decked boats should be built, with which
> 2. the northern coasts should be explored, whether, because the end itself is not known, they are connected with America. And when this has been done,
> 3. a port somewhere or other which belongs to Europeans should be sought or a European ship encountered, and men should be sent forth to inquire about the land and the location of the coasts discovered. An accurate journal of all this should be kept and brought back to St. Petersburg.[35]

34. Until 1823, when Berkh published the instructions as Peter wrote them, Müller's version, as it appeared with some variations in his "Lettre" and *Nachrichten* and the Russian, French, and English translations thereof, was the only published version.

35. 1758a, pp. 111–12. In the Russian translation (1758b, 7:388) paragraphs 2 and 3 are compressed somewhat: "(2) examine the northern coast, whether or not it is joined with America, and then (3) look for a landing place or try to encounter a European vessel. Also send men ashore for information about the newly discovered land in order to certify its name and location." The last sentence of the original third paragraph is then detached and made paragraph 4. In paragraph 2 the qualification "because its end is not known" is omitted. Thus it appears that finding out whether Asia along its northern coast is joined with America is made to appear as the main purpose, the one traditionally accepted, while the task assigned in paragraph 3 is made to appear secondary and independent of whether or not Asia and America are found to be joined, the contrary of what we have been arguing. Where the landing place is to be sought or a

The significant differences between Müller's version and Peter's are in paragraph 2. In Müller's version Peter's "land which goes to the north" has become the "northern coasts," or as Müller words the phrase, in his "Lettre" (1753, p. 54) "the northern extremity of the coasts of Siberia to the east." Bering is to examine them to determine "whether, because the end itself, is not known, they are connected with America." Here, as we have seen elsewhere, the northward-going land is identified with the coasts north of Kamchatka, not the unnamed land on the Homann map; and the purpose now is to find out whether these coasts are connected with America rather than whether the unnamed land was connected with America. How Bering finally interpreted this part of Peter's instructions shines through here.[36]

Later Müller was to accept completely the idea of the existence of a northern cape and to conclude that if there were a land connection with America, this cape or isthmus would have provided it. Müller says this in his commentary about the point at which Bering turned back on 16 August:

> Now one must admit that the understanding on which Captain Bering based his decision [to turn back] was false. For afterwards it was learned that this same cape [where he turned back] is the one which the inhabitants of Anadyrsk ostrog call Serdtse Kamen because of the heart-shaped peak on it. Although beyond it the coast turns west, this bending forms only a large bay, in the innermost curving of which, according to the above-mentioned information of the cossack Popov, the rock Matkol appears.[37] From there the coast again takes on a northern and northeastern direction until the real Chukotskii Nos in the form of a large peninsula appears at a polar elevation of 70° or more where to begin with it could have been said with foundation that no connection between both parts of the world is found. Nevertheless, who on the vessel could know this? Really authentic information about the land of the Chukchi and the land's end named after them was due to my geographical investigations made in Iakutsk in 1736 and 1737. It is enough to know that no mistake was made in this matter and that actually Asia is separated from America by a channel which connects the Arctic with the Pacific Ocean.[38]

Müller also gave graphic expression to this understanding of the geography of Chukotka on a map he drafted sometime between 1737 and 1743[39]

European vessel encountered is left indefinite. Certainly this inaccurate translation must have served further to obscure the intended destination and purpose of the voyage, and it makes Müller appear less knowledgeable about the voyage than he was.

36. Even with the publication of the official text of the instructions by Berkh in 1823, it is doubtful that without the new information presented by Varep in 1959 about the origin and date of printing of the Homann map of 1725 a close textual examination of the official version would have changed the established interpretation of it.

37. Popov's report is in *PSI*, 1:456–59, and his journey is described by Müller in 1758a, pp. 56–60 and 1758b, 7:200–2.

38. Translated from 1758a, pp. 118–19. Other translations are in 1758b, 7:394–95 and 1761, p. 48.

39. *Atlas*, no. 79 and pp. 52–53. On p. 52 it is titled "Map of the Places Lying between Iakutsk and the Chukotskii Nos and the Mouth of the Anadyr River." By whom it is not said.

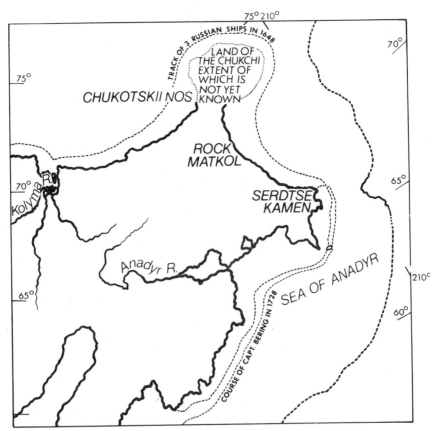

Fig. 30. Müller's Academy Map, 1754, 1758 (detail), from Müller 1761, frontispiece

and on the Academy map, which he published in 1754 and 1758 (fig. 30).[40] From these maps we can see that he adopted the concept of the mythical Shalatskii promontory expressed in Chirikov's statement. To be sure, he changed its configuration from Baer's bull's horn to a mushroom shape and placed it so that its eastern face lies longitudinally slightly east of Serdtse

40. The full title of the map is "Nouvelle carte des découvertes faites par des vaisseaux russiens aux côtes inconnues de l'Amerique septentrionale avec les pais adjacents. Dressée sur les mémoires authentiques de ceux, qui ont assisté à ces découvertes et sur d'autres connoissances, dont on rend raison dans un mémoire séparé (St.-Petersbourg: l'Académie impériale des sciences, 1754). It is reproduced in Efimov 1949, facing p. 74; 1950, pp. 195, 197; and in Orlova, comp. 1951, map no. 11 (see p. 543). It is described in Cahen 1911, pp. 270–72. An English translation of it appears in Müller 1761, frontispiece. It is from this latter version that figure 30 has been adapted. The map was reissued in 1758 under the same name, but with some corrections and revisions (Andreev 1959, pp. 7–8; Breitfuss 1939, pp. 94–95).

Kamen;[41] and he designates this imaginary cape Chukotskii Nos, though in a statement to the Admiralty College in 1737 regarding Dezhnev's voyage and again in his account of the Russian voyages he also calls it Shelaginskoi or Shalatskoi Nos.[42] Nonetheless, it is the Shalatskii promontory in changed guise. We can attribute Müller's changes to his discovery of Dezhnev's reports with their description of a "great rocky cape," which extended far into the sea, which lay between north and northeast, on which many Chukchi lived, and opposite which were two islands inhabited by natives who wore "fishbone teeth" in their faces (i.e., labrets).[43] It is these features too that led Müller to find in Dezhnev's description of this nos confirmation of the existence of the northern promontory, to assert that Bering did not reach it (Baer 1849, p. 249), and to identify that promontory and not the eastern extremity of the Chukotsk Peninsula as Dezhnev's cape. Dezhnev's reports also bore out Bering's conclusion that America and Asia are separated, although Müller realized that the northern promontory had offered the only possibility of a union between the two continents: only when it was known that this promontory was not connected with America could one be certain of the separation.

Müller not only came to the support of Bering's depiction of the coast between the Kolyma River and the easternmost tip of Asia, which the Admiralty officials had doubted, but he also gave new life to the concept of a northern promontory, providing it with the support of seemingly unimpeachable evidence. The concept continued to be accepted until Captain James Cook's third voyage into the Pacific.[44] Cook's two vessels cruised the waters north of Bering Strait in the summer of 1778 before his death, and again in the summer of 1779 after his death. Both Cook and Captain James King in their respective parts of the account of the voyage state that no signs of Müller's promontory were found; and they concluded, correctly, that it

41. Cf. Efimov 1950, pp. 66–67. The real Serdtse Kamen is ninety miles west of East Cape. Müller's concept of the rounded outline of the promontory was no doubt derived, as Polevoi points out (1970b, pp. 151–52), and Belov agrees with him (1973, pp. 186–87), from an error in copying Dezhnev's statement that the great rocky nos "turns abruptly to the south toward the Anadyr." It was made to read in the copy that Müller took to St. Petersburg "turns around and under toward the Anadyr" (Polevoi 1962b, p. 149; 1965a, p. 102, 1970b, p. 151; Belov 1952, p. 132).

42. 1758a, p. 52; 1758b, 7:195–96; Efimov 1950, pp. 258, 259; Belov 1973, pp. 185–86. Gmelin (1751, p. [4]) makes the same identification, as does Chirikov in a proposal to the Admiralty College, 12 February 1733, in which he refers to the "Northern Chukotsk corner" at the 73rd parallel on the map (*EB*, p. 205). This, obviously, is not Bering's Chukotsk corner near 64° 30′ north latitude.

43. Efimov 1950, p. 258. On his earlier and, until 1964, unpublished version of the map, that of 1737–43, Müller placed two "teeth islands" off the northwestern coast of the nos, but omitted them on the map of 1754.

44. Cf. the map of 1774 of Jacob Stählin von Storcksburg (*Atlas*, no. 157 and p. 105).

did not exist. From their observations of the Chukotsk Peninsula they decided that the features Dezhnev attributed to the great rocky cape fitted East Cape, the name they gave to the easternmost cape at the end of the Chukotsk Peninsula. Though this identification of Dezhnev's cape by Cook and King was not immediately accepted by others, not, indeed, until the late nineteenth and twentieth centuries, their exploration of the Arctic waters north of the Chukotsk Peninsula effectively disposed of the mythical Shalatskii promontory.[45]

IX

Be all this as it may, between the end of the voyage and the next summer Bering appears to have had some second thoughts about his conclusion and action of 16 August, for in the succeeding months he changed his mind. His proposal for his second voyage is the classic proof of this change. Indeed, Müller informs us that Bering confided to him his awareness that he had not fully carried out Peter's instructions (1753, p. 60; 1754, p. 12). But the failure to which Bering admitted was not the failure to bring back scientific and irrefutable proof of the separation of the two continents, to demonstrate the feasibility of a northeastern passage, but the failure to find the way to America, the primary objective of the voyage (*EB*, p. 21). Of the separation of the two continents he was convinced, and so it must have soon occurred to him that not having found any land junction with America in the north, as presumably the information obtained at Iakutsk had led him and others to believe, the way to America would have to be found by going east from Kamchatka, the view which, we suspect, Bering had first held.

That Bering reached this conclusion before he departed from Kamchatka is indicated by the short eastward excursion he made in June 1729 after leaving Nizhne-Kamchatsk. According to Müller, after Bering had returned to Kamchatka, he learned from the local inhabitants, presumably those at Nizhne-Kamchatsk, of the existence of land not far east of the peninsula.[46] Müller does not say when Bering learned this, before or after his voyage, but he places this item of information in that part of his narrative that deals with the period after the voyage (1758a, p. 120; 1758b, 7:395–96). This information

45. Cook 1784, 2:470; 3:262–64. It was King who made the detailed statement explaining their selection of East Cape as Dezhnev's cape. The geographical feature that Cook and King called East Cape is not the Cape Dezhnev of today, but the small peninsula at the end of the Chukotsk Peninsula, a rocky hill and headland connected with the main part of the Chukotsk Peninsula by a low-lying stretch of land, which they saw as an isthmus (thus it extended far into the sea). Cape Dezhnev is the easternmost tip of that headland, flanked by capes Peyek and Iugven (U. S. Hydrographic Office 1952, p. 55). Recently Polevoi advanced the conclusion that Dezhnev's great rocky cape is actually the Chukotsk Peninsula itself (1962b and 1965a). He argues his case convincingly, as I indicate in my article of 1973 (pp. 18–22).

46. Grekov (1960, p. 38) thinks that this information applies to Bering Island, which can be seen on a clear day from the Kamchatka coast.

brought the focus of the search for America from Chukotka back to Kamchatka, where Peter, as well as Bering, had put it in the first place. If Bering's native informants were right, Peter's unnamed land might exist after all. On the basis of this information and evidence of his own observation—evidence which he mentions in his proposal for a second voyage—Bering sailed in the *Sviatoi Gavriil* from the mouth of the Kamchatka River on 5 June 1729 and went about 130 miles east looking for the land alleged to be in that vicinity. He found none, however, and no sign of it, and so, checked by fog and adverse winds, he turned southwestward on 8 June and headed for Bol'sheretsk. From there he crossed the Sea of Okhotsk to Okhotsk where he began the long river and land journey back to St. Petersburg.[47]

This excursion makes sense only in relation to a search for a route to America; otherwise it seems irrelevant and unnecessary.[48] Certainly it was not intended to prove the separation of Asia and America in the vicinity of the Chukotsk Peninsula. To be sure, a three-day search seems halfhearted, but in all likelihood the *Sviatoi Gavriil* was not designed or provisioned for more than a tentative transoceanic voyage. To carry out Peter's instructions by sailing east would require a more ambitious enterprise than Bering could mount at that time.[49] In this brief foray to the east, therefore, we see at least part of the genesis of the second Bering voyage, the objective of which was to finish what he had been able only to begin on his first voyage.

X

On the basis of the evidence from the voyage itself, we have found that the reason Bering sailed north along the Siberian coast through the Bering Strait was that he had come to believe in the existence of a northward–going promontory, which he took to be Peter's "land which goes to the north" and which might, its end not being known, connect with America. This promontory could turn out to be an isthmus or in close proximity to America. Here would be found the place where the search for a city of European possession would begin. This conclusion is far more consistent with the evidence when scrutinized closely and carefully than is the traditional interpretation that Bering sought a strait or water passage.

We say this despite the fact that Nartov quotes Peter the Great as speaking about "an open route called Anian" and the fact that the announcement of

47. Polonskii 1851, p. 22; *EB*, p. 87. Bering states in his journal that he went east about four degrees of longitude or about 200 versts.

48. Only Pokrovskii (*EB*, p. 21) and Polevoi (1967, p. 118) appear to have grasped the meaning of this episode.

49. See chapter 5, note 28. Waxell (1952, p. 49) wrote that the first expedition suffered from a shortage of provisions and other necessary items.

Bering's voyage in the *Sanktpeterburgskiia Vedomosti* alludes to the question of "an open water passage" between Asia and America. When one studies the documents written by the participants of the expedition, one finds no reference to a water passage between the Arctic and Pacific oceans, no reference to a strait between Asia and America, and no mention of a search for a passage or strait. Later, in deciding to turn back after reaching 67° 18′ north latitude, Bering, it is generally agreed, accepted the Chukchi's information that the sea extended all the way to the Kolyma River from the end of the Chukotsk Peninsula. Thus in a sense he repeated Dezhnev's discovery of the water passage from the Kolyma to the Anadyr River, but Bering does not refer to this discovery of his in explaining his decision or as constituting the fulfillment of his mission. He says only that the land no longer went north and that he had seen no land elsewhere, remarks that imply the search for an isthmus more than for a strait. Had proof of the existence of an Arctic–Pacific water route been his objective, one could expect more than this by way of a statement. One would expect him to stress the fact that the coast turned west. His proposal for a second voyage does not, as we shall see in the next chapter, call for a scientific demonstration that the information obtained from the Chukchi was correct and thereby finally prove the existence of a water passage. Rather, it called for a voyage eastward to America, which would neither prove nor disprove the existence of such a passage. In other words, where Bering might be expected to mention the finding of this passage as the fulfillment of his task, he says nothing as to success or failure.[50]

Further, five items of evidence are difficult to reconcile with the traditional view of the purpose of the voyage: (1) Peter's designation of a European city in America as the expedition's destination; (2) his statement that the northward-going land was thought to be part of America; (3) the reference to the extension of land in the question to the Chukchi and in Chirikov's 13 August statement; (4) his remark in that statement about the belief that "that land" was joined to America; and (5) Bering's brief voyage eastward in June 1729. One can reject both Polevoi's thesis about the unnamed land on the Homann map and our thesis about why Bering sailed north, neither one of which is airtight, given the meagerness and nature of the evidence; but one is still left with these five items of evidence to be explained, and the traditional view does not explain them.[51] Indeed, it

50. The only mention of a strait to be found in the documents we have examined is the entry for 9–11 August 1728 in Bering's journal which Polonskii quotes (1851, p. 19). The strait is mentioned in passing: ". . . we passed around the Chukotsk cape and saw the island called St. Lawrence, about which the Chukchi had spoken. . . . Then we went NE along a strait." Since this island was the only land he reported seeing to the east of his course, one has to conclude that the strait was the passage between the island and the Asiatic shore.

51. Kushnarev (1976, pp. 86, 144–45) is a recent exception in that he tries to deal with the first and fifth items.

ignores them, whereas the two new theses do try to come to terms with them.

So much in the evidence points to America and so little points to the Bering Strait as the destination and concern of the leaders of the expedition that we must conclude that the version of the origin of the voyage and its purpose embodied in the episode related by Nartov and in the announcement in the *Sanktpeterburgskiia Vedomosti* is inaccurate at best or a deliberate misrepresentation to conceal the real objective of the voyage, as Polevoi claims. Grekov, faced with the contradiction, does not go so far as Polevoi, but he rejects the story. Noting what the modern editor of Nartov's stories, L. N. Maikov, has to say—that Nartov was not an eyewitness to all he reported, that he took some of his stories from other written accounts, and that an uncertain number of them were reworked by his son in the 1770s (Nartov 1891, pp. xi–xv)—Grekov concludes that the story is inaccurate and has to give way to more reliable evidence.[52]

A few of the details in the story do raise doubt about its accuracy. In the second paragraph (quoted in chap. 2, beginning of sec. II), Nartov states that he saw Peter draft the instructions to Bering while the latter was confined to his living quarters by his final illness. This places the time of the episode in January 1725, according to Grekov. Peter, Nartov says, was in a hurry to draft the instructions and having summoned Admiral Apraksin, handed the instructions to him with the order to see that they were carried out. The picture sketched here is that Peter, having mulled over the matter for some time, finally wrote the instructions in Nartov's presence and turned them over to the admiral without apparently having discussed the project with him, although after all Apraksin was head of the Admiralty College. The picture does not quite square with the December date usually assigned to the writing of the instructions or take account of the Admiralty College document on which Peter made notations. At best the story oversimplifies the genesis of the expedition. It leaves one with the suspicion that it was written after Bering's return to St. Petersburg and rests on what was announced in the *Vedomosti* and what was then believed about the purpose of the voyage.

The acceptance historically of the view embodied in Nartov's story is not hard to understand. Bering's voyage did produce at least a tentative answer to the question of a strait between Asia and America, a matter in which Europe had been and still was very much interested. The real goal of Bering's voyage the Russian government did not wish to reveal lest other powers become suspicious.[53] Although the announcement in the *Vedomosti* prom-

52. 1960, p. 21. Efimov (1950, p. 21) likewise is unwilling to take this story at face value.
53. One might think that the members of the Academy of Sciences associated with the

ised more information, not long thereafter plans for the Second Kamchatka Expedition were begun, and the secrecy enjoined about them probably explains why no additional information about Bering's voyage was released. Meanwhile, there can be little doubt that Bering himself contributed to the establishment of the traditional view of the objective of the voyage by his interpretation that Peter's "land which goes to the north" was the coast north of Kamchatka.

We have earlier noted that Bering was criticized in the Admiralty College for not exploring "where the Kamchatka land joined America." To answer his critics, he must have had to explain that from the information he obtained in Siberia he could conclude only that Peter's northward-going land was the eastern coast of Asia to the north. From such an explanation it must have been easy for others to conclude that Peter had sent Bering to explore the "northern" coast of Asia, as Müller later wrote or to examine the frontiers of Siberia "to the northeast," as Du Halde worded it in his earlier account,[54] especially if America as the intended final destination was an item of information kept concealed for reasons of state when publicizing Bering's discoveries. Those who sought a northeast passage would naturally focus their attention on the fact that his discoveries pointed to the strong probability of the existence of such a passage and, ignorant of the content of the third paragraph of the instructions, would conclude that Peter had sent Bering to settle the geographical question. In the absence of information to the contrary, it was natural for savants and others to conclude that the information Bering was reported to have brought back was the information he was sent to get, and thus the result of the voyage was mistaken for the purpose.[55]

Second Kamchatka Expedition would have learned something of the real purpose of Bering's voyage. It must be remembered, however, that Müller and the others were not members of the inner governing circle; they were academicians serving the state, not politicians. Also many of them were foreigners subject to skepticism on the part of the Russians about their loyalty (justified in the case of Joseph Delisle). Thus, one cannot expect that they would be privy to the motives existing in the innermost councils of state.

54. 1735, 4:452. The "Relation du voyage fait par le Capitaine Beering. . . ," added to the French translation of Strahlenberg's work (see app. 1), has Bering writing in the first person that "I was ordered . . . to find out among other things the limits of [Siberia] and particularly if the eastern corner of Asia is separate from America (1757, 2:264). In his "Short Account" Bering indicates his assignment simply by quoting Peter's instructions. Thus the "Relation" incorrectly attributes to Bering a statement he never wrote.

55. In both this chapter and the preceding one, we have accepted Polevoi's thesis that Peter's phrase "the land which goes to the north" referred to the unnamed land east of Kamchatka on the Homann map. But it must be admitted that that description can apply as well, if not better, to the finger of land north of the unnamed land and east of the Chukotsk Peninsula in the upper right corner of the Homann map. It too goes to the north, and since its northern end is left open, its end is not known. Could this be the northward-going land Peter had in mind? If it were, then he must have wanted Bering to sail north along the east coast of this land to its supposed union with America and thence south to a city of European possession. This would mean presumably that Peter thought the unnamed land east of Kamchatka was an island. Such a route to a city of European possession would have been quite roundabout and therefore longer than the one

Up to this point we have concerned ourselves mainly with where Peter wanted Bering to go and why Bering went north. We have not yet considered the more important question: Why did Peter want Bering to go to America? This question is better dealt with in another chapter, but first we must turn to an examination of the origins and objectives of Bering's second voyage and of certain aspects of the Second Kamchatka Expedition, of which this second voyage was a part.

south and then east along the southern coast of the unnamed land. This variant identification of the land which went north raises more questions than it answers. Polevoi's simpler explanation is to be preferred. Moreover, the documents we examined in this chapter give scarcely even a hint that Bering and his officers thought this open-ended peninsula or island was the land Peter had in mind. According to Chirikov, it was the land opposite the Chukotsk Peninsula and that was all. But even in the unlikely event that this was Peter's northward-going land, the intended destination for Bering remained the same—America, not an Arctic–Pacific water passage.

5

Bering's Proposals

BERING'S SECOND VOYAGE, unlike the first, poses no problems as to the certainty of the destination or any ambiguity of instructions. Where Bering was to go and what he was to do when he arrived there are carefully spelled out in the plans and instructions. Our task in this and the next chapter is therefore simpler: to answer the question, What did the planners of the second voyage hope to accomplish by it? To answer this question considerable information is available, though outside the Soviet Union some of it appears to be little known, certainly little used, and even Soviet scholars have not made as much use of it as they might. At the same time some of this information, most of it from Bering himself, serves to reinforce the conclusions reached in the two preceding chapters, and accordingly, we will consider that aspect of the information first.

The reader will note that in this and the next chapter the term "Second Kamchatka Expedition" is often used rather than "Bering's Second Voyage." In fact, the former term is part of the title of the next chapter. Nevertheless, we still are primarily concerned with Bering's second voyage, but this voyage was a part—and the most consequential part—of what became known as the Second Kamchatka Expedition; and although the several parts that made up this most ambitious enterprise were executed separately, they were connected in their objectives and planning, particularly the American, Japanese, and Arctic expeditions. For this reason these other parts of the expedition enter our story and have a bearing on our analysis and interpretation as presented in this and the next chapter.

On the other hand, it should be noted that the label "Second Kamchatka Expedition" has not been universally accepted. No unanimous agreement exists as to what it should be called. The officials who brought it into being never gave it an official name. The one most commonly encountered in the documents is the Kamchatka or the Second Kamchatka Expedition; less commonly it is called the Siberian Expedition, and sometimes the Siberian and Kamchatka Expedition.[1] Müller also terms it the Kamchatka Expedition (1753, pp. 47, 50; 1754, pp. 2, 4; 1758a, p. 138). The fact, however, that the geographical embrace of the name Kamchatka excludes hinterland Siberia and the Arctic Ocean, where several of the expedition's voyages and activities were carried on, gave rise to other names. Aleksandr P. Sokolov, who wrote the first detailed account of the expedition, calls it the Northern Expedition (1851b, pp. 190–91), and Belov follows his example (1956, p. 264, n. 1). It has also been given the double-headed name the Siberian–Pacific Ocean Expedition,[2] and even the triple-headed name the Great Northern, Second Kamchatka Expedition of Bering (Gnucheva, ed. 1940, pp. 38–39). Pokrovskii and Berg, on the other hand, employ the designation Bering's Expeditions in the titles of their respective works, although they also use the name Kamchatka Expeditions in their texts.[3] We prefer to go along with Grekov and Lebedev and use Second Kamchatka Expedition.[4] It has the sanction of early official use and tradition, and it has the advantage for us of a meaning well known and of relevance, since the vessels used on Bering's second voyage—the American expedition, as it is also called—embarked from and returned to Kamchatka.

I

The Second Kamchatka Expedition, with its component the American expedition, was the brainchild of Bering, though midwifed and nourished by others. It is proper then to begin with two sets of proposals dated 30 April 1730 that Bering presented to the Admiralty College after his return to St. Petersburg from his first voyage. The proposals were put before the Senate later that year, in December, when Bering was sent to Moscow[5] "to present information that is considered useful to the state in the eastern regions."[6]

1. E.g., *EB*, pp. 83, 90, 118, 386, 391; Imperatorskoe russkoe istoricheskoe obshchestvo 1898, p. 540; 1899, p. 275; Efimov 1950, p. 289; *Materialy dlia istorii russkago flota*, 5:345, 508, 7:307, 508, 8:194, 331, 706; *PSZ*, vol. 9, no. 6351, p. 63. Chirikov referred to it as the Kamchatka Expedition (*EB*, p. 205). Bering's first voyage was also put under the rubric "Kamchatka Expeditions" and came to be called sometimes the First Kamchatka Expedition, though in his "Short Account" he refers to it as the Siberian Expedition.

2. Efimov 1950, pp. 163, 182; *Atlas*, ix; Divin 1953, p. 16, n. 1; 1971, pp. 42, n. 1, 89.

3. *Ekspeditsiia Beringa* and *Otkrytie Kamchatki i Ekspeditsii Beringa*.

4. Grekov 1960, pp. 347–48, n. 1; Lebedev 1951, pp. 6–7, n. 1, 15; 1957, p. 192, n. 1; Lebedev and Grekov 1967, p. 178; Lebedev and Esakov 1971, pp. 198, 290, n. 29.

5. Unlike the Admiralty College, the Administrative Senate had been moved back to Moscow with the return of the central government to the old capital late in 1727 and in 1728. The move of the central government back to St. Petersburg occurred at the end of 1731 and early in 1732.

6. Baer 1872, p. 64; Andreev 1943a, p. 12; Berg 1946, p. 119, n. 4; Berkh 1823a, p. 99. Berkh found these proposals among the papers of Admiral A. N. Nagaev, the eighteenth-century naval cartographer of the Bering Sea. They are titled "Two Proposals of Vitus Bering" and bear the date 30 April 1730. Kirilov says in his "Memorandum" that Bering "had his proposals after he returned from his first expedition . . ." (app. 2; Efimov 1950, p. 290 or Andreev 1943a, p.

The first set of proposals, consisting of fifteen paragraphs or sections, makes suggestions for improvement of the administration of the easternmost regions of Siberia and for utilization of the natural resources there. The second set is much shorter, comprising five paragraphs. In them Bering suggests that voyages be undertaken eastward to America and southward to Japan for the purpose of opening up trade with each, and that the Arctic coast of Siberia be charted between the Ob and Lena rivers (Grekov 1960, p. 56). Too, he had indicated his willingness to undertake the voyage to America, as had Chirikov and Spanberg (1758a, p. 138; 1758b, 8:9).

Both sets of proposals were favorably received by the Senate, which soon began to act upon them. During the next twenty-seven months it issued a succession of orders putting them into effect. The Senate's attention went first to the first set, since implementation of these proposals was necessary for the realization of the second set. In February 1731 Empress Anna ordered the Senate to transfer Grigorii G. Skorniakov-Pisarev, who was then living in exile at Zhigansk north of Iakutsk on the Lena River, to Okhotsk as commandant, which the Senate formally did on 10 May (Novlianskaia 1964, pp. 88–90; PSZ, vol. 8, no. 5753, p. 461). Skorniakov-Pisarev had held high positions in the army and at court and had been *ober-prokurator* of the Senate until his exile following the fall of Prince Aleksandr Menshikov from supreme power in 1727. In exile he drank much, became quarrelsome and denunciatory, and neglected his responsibilities. He did not reach Okhotsk until 1735 and left in 1740. He was a trial there to Bering (*EB*, p. 16; Sokolov 1851b, p. 202). On 30 July the Senate issued an ukaz instructing Skorniakov-Pisarev to put into effect several of the recommendations of Bering for the Okhotsk region and Kamchatka (*PSZ*, vol. 8, no. 5813, pp. 520–24; Divin 1953, pp. 61–66).

Early in 1732 the government began to move on Bering's second set of proposals. In March Her Majesty's Cabinet commissioned the Senate to examine Bering's suggestion for a second expedition, and on 17 April a short imperial ukaz was issued to it ordering Bering to Kamchatka for the second time. The Second Kamchatka Expedition had been accepted in principle at the highest level (Grekov 1960, p. 57; PSZ, vol. 8, no. 6023, p. 749). Two weeks later, on 2 May, the Senate issued two ukazes. The first and longer one contained instructions regarding the preparation of the Second Kamchatka Expedition and its support—personnel, materials and equipment, provisions, various supporting activities, and the responsibilities of central agencies and local authorities. This ukaz and the earlier one issued to Skorniakov-Pisarev authorized the implementation of all of Bering's sugges-

35), which seems to be as much as is known about the moment when they were written. The date often assigned to them is 4 December 1730, the date of their presentation to the Senate and the date found on the copy in TsGADA, *f.* Senata, *kn.* 664 (Andreev 1943a, p. 37, n. 8).

tions in his first set of proposals. The ukaz also ordered the exploration of the Arctic coast from the Ob River to the Lena River and Kamchatka (item 21) (*PSZ*, vol. 8, no. 6041, pp. 770–74). The second ukaz ordered that vessels be built in Kamchatka in which to look for lands between Kamchatka and America, for islands south of Kamchatka, and the Shantarskie Islands; and that the passage by sea to the mouth of the Amur River and beyond to the Japanese Islands be explored (*PSZ*, vol. 8, no. 6042, pp. 774–75). On 19 June the decision to add to the expedition a contingent of professors from the Academy of Sciences to carry on scientific investigations in Siberia was formalized in an ukaz (Gnucheva, ed. 1940, p. 40). On 16 October the Admiralty College reported to the Senate the instructions it had drafted for Bering and the other commanders regarding personnel, equipment, provisions, and the like (*EB*, p. 89). All of this planning was brought together at the end of the year in a report (*doklad*) of sixteen articles submitted by the Senate to the empress and dated 28 December 1732. In it the plans for the several parts of the Second Kamchatka Expedition were set forth. It was approved on that date.[7] Three days later, on 31 December, the Senate issued the report, virtually unchanged, as an ukaz to the Admiralty College.[8] On 5 January 1733 officials of the Admiralty College heard a reading of the Senate's ukaz and took immediate steps to put it into effect.[9] Study of the ukaz led to some modifications in the plans for the voyage to America, and supplementary instructions were issued: an ukaz of 21 February 1733 from the Senate to the Admiralty College; instructions from the Admiralty College to Bering on 28 February 1733; and an ukaz from the Senate to Bering on 16 March 1733.[10] We turn now to a more detailed examination of Bering's proposals.

II

Most writers on Bering's voyages have seen little relevance to the voyages of the first set of proposals, having been content to mention them briefly

7. Imperatorskoe russkoe istoricheskoe obshchestvo 1898, p. 540; *PSZ*, vol 8, no. 6291, pp. 1002–13. An abridged and in places incorrect English translation is in Golder (1922, pp. 29–32). This report has commonly been regarded by scholars as the ukaz containing the orders to the expedition. For practical purposes this is true, but it should be noted that the document, as it appears in *PSZ*, technically is a report, not an ukaz, though it acquired the effect of one once approved by the empress.

8. *EB*, pp. 90–97, 376, 378–79, n. 16. The instructions in most particulars literally repeat the earlier report. Hereafter reference to these instructions will be to them in the report, but it should be understood that such references include the official instructions of 31 December 1732 as well.

9. *Materialy dlia istorii russkago flota*, 7:502–9.

10. The ukaz of 21 February is in Waxell 1940, p. 161, n. 40 (cf. Grekov 1960, pp. 57, 61); the instructions of 28 February are in *EB*, pp. 151–73 and Gorin, ed. 1935, no. 5, pp. 160–80; the ukaz of 16 March is in *EB*, pp. 126–50; Gorin, ed. 1935, no. 4, pp. 146–67; and *PSZ*, vol. 9, no. 6351, pp. 63–69.

and then dismiss them.[11] Yet a study of his proposals reveals that he had learned much from the organization and preparation of his first voyage and saw what needed to be done to carry out his recommendations in his second set of proposals. In the first set Bering recommended the introduction of agriculture and cattle raising in the Okhotsk region and Kamchatka, the development of such natural resources as the iron ore deposits near the Angara River and Iakutsk and the pitch in the pine forests along the Iudoma and Uda rivers; salt could be boiled if kettles were provided. Such measures would reduce the need to transport necessary items great distances. He recommended improvements in the living and working conditions of the service personnel and natives, protection of the Koriaks and other natives from raids by the Chukchi, and transfer of artisans to Okhotsk and Kamchatka, the establishment of local authorities in Kamchatka in place of agents from Iakutsk, the establishment of a port at Okhotsk, improvements in transportation, and other measures. In a word Bering saw the kind of support system needed on the Pacific seaboard if exploration on the scale he proposed was to be carried out, overseas trade developed, and Russia's hold on its far eastern territory strengthened. They reveal Bering to have been well informed on local conditions in eastern Siberia and to have had a broad grasp of Russia's requirements there even if he underestimated the costs and difficulties.[12] He had, we can believe, involved himself wholeheartedly and intelligently in the project on which Peter had sent him and which he was now prepared to continue.

Bering designated his second set of proposals "A most humble plan, not on command [i.e., unsolicited], should the intention begin to take form to send out an expedition especially from Kamchatka to the east" (Grekov 1960, p. 56; Andreev 1943a, p. 12). Paragraphs 1, 3, and 5 deal with exploration; paragraphs 2 and 4, with logistics and cost. They are translated as follows:

> 1. While exploring I discovered that farther east the ocean waves rose lower and also that large pine trees which do not grow in Kamchatka had been thrown ashore on Karaginskii Island.[13] From this I concluded that America, or other lands lying this side of it, would be not very far from Kamchatka, perhaps 150 or 200 miles. If this is indeed so, then it will be possible to establish trade with the lands discovered there, to the advantage of the Russian Empire. It will be possible to search for this route directly if a vessel is built of a size, for example, of 40 or 50 lasts [80 or 100 tons].

11. Pokrovskii (*EB*, p. 16) is an exception.

12. Andreev 1943a, p. 14; Grekov 1960, p. 56; Bodnarskii 1947, p. 122; Znamenskii 1929, p. 8; cf. Divin 1957, pp. 157–75. To what extent Chirikov contributed to Bering's proposals is not known. He had probably the best analytical mind among the top three: Bering, Spanberg, and himself. After the Second Kamchatka Expedition, in 1746, he was asked by the Admiralty College to submit his views on strengthening the defense of the far east (Divin 1953, pp. 207–23; see chap. 7, n. 28).

13. Müller (1758a, p. 67; 1758b, 7:208) explains that these "large beams of pine and fir" were used by the inhabitants in building their winter dwellings.

2. This vessel ought to be built in Kamchatka because the timber needed for construction can be obtained there in quantity and suitability better than elsewhere. Besides, fish and hunted animals can be more readily and cheaply obtained there as food for the workers, and more help can be obtained from the Kamchadals than from the inhabitants at Okhotsk. Furthermore, vessels can sail better on the Kamchatka River because of its depth than on the Okhota River.[14]

3. It would not be without advantage to explore the water passage from Okhotsk or Kamchatka to the mouth of the Amur River and farther to the Japanese Islands. I have the hope that noted places[15] can be found there and trade established with them. Also if the possibility of carrying on trade with Japan permits, no small profit may develop for the Russian empire in the future. Because of the lack of vessels [coming?] from these places any Japanese vessel that might be met could be seized.[16] For this [undertaking] a vessel of the same size as that mentioned above, or even a smaller one, could be built in Kamchatka.

4. The expenses for this expedition, except for salaries and provisions, as well as the materials for both vessels which can not be obtained there, but would have to be transported from Siberia could, with transportation, amount to ten or twelve thousand rubles.

5. If it is considered desirable, it is possible to explore unhindered the northern lands or the coast of Siberia from the mouth of the Ob River to the Enisei and from there to the Lena River in boats or by land because these lands are under the high authority of the Russian empire.[17]

The evidence that convinced Bering land was to be found not far east of Kamchatka is told in more detail by Delisle, who was drawn into the planning of Bering's second voyage. In his memoir "Explication de la carte de la mer orientale dressée pour montrer le plus court chemin de l'Asie à l'Amerique," which he read before the Academy of Sciences and presented to the Senate, he listed these observations by Bering:

1. That by moving away from the coast [of Kamchatka] he found only the small depth and low waves which are customary in narrow seas, much different from the high waves which occur along the coasts facing a vast ocean.

2. That he found pine and other trees which did not grow in Kamchatka ripped out by the roots and carried by an east wind.

3. That he learned from natives that the wind could bring the ice in two or three days, but that the wind had to blow four or five days from the west to carry the ice away from the shore in northeast Asia.

4. That every year birds in pretty much the same months fly from the east and after spending several months on the shores of Asia return also pretty much at the customary time.[18]

14. Actually the vessels were built at Okhotsk and then moved to Avacha Bay (Petropavlovsk) preparatory to sailing to America.

15. Grekov (1960, p. 56) translates it as "rich;" Lensen (1959, p. 45), as "suitable."

16. Probably Bering means that such a vessel might forcibly be detoured to a Russian port for an exchange of goods rather than captured (Baer 1872, p. 63, n. 1.)

17. Sokolov 1851b, pp. 435–36; Vakhtin 1890, pp. 109–10. Golder's translation (1922, p. 26), repeated by Tompkins (1945, p. 28), is inaccurate in places.

18. 1752, pp. 5–6; also in Golder 1914, pp. 304 (French original) and 305 (English translation); Divin 1953, p. 55.

Müller gives essentially the same information and adds that it was concluded from this evidence that the "continent" which lay opposite the Chukotsk Peninsula stretched south past Kamchatka, that the land situated east of Kamchatka and the Chukotsk Peninsula was not just a big island, but the continent of North America itself.[19]

III

Certain Soviet and American scholars who hold the traditional view of the purpose of Bering's first voyage see in these proposals an attempt by Bering to get another chance to settle the geographical question he was accused of failing to solve and to establish with finality the relationship of Asia to America. Berg writes that the Senate was not assured regarding the separation of Asia and America, that Bering recognized his failure to answer the question fully, that his voyage had not obtained data that permitted an answer as to how far America is from Asia, and that accordingly Bering proposed an expedition to find America, which he believed to be not far from Asia (1946, pp. 119–20; cf. 1942, pp. 7–8). Ogloblin, Andreev, Gnucheva, and Nordenskiöld express similar views.[20] G. V. Ianikov states that full assurance of the separation of America from Asia was lacking; that Bering, not seeing the coast of America, did not suspect he had passed through the strait separating the two continents; and that recognizing his failure to fulfill the assignment set for him, he advanced his proposals (1949, pp. 15–16). Golder and Tompkins go further and see Bering's proposals as a petition for a chance to redeem himself. Golder expresses his views quite forcefully:

> Soon after his arrival at the capital Bering submitted his report to the empress and Admiralty College . . . and Senate. The account of his achievement did not elicit any great amount of praise. Many called his mission a failure, saying that at the most he merely determined the northern limits of Kamchatka. His superiors, at least a number of them, held a similar view. . . [1914, p. 165]. The doubters maintained that as long as the coast and the waters between the Kolyma River and East Cape were unexamined the problem of the relation of Asia to America was unsolved. . . . They called attention to the numerous Siberian rumors that a large body of land (*bolshaya zemlya*) existed north of the Kolyma River and another east of the East Cape. Were these two or more distinct continents or islands or were they one? Were they part of Asia or America? . . . Bering was expected to answer [these questions] but could not answer them satisfactorily [1922, p. 25].

19. 1758a, pp. 66–69; 1758b, 7:207–9. He also mentions the report of a "foreign" native in 1715 who had lived in Kamchatka and who had come to Karaginskii Island from a land to the east where tall cedar trees grew with nuts unlike those in Kamchatka and from which big rivers emptied into the Kamchatka Sea (Pacific Ocean). He had fled to Kamchatka after his companions had been killed on Karaginskii Island.

20. Ogloblin 1890, p. 30; Andreev 1943a, p. 11; Gnucheva, ed. 1940, p. 39; Nordenskiöld 1881, 2:182–83.

Further on, Golder also states that the important question the Second Kamchatka Expedition, like the first one, was to answer—its *raison d'être*—was whether Asia and America are united.[21] Tompkins, somewhat hyperbolically, avers that Bering was stung by a sense of failure to settle the geographical question, and in an act of self-exculpation he recommended and offered further exploration, a series of voyages that would end all uncertainty. His most striking proposal, writes Tompkins, was to push boldly into the uncharted waste of the Pacific in search of the American continent.[22]

There are ambiguities and unexplained lacunae in the statements of these men, in part because they have not considered the objectives of the American expedition apart from the objectives of the Second Kamchatka Expedition in the aggregate. How sailing east to find America would answer the question of a land connection between Asia and America farther north is not said. Whether the voyage to Japan was intended to help answer the question, and if so, how, are not explained. These men recognized that some of the objectives of the Second Kamchatka Expedition were added by the Senate, but whether or not and how they grew out of Bering's proposals they do not make clear. And to say that Bering proposed to strike boldly into the wastes of the Pacific is to imply that Bering knew a vast ocean lay ahead of him when in fact he had first expected to sail only a couple of hundred miles or so to reach America (cf. *PSZ*, vol. 8, no. 6042, p. 774). Moreover, in arguing that Bering was in considerable disfavor at St. Petersburg because of his "failure," Golder is hard put to justify Bering's promotion to the rank of captain-commander, the fourth highest rank in the imperial navy, "by highest command" and the payment to him of a reward of 1,000 rubles, twice the amount

21. 1914, p. 248; 1922, p. 328. In fairness to Golder it should be noted that at one point he makes a passing bow to the presence of other motives behind Bering's second voyage: "The desire to determine the relation of Asia and America was not the only argument advanced in favor of the expedition. Some of the reports on that subject submitted to the Empress pointed out the benefits to be derived from territorial and commercial expansion, additional naval bases, and the discovery of precious metals. No doubt all these reasons had their weight with those in authority" (1922, p. 26). But Golder sees solution of the geographical question as paramount and goes no further. He brushes aside the other benefits to be derived from commercial and territorial expansion as secondary and never once considers that these benefits might be the real reason for the voyage rather than "the efforts of the Russians to determine the relation of Asia and America." Golder's case is a good illustration of the degree to which the traditional view of Bering's voyages, especially the first, had so pointed minds in one direction that other directions were not noticed.

22. 1945, pp. 27–28; Tompkins and Moorhead 1949, pp. 56–57. Sokolov, whose account of the Northern Expedition is still a basic one because of his use of material in the Marine Archives (Andreev 1943a, p. 16), was content to note Bering's proposals and to add that a combination of circumstances—a peaceful reign, the presence of strong proponents of learning in the State Cabinet and Admiralty College and of foreign academicians anxious to study their new country—made it possible not only to gain acceptance of Bering's proposals, but to broaden them (1851b, p. 203).

usually paid to captains who had commanded on distant voyages.[23] He also ignores the fact that the Senate thought well enough of Bering's first set of proposals to adopt them.

Other writers have eschewed any failure-and-redemption explanation and have seen Bering's proposals as recommending further and expanded exploration of the North Pacific.[24] Though they do not ignore such ulterior motives as trade and mineral wealth, such writers have not made much of them.[25] The emphasis is on the exploration Bering proposed, presumably to clear up the questions raised by Bering's first and inconclusive voyage. Others go somewhat further. Mitrofan S. Bodnarskii and S. Znamenskii, who give Bering much of the credit for initiating the Second Kamchatka Expedition, see him as a man of broad vision who understood the need to make a wider swing in order to solve the great problems: that of sailing across the Pacific and following the contra-positioned American coast, that of completing the search for the route to the nearest neighbor, Japan, and that of surveying the Arctic coast of Siberia.[26] Belov insists that there were political and economic considerations of long-standing concern behind the mounting of the expedition (1956, p. 265). Bancroft expressed the opinion that the Russians wished to know more of the vast undiscovered region from Cape Mendocino to the Strait of Anian in the hope that it might yield valuable metals (1886, pp. 44–45). That the Senate expanded Bering's proposals is generally noted too. Nevertheless, such recognition of larger purposes has not been followed by an examination in depth of his proposals for the Second Kamchatka Expedition, and for that matter, of the elaboration of them by the central authorities at St. Petersburg. It is, therefore, with the failure-and-redemption thesis and the less than thorough explanation of the origins of the expedition in mind that we turn now to look at Bering's proposed explorations.

IV

In the first paragraph of his second set of proposals, recommending a voyage to America,[27] Bering is quite explicit about the purpose or objective

23. *Materialy dlia istorii russkago flota*, 7:307–8; Imperatorskoe russkoe istoricheskoe obshchestvo 1898, pp. 288, 290. Bering's junior officers also received promotions (Andreev 1943a, p. 1; Grekov 1960, p. 343, n. 43). Müller (1753, p. 60; 1754, pp. 11–12) reports that the promotions were the reward given Bering and his officers for offering their services for the second expedition.

24. Andreev 1943a, pp. 11–12; Sokolov 1851b, pp. 190–91; Lauridsen 1889, p. 62; Müller, 1758a, p. 138; 1758b, 8:9–10; Nordenskiöld 1881, 2:182–83.

25. E.g., Stejneger 1936, p. 236; Lebedev 1957, p. 193; Lebedev and Esakov 1971, p. 199.

26. Bodnarskii 1947, p. 122; Znamenskii 1929, pp. 83–84. The three paragraphs on p. 122 of the former are identical with three paragraphs on pp. 83–84 of the latter.

27. To avoid any confusion with the first set of proposals, I refer hereafter to the individual proposals of the second set as recommendations.

of such a voyage: finding the way to America so as to establish trade with its inhabitants. He says nothing that can be interpreted as an indication of interest in the geographical question for its own sake, of seeking to determine the relationship between the two continents or charting the American coast. Obviously, if he found the route to America, it would help reveal that relationship, but scientific inquiry does not appear to have been Bering's concern, certainly not his primary concern, despite the fact that he had been criticized in St. Petersburg and Moscow for not displaying enough of such interest on the first voyage. Müller's statement that "the intention of the first expedition did not come under discussion again here [i.e., in the Second Kamchatka Expedition] because by then it was considered as already fulfilled" (1758a, p. 138; 1758b, 8:9) appears to confirm this conclusion, though his statement is contradicted in article 2 in the Senate's report to the empress, which is devoted to plans for Arctic exploration (see chap. 6, sec. IV). Manifestly Bering's first recommendation is a suggestion to undertake for a second time the effort he made tentatively in June 1729 to reach Peter's objective, America, by sailing east, this time with more adequate means— two vessels, each larger than the *Sviatoi Gavriil*.[28] The second voyage would fulfill Peter's instructions as the first one had not (Polevoi 1964a, p. 92). And if trade was the objective Bering set forth now, is it not reasonable to conclude that he did so because he understood this to have been Peter's purpose in sending him to find the route to America in the first place?

The third paragraph of Bering's recommendations, about discovery of the route to Japan, does not appear to be designed to clarify the relationship between Asia and America. In fact, there is evidence that indicates he developed the idea of this recommendation before his first voyage: in response to the great interest in developing trade with Japan expressed to him by Kozyrevskii during their meeting at Iakutsk in 1726, Bering promised that on his return to St. Petersburg he would broach there the matter of exploration toward Japan.[29] Conceivably such a voyage might clear up the uncertainties about such islands as Company Land and State Island, but not the questions whether Asia and America are connected or how far America is from Asia. There is, however, no hint in Bering's recommendation of such an objective. On the contrary, Bering states quite clearly why he advocates search for the route to Japan: not to clarify the geographical questions, but to

28. Bering's vessel on his second voyage, the *Sviatoi Petr*, was 80 feet long and 20 feet wide with a draft of 9½ feet; it carried a complement of 76 men, 102 barrels of waters, and more than 150 tons (6000 puds) of freight. Chirikov's vessel, the *Sviatoi Pavel*, was almost identical in these respects. The *Sviatoi Gavriil* was 60 feet by 20 feet with a draft of 7 feet, and carried 44 crew members and 23 barrels of water (Golder 1914, pp. 140, 178; 1922, pp. 34, 48, 341; Berg 1946, p. 188; Grekov 1960, pp. 28, 110; Berkh 1823b, p. 46).

29. Sgibnev 1869a, p. 43; Znamenskii 1929, pp. 74–76; Lensen 1959, p. 44; Polonskii 1871, pp. 396–97, 398.

open up trade with that country. His preoccupation with the development of trade is unequivocal in both the first and third paragraphs.

The recommendation in the fifth paragraph, exploration of the Arctic coast of Siberia, is on first reading not so clear in its intention. It can be seen as being directed toward settling the question of a land connection between the two continents, as Baer so interpreted it (1849, p. 242; 1872, pp. 63–64) and as later it was indeed expanded to do. Golder characterized the recommendation as a "weak and half-hearted suggestion," which it was, if, as Golder seemed to think, it was aimed at solution of the geographical question (1914, p. 169). But there is no indication that such was Bering's intent. It was not as weak and halfhearted a suggestion as Golder thought.

What Bering proposed was the exploration not of all the Arctic coast of Siberia, but only of that portion between the Ob and Lena rivers. He says nothing about exploring the coast east of the Lena River, let alone east of the Kolyma River. It was this latter stretch of coast, to the point of land last seen by Bering in August 1728 on his northbound voyage, that would have to be explored if the separation of the two continents was to be proved or disproved conclusively—the point Chirikov had made in his 13 August statement. What Bering had in mind was something else. As the Senate later stated in article 2 of its report to the empress in December 1732, several parts of the route between the Ob and the Lena were not known.[30] Bering perhaps first became aware of this during his visit to Arkhangelsk in 1719. Also, it was a stretch of coast that the Russians controlled and as such could be surveyed safely or, as Bering notes, "unhindered." On the other hand we have evidence that he believed the coast east of the Lena, at least part of it, unsafe for exploration. Chirikov later pointed out that the stretch from the Kolyma River to the Chukotskii Nos was controlled by the hostile Chukchi (*EB*, 206), a people to whose dubious mercies Bering had been unwilling to expose his crew and vessel over the winter of 1728–29. Had Bering had in mind charting the coast east of the Lena or Kolyma, he would hardly, under these circumstances, have suggested exploration by land as an alternative as he did in the case of the Ob–Lena sector. Bering's recommendation, it becomes evident, was not directed primarily toward a solution of the geographical question.

There is another, but unspecified, reason why Bering did not include the Lena–East Cape sector in his recommendation. As we saw in the last chapter, Bering had become convinced on the basis of what he had learned at Iakutsk and from the Chukchi that there was a water passage between the Chukotskii Nos and the Lena, that Asia was not connected with another continent. Moreover, among the things he must have also learned at Iakutsk is that on several occasions from the 1630s to the end of the seventeenth

---

30. See chapter 6, section IV; *PSZ*, vol. 8, no. 6291, p. 1005; cf. Lomonosov 1952, pp. 119–20; Vize 1949, pp. 92, 93.

century Russians had sailed in kochi (deckless sailboats) from the mouth of the Lena as far east as the Kolyma.[31] This knowledge and the Chukchi report of a water route from East Cape to the Kolyma and the report of the voyage from the Lena to Kamchatka were sufficient evidence for Bering that there was no need to survey the part of the coast east of the Kolyma. His recommendation, then, instead of being aimed at solution of the geographical question that he had allegedly been sent originally to answer, was made on the assumption that the question had been answered; it was directed toward another objective.

In proposing voyages to America and Japan, Bering is quite clear as to the goal to be reached—opening of trade with the inhabitants of those countries. But he says nothing comparable about the exploration of the Ob–Lena segment of the Siberian coast. For all he says, his proposal could be interpreted as being intended to serve scientific curiosity; but the most likely purpose is that mentioned in article 2 of the report of 28 December 1732, that is, finding a northern sea route to the Pacific. We have earlier noted (see chap. 2, middle of sec. I) that this was an idea abroad in official circles, exemplified in the Saltykov proposals, in Peter's remark to John Perry, and in the report in 1719 of the French ambassador Compredon. Bering himself had had firsthand experience with the difficulties and expense involved in reaching the Pacific coast by land across Siberia. The Dutch and English efforts to find a northeast passage were known to Bering and the others, and the Russians themselves had long sailed the Arctic coast from the White Sea to the Iamal Peninsula. Bering had evidence convincing him that the Lena–Kamchatka water route existed. All that remained to be determined was the Ob–Lena segment. Even if the Iamal Peninsula west of the Ob Gulf proved difficult or impossible to circumnavigate, the finding of a water route from that gulf to the North Pacific would, it was believed in ignorance of the formidable obstacles to Arctic navigation, circumvent several thousand miles of time-consuming and burdensome transport in Siberia. A water route to the North Pacific would greatly facilitate the trade with America and Japan which Bering hoped would follow from the success of the other two voyages he was proposing. Perhaps this is why he placed this recommendation last rather than first, as he could be expected to have done if vindication of his discovery of the separateness of the two continents had in fact been his intent. But neither vindication nor scientific-geographic goals were what Bering had in mind. His objectives were pragmatic and economic. Thus the failure-and-redemption thesis turns out to be without substance, and our conclusion developed in the two preceding chapters that the purpose of the first voyage was to find the route to America is not contradicted.

31. Belov (1956, pp. 328–29) in a list of voyages between the Lena and points east notes sixteen between the Lena and Kolyma in the period 1633–89. Vize (1948, p. 70) notes twenty-four in the period 1633–1702.

6

The Second Kamchatka Expedition:
Plans and Objectives

BERING'S RECOMMENDATIONS tell us what he had in mind regarding a second voyage and suggest what he understood the objective of his first voyage to have been, but they do not tell us how the officials in the Admiralty College and Senate viewed the goals of his second voyage and of the Second Kamchatka Expedition. It was they who officially set the objectives and determined the scope of the Second Kamchatka Expedition. It is with those objectives relating to Bering's second voyage, to the American expedition, that this chapter will deal.

I

The role of the Senate and Admiralty College was central in the planning of Bering's second voyage and the rest of the Second Kamchatka Expedition, as it had not been for his first voyage (cf. *PSZ*, vol. 8, no. 6291, art. 1). Bering's first voyage had been conceived and initiated by Peter, to the extent that he himself wrote the instructions for it, though his failing health and death precluded any further connection with the enterprise. His successors, particularly the first two, his widow Catherine I and his young grandson Peter II, reigned rather than ruled. Neither they nor Anna (1730–40), who was empress for most of the period of the Second Kamchatka Expedition, were initiators and movers like Peter the Great. It fell accordingly to certain men of state affairs to push the project and set its goals, and to sustain it during its later difficult days. Three men in particular were the main shapers of the Second Kamchatka Expedition. They were Andrei I. Osterman, the founder and dominant member of the Empress Anna's three-man Cabinet of Ministers; Count Nikolai F. Golovin, vice-admiral and a member of the Admiralty College and after April 1733 admiral and its president; and Ivan K. Kirilov, senior secretary of the Administrative Senate, the body where the effective, though not formal, final decisions were made (Andreev 1943a, p. 13; 1944a, p. 61; *EB*, p. 17). These men had risen to positions of influence and authority under Peter, and one can believe that something of the boldness and sweep of concept that characterized many of Peter's undertakings and his concern for the advancement of Russia had rubbed off on them. One may not be able to document Peter's influence on the Second Kamchatka Expedition, but one senses strongly that it was there (cf. Sokolov 1851b, p. 203).

Osterman's role appears to have been not so much that of active planner as of advocate for the project before the throne through his membership in the Cabinet. That he believed in it wholeheartedly is evidenced by the support he gave Bering in later phases of the Second Kamchatka Expedition when Bering came under strong criticism because the expedition was taking so long to mount (Andreev 1943a, p. 13; Grekov 1960, p. 69; *EB*, p. 40). It was the Cabinet that in March 1732 commissioned the Senate to examine Bering's second set of proposals (Grekov 1960, p. 57), and it was the Cabinet that approved the final plans. Obviously Osterman was best placed of the three men to obtain "highest" approval.

It is more to Golovin and Kirilov that one looks for the shaping of the Second Kamchatka Expedition. They were the active planners, as well as advocates before higher authority. The initial stage of the planning for the expedition itself, as we have noted, occurred in the early months of 1732. At that time Golovin was still a year away from elevation to presidency of the Admiralty College, a position to which he was appointed in April 1733 and in which he served until his death in 1745 (*EB*, p. 17; Amburger 1966, p. 350), but the position had not been filled since the death of Admiral Apraksin in 1728, and Golovin stood high in the college, being appointed to a special commission in January 1732 to study and reorganize the navy and being made inspector-general of the navy and admiralty in April. He brought to that department a background of experience abroad, for he had visited the Netherlands in 1708, had spent eight years in England where he served in the British navy and assisted Saltykov in the purchase of vessels, and had served six years as ambassador to Sweden before joining the Admiralty College. His appointment to its presidency indicates he had played a leading role in its affairs.[1] His role in the planning of the Second Kamchatka Expedition is less clear than in the execution of the plans; in this area he was a staunch backer of Bering during his many moments of travail and exposure to criticism in Siberia—evidence of Golovin's strong commitment to the expedition (Andreev 1943a, p. 13). It is believed that the Admiralty College reflected his ideas when it expanded Bering's recommendation of a survey of the Ob–Lena section of the Arctic coast to include the whole Arctic coast

1. Amburger 1966, pp. 349, 350, 443; *Materialy dlia istorii russkago flota*, 7:273–74; *Entsiklopedicheskii slovar'*, vol. 10, chast' 1, 71.

from the White Sea in the west to the tip of the Chukotsk Peninsula and south to Kamchatka.[2] His association with Saltykov may well have led to an interest in such a passage (Grekov 1960, p. 349, n. 10; Ianikov 1949, p. 138). We know that in October 1732 Golovin proposed sending a naval supply expedition from Kronshtadt to Kamchatka to support Bering's activities there, though it was not approved. The memorandum in which he advanced the proposal reveals his bold and sweeping intentions for advancing Russian interests in the Pacific.[3]

Of the three men, however, it is Kirilov who appears to have had the most to do with giving form and substance not only to the enterprises recommended in Bering's second set of proposals, but also to the recommendations in the first set. Müller tells us that Kirilov was the "foremost moving force" in the Second Kamchatka Expedition, that he "worked especially hard in this matter so that the expedition could quickly achieve the desired success,"[4] and that he drew Bering into the planning. The Soviet scholar Andreev, after examining much of the correspondence in the archives concerning the planning of the expedition, confirms Müller's appraisal of Kirilov's role (1965, p. 63; 1944a, pp. 56–57). Too, it was Kirilov who wrote a memorandum about the Second Kamchatka Expedition which tells us more than any other source the purposes behind it, as we shall see later (see this chap., end of sec. II, and app. 2).

Kirilov was one of those able men of uncertain social origin who were drawn into service around Peter and rose to high position. He combined unusual ability with inexhaustible energy, varied interests, and wide knowledge; for his time he was a well-educated man, even though largely self-taught. Entering the chancellery of the Senate as a clerk, by 1727 he had been advanced to senior secretary of the body. His service there brought him into contact with Peter the Great, whose influence on him was strong. In 1727 he was also made secretary of the new Commission of Commerce established by the Supreme Privy Council and headed by Osterman. In these two posts he gained a diversified experience and familiarity with the problems and resources of the state. His particular interests were geography and cartography, especially of Siberia, Tartary, "Edso-Land," Kamchatka, India, and Persia. He was put in charge of the center for topography set up by the Senate in 1720 to begin a survey of the country, and he guided the

2. Grekov 1960, p. 62. Beaglehole (Cook 1967, pp. l-li) refers to one Cramond, a retired English merchant who had traded in Russia and Persia and who had been struck with the "Probability (I say Certainty)" of a northeast passage in 1730. Cramond had learned from "Count Gallowin, first lord of their Admiralty" of the Russians' determination to find it, "being assured by the Inhabitants of the Rivers in the North Sea that their Ancestors had frequently [!] gone through the Streights of Anian round to Kamchatka."

3. Divin 1953, pp. 66–71; Berg 1946, p. 122. Described at the end of the next section.

4. 1758a, pp. 138–39; 1758b, 8:10; *Materialy dlia istorii Akademii nauk*, 6:253.

work of the first Russian geodesists and the publication of their maps. We mentioned in chapter 3, Kirilov's map of Eastern Siberia and Kamchatka of 1724, and he was the prime mover in the preparation and publication of the "Atlas of the Russian Empire" of 1734, the first Russian atlas (Fel' 1960, pp. 148–70). Through such activity he became acquainted with the problems of the frontier areas of the empire (Donnelly 1968, p. 59). Like Peter, he was much interested in the extension of trade with other countries and with the acquisition of additional natural resources. At the time of his death in 1737 he was commander of the expedition that founded Orenburg and extended Russian rule over Bashkiriia, a position to which he had been appointed in 1734.[5] Given his experience and interests, it was natural for him to have become involved in the Second Kamchatka Expedition; and even though his association with it was not as long as that of Osterman and Golovin, his formative influence on it was great.[6]

In the hands of Kirilov and others Bering's second set of proposals was considerably expanded. We have already noted that Bering's suggestion of charting the coast from the Ob to the Lena was extended to include almost all of Russia's Arctic coast. The voyage to America was to be made in two vessels instead of one and was to be directed to a search for the islands believed to lie east and southeast of Kamchatka. Not only was the route to Japan to be sought, but all of the Kurile Islands were to be explored; and for this not one, but three vessels were to be built. In addition to the coast south of Okhotsk to the Amur River and the Shantarskie Islands, the rivers east of Lake Baikal were to be surveyed in the hope of finding a shorter route to the "Kamchatka Sea." And the Academy of Sciences was asked to survey the human and natural resources of Siberia, as well as to assist in planning Bering's route to America. Thus did Bering's superiors accept and enlarge his proposals. Parenthetically, one is constrained to comment that here is evidence that Bering's thinking was quite in harmony with that of the officials at St. Petersburg—evidence that belies the conclusion of Golder and others that Bering was rather out of favor with them for his supposed failure to settle the geographical question of the relation of Asia to America. Indeed, the planners turned to Bering for advice and counsel.

II

To understand what these men in the Senate and Admiralty College and their staffs sought to achieve through Bering's second voyage we do best to begin with the Senate's report of 28 December 1732 to the Empress Anna.

5. Donnelly (1968, chap. 6) gives an account of this part of his activities. He died from tuberculosis (Novlianskaia 1964:116).

6. Novlianskaia 1964, pp. 7, 11–17, and *passim.* Her short biography helps to rescue Kirilov from a relative obscurity not justified by his achievements. See also Andreev 1965, pp. 12–13.

Articles 4, 6, and 11 of that report are the ones with which we are particularly concerned. Article 6, which we examine first, deals with Bering's voyage or the American expedition alone; articles 4 and 11 deal with it and with
the other voyages as well.[7]

> 6. Inasmuch as Captain Pavlutskii stated in his latest report [26 November 1730]
> from Kamchtka that serviceman Afanasii Mel'nikov,[8] who returned from the
> Chukotsk Peninsula, having been sent there from Iakutsk in 1725 to seek out and
> subject unconquered natives to the payment of tribute, reported that in April 1730
> when he was on the Chukotsk Peninsula, two men who had [pieces of] walrus teeth
> inserted [in their faces] near their own teeth, came to the Chukchi on the penin-
> sula from an island, and they told him that it is one day's journey from the
> Chukotsk Peninsula to their home island on which they have their dwellings, and
> that it is also one day's journey from this island to another one which is called the
> Big Land, where there are all kinds of animals—sables, foxes, beavers, wolverines,
> lynxes, wild deer—and where there are also forests of all kinds and a sufficient
> number of reindeer natives and "foot" natives. Although it is impossible to confirm
> such reports, nevertheless on the voyage inquiry is to be made of the Chukchi, and
> [the vessels] are to go to these islands if they are in fact on the route to America.
> Upon arrival [the Russians] are to behave with respect to the natives and other
> matters according to article 4. Then they are to sail to America and en route to look
> for islands and land, for there is no information beyond Pavlutskii's whether there
> are islands and land between the known Kamchatka coast and the American coast
> or only the ocean, which on the map made by Professor Delisle extends from the
> above-mentioned Chukotsk Peninsula about 45 degrees to the Spanish possession
> of the Province of Mexico.[9] When [the expedition] reaches the coast of America,
> then in accordance with the instructions of His Imperial Majesty Peter the Great
> given to Captain Bering in 1725 it is to go to a city or settlement of a European
> sovereign, or if it encounters a European vessel, it is to find out from it the name of
> the coast and to put it down on paper and to go ashore. Having obtained authentic
> information and having plotted it on a map, [the expedition] is to return to the
> coast of Kamchatka, meanwhile searching for other new lands or islands and being
> very much on guard so as not to fall into the hands of others and reveal to them the
> route to our country, which they have never heard of before [PSZ, vol. 8, no. 6291,
> p. 1007].

Although article 4 relates primarily to the exploration of the section of the
Arctic coast east of the Lena and Kolyma rivers, it contains a statement about
the treatment of natives wherever discovered, as indicated in article 6. The
article is therefore germane to the American expedition. It reads as follows:

7. Articles 4, 6, and 11 of the instructions of the Senate to the Admiralty College of 31
December 1732 are identical with the same numbered articles in the report (EB, pp. 92–93,
93–94, 96–97).

8. Regarding Mel'nikov's journey and report see Sgibnev 1868, pp. 138–39; Imperatorskoe
russkoe istoricheskoe obshchestvo 1899, p. 207; Grekov 1960, p. 54; Efimov 1950, pp. 154–55.
His report is the third such concerning the islands and Big Land to the east of the Chukotsk
Peninsula, after those of Popov (1711) and Tatarinov (1718).

9. On this map the American coast is sketched from 15° to only 45° north latitude. It is not
shown in figure 31, which is a detail from the larger map, a map discussed in the next section.

4. There is indicated on the map an island in the Northern Sea opposite the mouth of the Kolyma River, which is reported to be presumably a big land. Some Siberians used to go there and saw people on it. Bering and his associates are to find out about it for certain in Iakutsk, and if it is true or they observe other islands and land from the sloops sent out to sea, they are to land on them and explore them as much as possible. If people are found there, they are to be treated kindly and in no way antagonized. They are to find out how big those islands and lands are and in what direction they extend, and upon what [the natives] subsist. Further, looking for an opportunity to extend the kindest treatment, [the Russians] are to give them small gifts, which according to Siberian custom are given to the chieftains and other natives in such first encounters. Should they wish of their own will to become our subjects, they are to be accepted as such. They should be treated especially with kindness and if necessary given protection and not burdened in any way. Unless they allocate tribute among themselves and begin to pay it of their own accord, [the Russians], however, are not to linger long because of this, but to depart in order not to lose by delay the time favorable for navigation . . . [*PSZ*, vol. 8, no. 6291, p. 1006].

Article 11 contains instructions for the commanders of all the vessels being sent on voyages:

11. On all the above-mentioned voyages along the new lands and islands look carefully for places suitable for landing and for havens in time of ocean storms or ice, and for places where trees suitable for the repair of vessels grow so that with such information ocean vessels in the future can hope to go to such places safely for refuge and other needs. Further, where it is possible and circumstances permit, the assayers previously mentioned [in article 1] are ordered to examine the land itself with an adequate guard to see if valuable minerals and metals are there. If they are, then the ore should be taken and broken up and in light of expectations and the evidence, large samples made, and such localities in particular described. If there is discovered in localities subject to Russia subsurface wealth which from a large sample gives evidence of profit, notify the commandant at Okhotsk upon return or other commandants elsewhere without letting it be known afar. They are to send in special vessels the artisans sent out [to Siberia], and with them the necessary number of men for protection and work, and tools, supplies, and provisions. In this activity they are to undertake to produce in every way a profit for the benefit and interest of Your Imperial Majesty. When accomplished, this is to be reported to the Senate and the ore samples forwarded [*PSZ*, vol. 8, no. 6291, pp. 1009–10].

Turning our attention back to article 6, we note first that what the officials in the Senate were asking Bering to do was the same, with one major difference, as what Peter had ordered him to do. He was to sail eastward to America, then turn south toward Mexico, and seek a place under European sovereignty, or a European vessel, from which information could be obtained about the west coast of America. But instead of approaching America by sailing along the southern coast of the land which went north, as Peter had indicated, Bering was to sail northeast to the land of the Chukchi, i.e., to the Chukotsk Peninsula, and then east to the Big Land, believed to be the part of America closest to Asia and to be rich in fur-bearing animals. From there he would then proceed to complete the unfinished part of the task assigned to him by Peter. Here is further confirmation of the real intent of Bering's first voyage.

The Senate's instructions, however, go much beyond Peter's and required Bering to undertake other tasks. Bering was not merely to search for the route to America; he was to look for any islands that might lie between Kamchatka and America. These islands and any other new lands discovered were not just to be found and described; their human and natural resources were to be investigated. This we see in all three articles quoted. In article 6 it is noted that the Big Land beyond the island opposite the Chukotsk Peninsula is reported to have all kinds of animals—"sables, foxes, beavers, wolverines, lynxes, wild deer"—and to have "forests of all kinds and a sufficient number of reindeer and foot [sedentary] natives," which the Russians saw as a source of income to be tapped by persuading the natives to pay tribute, in the manner prescribed in article 4. Article 11 required that Bering and the other commanders look for metals and minerals and that the first steps toward their exploitation be taken. In other words, it was intended that the voyages, including Bering's, were to bring material benefits to the state, an intention declared at the beginning in the Senate ukaz of 17 April 1732, which first ordered Bering to Kamchatka and which states that his expedition from there was to be undertaken "for the benefit of the state and the augmenting of Our [the sovereign's] interests" (*PSZ*, vol. 8, no. 6023, p. 749). This purpose was reaffirmed in the second ukaz of 2 May 1732, which calls for attempts to be made "where there are unsubjugated peoples [i.e., aborigines] to effect the collection of tribute, looking to the profit and benefit of the state" (*PSZ*, vol. 8, no. 6042, p. 774). Nothing, it may be added, is said about answering geographical questions.

Bering and the other commanders were given instructions how to go about accomplishing these objectives. In articles 4 and 9 (which we have not quoted) they were told to make efforts to persuade the natives to accept Russian sovereignty and to pay tribute. This was to be done by treating the natives kindly, by refraining from force, and by presenting small gifts to them, especially in exchange for furs. The commanders were to be provided with such items as colorful cloth, glass beads, needles, trinkets of various sorts, and particularly Chinese tobacco, called *shar*, which Bering had observed to be in great demand by the Kamchadals (*PSZ*, vol. 8, no. 6291, pp. 1006, 1009; *EB*, pp. 96, 167). Two thousand rubles were allocated for the purchase of such gifts, which were in fact acquired, part of them going to Iakutsk for use by the Arctic expeditions, the rest to Okhotsk for the Pacific expeditions.[10] In later instructions, the supplementary ones of 16 March 1733 to Bering, the Senate went further and stipulated that in the case of native tribes that accepted Russian rule, nonviolent efforts were to be made to persuade them to give hostages and to send young men to Russia to learn the Russian language.

> 22. When through the good fortune of Her Imperial Majesty you and the other naval officers in the course of sea journeys find new islands and lands subject to no one and the people there, by force of Her Imperial Majesty's exalted ukaz and through your diligent efforts, accept subjection of their own free will, you are to treat them kindly and not to resort to violence or act with brutality but to use persuasion to the end that they will send one of their best men with you to Her Imperial Majesty. You are to explain that they will not be harmed or detained, that above all on the journey both here and back to their country they will be conducted with every convenience and will be rewarded by Her Imperial Majesty's mercy. Further you are to try to obtain such people as are disposed toward this from those young people in your presence who while with you and while travelling are to be persuaded to study the Russian language and to record their language, at least the necessary expressions and the names of things.
>
> 23. If, as mentioned above, such people risk going and you are still occupied with your own business, do not detain them long, but as soon as you reach our Kamchatka outposts or other inhabited places, turn them over to the local commandant for immediate despatch to Siberia and Moscow, providing written instructions as to how to conduct them from place to place and to meet their needs, taking into account their eminence and inclination. However, besides this there should be put in charge all the way to Moscow one or two of your men who in dealing with them can accustom them to the above indicated study, expressions, and writings [*EB*, p. 149; *PSZ*, vol. 9, no. 6351, pp. 68–69].

These procedures stipulated by the instructions were, it should be observed, not new. The same or similar procedures are outlined in the instructions from the officials in Moscow to the men in the field in the course of the conquest of Siberia in the seventeenth century. The search for "new lands" to be brought under the "exalted hand of the sovereign" to the end of making a "profit" for him was a constant. Tribute in furs was to be imposed and hostages to be taken from among the "best" men of the tribe to assure its payment. Where the possibility of subjugation of the natives by force was minimal or absent, as in the case of nomadic natives who could not be pinned down to a given locality, peaceful persuasion was to be used, reinforced by the giving of gifts. Because the Russian exploratory maritime expeditions would be poorly placed to use force against reluctant natives, it was this latter technique of persuasion that the planners in St. Petersburg envisaged

10. *EB*, pp. 167–68, 389, para. 7. A list of items for gifts is given in ibid., p. 377; cf. p. 376, n. 16.

in the forthcoming expeditions. Like the instructions to Bering, those of the seventeenth century stress kind and fair treatment of the natives, from a sense of enlightened self-interest—instructions unfortunately honored in the breach as much as in the practice. To anyone acquainted with the Russian administration of and relations with the natives in the conquest of Siberia, the foregoing instructions to Bering and his commanders have a very familiar ring.[11]

Another major objective of the several expeditions, set forth in article 11, was the discovery of minerals and precious metals. In article 1 of the report, as well as in article 15 of the Senate's instructions of 16 March 1733 to Bering, it was stipulated that two or three assayers were to be sent from the metallurgical works at Ekaterinburg in the Urals to eastern Siberia, in addition to another assayer named Simon Gardebol', who had been sent to Kamchatka in 1727 with Captain Dmitrii I. Pavlutskii. These men were to be assigned where needed in the several parts of the Second Kamchatka Expedition.[12] Actually none of these men was available in 1741 when preparations for Bering's second voyage were nearing completion, so he asked Georg W. Steller, the noted German naturalist who had joined the academic section of the Kamchatka Expedition and whose later account of the voyage is one of the principal sources of information about it, to take on the duties of assayer or mineralogist and accompany him on the *Sviatoi Petr* (*EB*, pp. 141–42, 169; Stejneger 1936, p. 236). Bering reported to the empress the appointment of Steller in a document dated 18 April 1741:

> However, Steller, the adjunct in natural history sent from St. Petersburg, is now here, and he has stated in writing that he has the necessary skill in searching for and assaying metals and minerals. For this reason the captain commander and the expedition's officers decided to take Steller with them on the voyage. In this matter Steller stated that besides this he would, in accordance with his responsibility, make various observations on the voyage concerning the natural history, peoples, conditions of the land, etc. If any ores should be found, adjunct Steller will assay them [*EB*, p. 142].

As for Steller himself, he makes clear in his account of the voyage that assaying alone was his official assignment.[13]

11. Fisher 1943, pp. 33–34, 40, 49–61, 71–74; Lantzeff 1943, chap. VI and pp. 123–32; Bakhrushin 1955, pp. 137–60 *passim*; 1959, pp. 45–53. Orlova (1951, pp. 236–38) reproduces an instruction regarding the treatment of natives that is typical of those issued by the Siberian authorities.

12. *PSZ*, vol. 8, no. 6291, p. 1003; vol. 9, no. 6351, p. 67; *EB*, pp. 89, 141–42.

13. Golder 1925, pp. 16, 40–41, 57. Bering saw an additional benefit in Steller's appointment in the latter's ability to serve as his physician, for his health was failing. Steller accepted it because it afforded him an unprecedented opportunity to examine the flora and fauna of the new world, the desire closest to his heart. Most students of the voyage, except Stejneger (1936, pp. 236, 242, 273), have lost sight of the official and primary reason for Steller's presence on the voyage, and even Stejneger missed the full significance of it.

There is another bit of evidence that the search for minerals and metals was one of the expedition's tasks and that it was taken seriously. In a communication of 12 February 1733 to the Admiralty College raising questions about the route to be followed, Chirikov, who was to command the second vessel of the American expedition, remarks:

> There are islands at 67 degrees and higher, but I do not expect that they are habitable because they are cold and unpopulated, and it is unlikely that on these islands real ores can be obtained. It would be better, I confess, to look for islands in America between the 50th and 65th parallels where the climate is suitable for inhabitants and the land may not be empty [*EB*, p. 207].

A final task of the several maritime expeditions is briefly mentioned in the report of 28 December, also in article 11, and again in the Admiralty College's instructions to Bering of 28 February 1733 (article 14) (*EB*, p. 168). The ship commanders were to look for harbors suitable for refuge from storms and for the repair of vessels, in anticipation of continuing contact with the lands to be discovered. This suggests that the planners of the Second Kamchatka Expedition hoped the American expedition, among the others, would provide opportunities in the new lands for future exploitation. In short, the satisfaction of scientific curiosity was secondary or incidental; exploration was to be the means to an end, not the end itself.

In the documents from which the evidence about the objectives of the American expedition is obtained, mention of one objective is conspicuously lacking—trade. Bering himself had advanced trade as the justification for a second attempt to reach America, but the documents issued by the Admiralty College and Senate, with one exception, do not. It is possible that in the earlier stages of planning the officials of the two agencies had trade in mind. In the Senate ukaz of 2 May 1732 ordering Bering again to Kamchatka, his evidence that America is probably not far from Kamchatka is restated and what he had to say about trade is also repeated: ". . . and if this is true, then it is possible to establish trade with the lands discovered there to the profit of the Russian Empre" (*PSZ*, vol. 8, no. 6042, p. 774). In Golovin's memorandum of 1 October 1732 trade is hinted at as desirable.[14] Too, there is a statement in a later document that perhaps suggests trade as an objective. In a request of the Admiralty College to the Senate, dated 16 February 1733, to change certain parts of the instructions to Bering about sailing to America, note is taken that the Spanish colonists do not carry on trade with any other power than Spain without permission from the king (*EB*, p. 30). This might be interpreted to mean that establishment of trade with the Spanish colonies had been intended, but was now seen as futile. It is more likely, however, that this statement was intended to explain that the Russians would meet a

14. Divin 1953, pp. 70–71, citing TsGADA, *f.* Gosarkhiva, *razr.* XXIV, *d.* 8, *l.* 9.

hostile reaction from the Spanish colonial authorities should they enter the latter's waters, and accordingly the effort to do so should not be made.

There was good reason, however, for the Russians not to think in terms of trade with America. We turn again to the ukaz of 2 May, to article 1:

> . . . the Administrative Senate has ordered: in ships which [Bering] is to build he is to go for the purpose of exploring the new lands which lie between America and Kamchatka, also the islands which extend toward Japan from the tip of Kamchatka, and especially the Shantarskie Islands, whose location was mentioned in 1731— going and determining reliably about the establishment of trade, or *where there are unsubjugated peoples, to effect the collection of tribute* [emphasis added], looking to the profit and benefit of the state [*PSZ*, vol. 8, no. 6042, p. 774].

Article 2 of the ukaz orders the search for the route to Japan in order to establish trade with the Japanese and cautions against giving any offense to them. Nothing similar is said in the ukaz about trade with America. In other words, lands inhabited by peoples not subject to any European or Asiatic power and presumably aboriginal in status were to be brought under Russian sovereignty and their economic resources exploited for the benefit of the state by the imposition of tribute in the manner previously described. With such peoples trade would be incidental, but in the case of the lands already under the rule of an established power like Japan or Spain, the imposition of tribute was obviously out of the question, and the benefits to be derived from contact with such lands would have to come through trade. To be sure, though the report of 28 December 1732 anticipated that the American expedition was to go to Mexico, to fulfill Peter's original instructions, the intent seems to have been only for purposes of obtaining information, and this particular destination was later deemed expendable. The areas that the Russians would be exploring prior to reaching Mexico would be aboriginal America, not yet under European jurisdiction. For that area traditional Russian practice would be to install the system of tribute, not to engage in trade between equals. That is why the opening of trade does not appear as an objective of Bering's second voyage.[15]

Thus far in determining the objectives of Bering's second voyage we have depended on documents of collective authorship issued by the Admiralty College and Senate. Two memoranda, one written by Golovin and the other by Kirilov, provide additional evidence confirming our conclusions. Golo-

---

15. Support for this analysis comes from V. A. Miatlev, appointed governor-general of Siberia in 1753. Charged by the Senate with reviving the Second Kamchatka Expedition so as to "discover more unknown lands and to use those acquired," he responded with a proposal for a varied and extensive program, one of whose parts was to obtain "information about the lands found by Bering east of Kamchatka. . . ." "[W]here possible we shall persuade these people to become subjects under the supreme power of H. I. M.; where it will not be possible to persuade them to do this and there is not the strength to compel [them], the conclusion of a commercial treaty with them will be required" (Makarova 1968, pp. 140–41; 1975, pp. 144–45, quoting *Senatskii arkhiv*, vol. 9 [Sanktpeterburg, 1901], p. 103).

vin's memorandum, dated 1 October 1732, is the one that advances the proposal to send a naval expedition, consisting of two frigates and a transport, from Kronshtadt to Kamchatka to supply and reinforce Bering there. In it Golovin expresses his concern over the deterioration of the Russian navy after the recent wars and over the possible threat the Anglo–French rivalry posed for Russia in the North Pacific. He saw in the Second Kamchatka Expedition a valuable means for strengthening Russia's position there. He was concerned lest the British and French, during the six years it would take to mount the American and Japanese expeditions, would strengthen their position there to the disadvantage of Russia. The despatch of two frigates and a transport as a supplementary means of transporting supplies for the expedition would accelerate its preparation and provide training and experience for naval officers and sailors. But most important in relation to our topic, the Russians would be enabled "without danger to go everywhere and look for lands and islands. . . ." If the proposed voyage were successful, Golovin notes, then two frigates should be sent annually not only for training purposes, but "for searching anew for lands, islands, passages, harbors, straits, and the like." And finally, he wrote: "In the exploration of America there may be the following great gains for the state: very rich mines, both gold and silver, are there which are still unknown, [and it is known] what profit the Spanish, English, and Portuguese kingdoms receive and how important the commerce and navigation to these regions are to these kingdoms now."[16]

Kirilov's memorandum was written sometime after the completion of the planning of the Second Kamchatka Expedition, but before May 1734.[17] At the same time that he was involved in planning this expedition, he was also deeply engaged in the planning of the Orenberg expedition to bring Bashkiriia, the region from the southern Ural Mountains to the Ural (Iaik) River, under Russian control (Donnelly 1968, pp. 62, 64, 94–95; Novlianskaia, pp. 101, 120). In his opening paragraph he states: "In the present prosperous reign of our sovereign Empress, by God's mercy and the fates and by her own good fortune, two undertakings are developing not only of great and immortal glory, but *for the expansion of the empire and for inexhaustible wealth* [emphasis added]. The first [and] well known one is the Siberian and Kamchatka expedition. The second [and] still not disclosed one is the Kirghiz-Karakalpak expedition. . . ." Further on he specifies the

16. Divin 1953, pp. 66–71, quoting TsGADA, *f.* Gosarkhiva, *razr.* XXIV, *d.* 8, *ll.* 6–9. Zubov 1954:1943. A photocopy of the "Propositions of Count Golovin" are in *Archives, Russia*, vol. 8, in the library of the University of Washington, Seattle.

17. The memorandum as printed is undated and without addressee. In it Kirilov refers to 1732 as the "past year." The empress responded to it on 1 May 1734, so we may assume it was addressed to her. It was published for the first time, in full, in Dobrosmyslov, ed. 1900, 1:1–49; the Kamchatka portion is in Andreev 1943a, pp. 35–37, and in Efimov 1950, pp. 289–92; and in English translation in appendix 2.

objectives of the Kamchatka expedition, "the like of which there has never been before." They include: "(1) to find out for certain whether it is possible to pass from the Arctic Ocean to the Kamchatka or Southern Sea. . . ; (2) to reach from Kamchatka the very shores of America, to some unknown place at about 45° of longitude; (3) to go from Kamchatka to Japan. . . ; (4) on that voyage and elsewhere *to search for new lands and islands not yet conquered, as many as possible, and to bring them under subjection*; (5) *to search for metals and minerals. . .*" [emphasis added]. Then he goes on to explain the thinking behind the voyage to America:

> The benefit to be expected is that from the eastern side Russia will extend its possessions as far as California and Mexico, athough it would not receive immediately the rich metals which the Spanish have there. However, without preparing for war, we can in time acquire them through kindness, though I know that the Spanish will not be pleased. Besides, the local people are greatly embittered against the Spanish and for that reason have to escape to unknown places farther away (and it appears that there are no other places except closer to us). Here on our side it is firmly established not to embitter such people. . . . To the south all the islands as far as Japan do not really belong to anyone, and already four islands have been brought under subjection by Pavlutskii's command. The same has to be reckoned about Esso and the land called "Company," that they can not escape Russian possession if only the assistance for the present beginning does not slacken in the future. Although God will nowhere disclose in any way what wealth the Japanese have, nonetheless the Japanese will not reject trade here for it is better for them to buy the needed goods from us directly than to repurchase them from the Chinese at higher cost. . . [Andreev 1943a, p. 36; Efimov 1950, pp. 290–91].

These passages from the memoranda of Golovin and Kirilov could hardly be more explicit about the intentions and goals of the leadership in St. Petersburg in organizing the Second Kamchatka Expedition in general and Bering's second voyage in particular. In the case of the second voyage the goal was no less than the beginning of a Russian intrusion into North America: the annexation of territory and the exploitation of the animal and mineral resources to be found there. Whether Bering in proposing voyages to America and Japan and along the Arctic dreamed of more than he proposed we can only speculate, but it is certain that in the hands of such men as Osterman, Golovin, and Kirilov, his proposals had been expanded into undertakings of potentially far-reaching consequences.

III

In the last stages of planning the American expedition, its ultimate destination was changed, and shortly before the expedition was to depart from Kamchatka, the decision about the route to be followed was finally made. Each of these matters in its own way serves to illustrate the pragmatic purposes behind Bering's second voyage.

It was Chirikov who nudged the Admiralty College and Senate into changing the intended final destination of the expedition. Of the two commanders
assigned to the American expedition he exhibited the more scholarly turn of
mind and scientific curiosity. Bering was more concerned with the administrative and logistical problems of the several components of the Second
Kamchatka Expedition (*EB*, pp. 17–18; Lebedev 1951, p. 20). Chirikov
found the instructions from the Admiralty College and Senate regarding the
route to be followed on the voyage less than clear and even contradictory.
According to article 6 of the Senate's report of 28 December 1732, the
expedition was to sail to the Chukotsk Peninsula, look for the islands opposite it and for America, and then to proceed to Mexico, a place of European
possession,[18] whereas later instructions, from the Admiralty College, called
for sailing northeast to 67° north latitude or farther.[19] Under date of 12
February 1733, Chirikov submitted a memorandum to the college in which
he called attention to this inconsistency, noting that the distance from the
"Chukotsk corner" at 64° north latitude to Mexico, below 25° north latitude,
was 45 degrees and that the distance from the Kamchatka River to 67° north
latitude was not less than 2,000 versts. It was not clear therefore to what
country the expedition was to go from Kamchatka, whether it was to go
"between north and east or south and east." Moreover, a voyage to both
places could not be made in one year (*EB*, pp. 206–7; Divin 1953, pp.
79–81). Chirikov then advanced a proposal of his own. There was no need,
he wrote, for the American expedition to go north to the 67th parallel. The
expedition from the Lena River to Kamchatka could determine whether Asia
is separated from America,[20] and in any event any islands found at 67° would
be uninhabited and too cold, thus preventing efforts to exploit any mineral
resources there. It would be better to look for islands near America between
the 50th and 65th parallels, where the climate would be better and the land
perhaps inhabited. Moreover, at the 65th parallel, America is probably not
far from Asia. But most pertinently, this approach would eliminate the need
to go to Mexico for verification, for if the expedition encountered uninter-

18. It should be noted that in the ukaz of 2 May 1732 warning is given that the Russian
vessels were "not to go to any American or Asiatic places" under European sovereignty or
belonging to the "Chinese Bogdykhan or Japanese Khan" lest suspicions be aroused or the route
back to Kamchatka discovered and the weakness of the Russian position there exposed. Yet in
the next paragraph the Russians are ordered to find the route to Japan and establish friendly
relations, and in the instructions issued at the end of the year Bering was ordered to go to New
Spain, a place of European possession. The first contradiction was either unwitting or ignored;
the second was later eliminated.

19. The instructions from the Admiralty College of 28 February 1733 (*EB*, pp. 151–73) do
not mention this, so it must be an earlier version to which Chirikov refers (*EB*, pp. 207, 398, n.
9).

20. Nowhere else does Chirikov suggest that determination of the separation of Asia and
America was on the agenda of the American expedition.

rupted coast for the fifteen degrees of latitude and the longitudinal position was correct, one could be sure that the coast was part of America. Finally, the expedition could not make the round trip to Mexico by such a circuitous route and then back to Kamchatka in one navigation season. For these reasons Chirikov proposed that the expedition go from Kamchatka to the Chukotsk Peninsula, pick up interpreters on the small island seen on the first voyage (one of the Diomedes), and then cross over to America, which he believed to be nearby, and there follow the coast south to the 50th parallel and thence back to Kamchatka (*EB*, pp. 207–8; Divin 1953, pp. 79–80).

The Admiralty College readily fell in with Chirikov's recommendation. The real objective of the voyage, it was noted in the minutes of the meeting of the college on 16 February, was to find the unknown part of the American coast, and how long that would take was not known. But once discovered, not only was the distance to Mexico and back too great to be covered in one season, but to make the voyage in two seasons was out of the question, for the ships could not carry enough provisions for two seasons and a long winter layover somewhere in America. Actually, it was not necessary to visit Mexico for the coast of America was known and mapped as far north as 40° north latitude, and it would be dangerous as well because Spain opposed the intrusion of foreign vessels into its colonial waters in order to protect its monopoly of its colonies' trade.[21]

With the elimination of the part of the voyage south of the 50th parallel, the college felt it necessary to specify that the expedition was to obtain from the inhabitants in aboriginal America the kind of information it was originally to have obtained from the cities of European possession. The Russians were to go ashore, find out who the people there were, what they called themselves, and whether their country was indeed a part of America. This information was to be put on a map, after which the expedition was to move farther along the coast and repeat the operation until such time as the change in season dictated the wisdom of returning to Kamchatka. Such an arrangement, it was stated, would not tie the hands of the commander of the expedition and risk producing the kind of fruitless results the first voyage had (*EB*, p. 30).

On the other hand, the Admiralty College was unwilling to adopt Chirikov's suggestion about the route to be taken by the expedition. Instead it chose to stay with the stipulation contained in article 5 of the Senate's report of 28 December that the route was to be determined by the professor assigned to the expedition by the Academy of Sciences in consultation with Bering and his officers. The college made this clear in its minutes of meeting of 16 February (ibid.).

21. *EB*, pp. 29–30; *Materialy dlia istorii russkago flota*, 7:523–24.

Under the same date the college sent to the Senate a report incorporating these recommendations. That body in turn issued an ukaz to the college approving them.[22] A week later, on 28 February 1733 the college issued a supplementary set of instructions to Bering, article 9 of which included the changes approved by the Senate.[23]

Thus Mexico, or New Spain, was eliminated as the final destination of the American expedition. This provision in the original instructions appears to have been prompted in the first place by a desire to realize the objective set up by Peter, whose influence persisted, and its inclusion emphasizes that the unachieved goal of Bering's first voyage was America. Mature reflection by the planners, however, made evident to them that realizing Peter's objective was neither feasible nor without great risks. It was expendable and so was discarded. It was not consistent with the objectives presented in article 4, 6, and 11 of the report of 28 December and in the memoranda of Kirilov and Golovin, namely, finding the part of America north of the Spanish possessions and assessing its potential for political acquisition and economic exploitation.[24]

By eliminating Mexico as the final destination, the new instructions also removed the dichotomy in the earlier instructions regarding the route to America, but the responsibility for choosing the route remained the same: a conference or sea-council composed of the professor from the academy and Bering and his officers. Its choice, when made, appears to have been an unexpected one, and because it had unfortunate consequences, was later much criticized. Nevertheless, it too underscores the practical purpose of the expedition.

A major reason for Bering's failure to reach America on his first voyage, as instructed by Peter, was the insufficiency and inaccuracy of his information about the geography of the North Pacific. Both the Admiralty College and Bering were of the opinion that a second expedition in search of America would more likely succeed if the Academy of Sciences were to provide it with the best available information about the lands and seas for which it was bound (Müller 1753, p. 60; 1754, p. 12). Formally established only a few days before Bering's departure on his first voyage, the academy had not yet assembled its intellectual resources. Now, eight years later, they were available. Consequently the academy was asked to provide the best information it could for planning the route to America. The first request was made early in the period of planning of the Second Kamchatka Expedition, at about the

22. Grekov 1960, p. 61; cf. pp. 57, 349, n. 12; text is in Waxell 1940, p. 161, n. 40.

23. *EB*, pp. 163–64. Article 10 granted permission to take a second year if necessary.

24. Pokrovskii (*EB*, pp. 28–30) thinks, and Lebedev (1951, p. 17) agrees with him, that the European diplomatic situation was the real reason for abandoning Mexico as the ultimate destination of the American expedition. By the end of 1732 relations between Russia and France and the latter's ally, Spain, had deteriorated badly.

same time that Bering's two sets of proposals were presented to and considered by the Senate. Sometime before or early in 1731 the Admiralty College called upon the academy to prepare a map of the North Pacific and adjacent lands. The academy turned the assignment over to Joseph N. Delisle.[25] It appears that long before formal approval of Bering's second voyage was given the Admiralty College was laying the foundation for the enterprise. In 1732 Delisle wrote a memoir to accompany the map, and it was this map (fig. 31)[26] and the memoir, copies of which were furnished to Bering, which provided the information and speculations on which the selection of the route to America was based.[27]

For its time Delisle's map was a good one and contemporary, based on a map made by his late older brother Guillaume in 1722; but it incorporated several of the inaccuracies and myths then believed about the lands of the North Pacific near Kamchatka (cf. Lebedev and Esakov 1971, p. 199). Specifically, it showed Esso Land (*Terre d'Eso*) just south of the island of Sakhalin and near the coast of Asia, a small States Island (*I. des Etats*) immediately east of the southeast corner of Esso Land, a larger Company Land (*Terre de la Compagnie*) in turn east of State Island and directly south of Kamchatka, and east of Company Land a much larger area described as "Land seen by Dom Juan de Gama," which shades off vaguely toward America. From his memoir it is manifest that Delisle had few doubts about the existence of these lands. This view was also shared by Kirilov, as evidenced by his

25. The early dating of the drafting of this map by Delisle is based on a map reproduced in Zhdanko (1916, facing p. 844). It is one of the North Pacific, titled "Vsei Karte," and dated "1731 in the month of February." It belonged to the Admiralty College, and the legend on it explains that it was "copied from a map prepared by Professor Delisle for the route of the new navigation." A copy of the French map, sent or brought back to Paris by Delisle and dated 1731, is reproduced in Golder (1925, facing p. 72), who discusses it on pp. 70–72, n. 148. Evidently this map was the basis of Delisle's claims (1752, p. 6) that he had presented the map to the empress and the Senate in order to stimulate further exploration in the North Pacific and that he had succeeded. Müller vigorously and repeatedly rejected this claim, stating that Delisle did not initiate the map, that on the contrary he had been asked by the Academy of Sciences to prepare it, and that the order was given after Bering had been ordered in April 1732 to Kamchatka and not before. Though Müller was right about the initiation of the map (it, incidentally, went to the Senate only, not to the empress), on the basis of Zhdanko's and other evidence he was wrong about the time of its composition (Grekov 1960, pp. 348–49, n. 4; Müller 1753, pp. 59–61; 1754, pp. 11–12; 1758a, p. 139; 1758b, 7:10).

26. Efimov (*Atlas*, p. 52) states that the original of the map was transferred to the Senate in 1732 and that a copy of it was given to Bering. A later, 1733, version is reproduced in *Atlas* (no. 78), and it is from this version that figure 31 has been adapted.

27. Müller 1758a, p. 139; 1758b, 8:10–11. In the accounts of the sea-council at which the choice of route was made, including Müller's (1758a, pp. 193–95; 1758b, 8:126–27), only the map is mentioned, not the memoir. But elsewhere Müller states (1753, p. 61; 1754, p. 12) that Bering was given a copy of both the map and memoir. The use of the word "map" in the context of the sea-council must have subsumed the memoir. The French original of the memoir and an English translation of it are in Golder 1914, pp. 302–13; a Russian translation is in Sokolov 1851b, pp. 437–45.

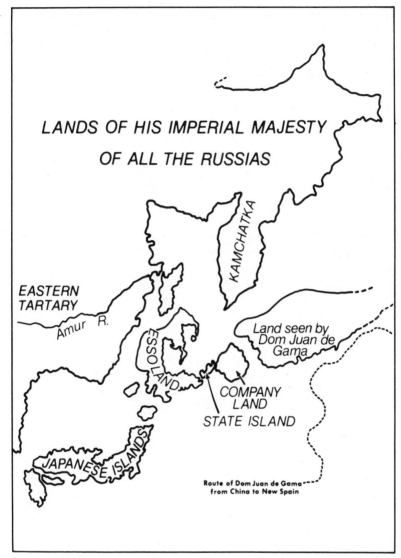

Fig. 31. J. N. Delisle's Map of the North Pacific, 1733 (detail), from *Atlas*, no. 78

memorandum and a general map of Russia, which represents these lands much the same as does Delisle's.[28] The myth of de Gama and other lands

28. This map appears in his atlas of 1733–34 and is reproduced in *Atlas*, nos. 71 and 72, pp. 48–49. Strahlenberg's map (fig. 18) with its depiction of Company Land likewise reflects the contemporary belief in the existence of these islands.

mentioned in chapter 3 was still very much alive. On the other hand, no land was depicted on Delisle's map between Kamchatka and the Chukotsk Peninsula in Asia and Baffin Bay and Hudson's Bay in North America, nor was the west coast of North America north of the 45th parallel shown, though in his memoir he stated his conviction that the higher the latitude, the more closely America approached Asia and that the distance between them in the latitudes earlier reached by Bering was small.

It was with this understanding of the geography of the North Pacific that Delisle pointed out in his memoir three possible routes "to discover the lands in the east nearest to Asia": (1) from the most northerly and easterly point of Asia, i.e., the tip of the Chukotsk Peninsula, which Bering had seen, between northeast and southeast to America, at the very most a distance of no more than 600 leagues; (2) from Kamchatka, where Bering had noted signs of land to the east, to that land, a shorter route; and (3) toward Juan de Gama Land, which one would perhaps find more quickly and certainly by sailing south. Delisle did not, however, specify a route from de Gama Land to America, maybe because he thought of it as being the westernmost extension of America. The route chosen finally was the third one: southeast toward de Gama Land. The choice was made at a sea-council held on 4 May 1741 at Petropavlovsk Harbor, in Avacha Bay, Kamchatka, whence the expedition departed a month later. The council consisted of Bering, his senior and junior officers, and Louis Delisle de la Croyère, the younger half-brother of Delisle and the professor assigned by the Academy of Sciences to the American expedition. He had arrived at Petropavlovsk a few weeks before the meeting with a copy of his brother's map. Whether he brought a copy of the memoir, in addition to Bering's, is not said.

Except for the references in Kirilov's memorandum, de Gama Land and the other alleged lands are not mentioned in the documents relating to the American expedition prior to 4 May 1741. The selection of this route thus leads one to ask if under the influence of Joseph Delisle considerations of a purely scientific nature entered into the decision—especially, the question whether Juan de Gama Land and the other islands existed or not. Or was the selection made with the objectives of the expedition in mind?

At the outset it can be said that in his memoir Delisle does not argue explicitly for the de Gama Land route, let alone urge it upon the naval officers with the objective of solving a geographical question. That he would have chosen the de Gama Land route had the choice been his alone can be inferred, however, from the fact that he devoted more attention to it in his memoir than to the other two routes, explaining why he located de Gama and the other lands where he did and stating that he could provide information regarding navigation in the area. He also pointed out that since no one had been on the lands seen by Juan de Gama, presumably no other power had taken possession of them.

Two of the participants in the sea-council left accounts in which they state the reasons for the choice. One of them is Lieutenant Sven Waxell, second in command on Bering's vessel, the *Sviatoi Petr*, whose journal did not come to light until 150 years after the voyage.[29] He writes:

> All winter the officers discussed a suggested course of east and east by north. . . . A consultation on this problem was held between all the officers and mates; this was also attended by a professor of astronomy, de la Croyère, who was with the expedition. . . . He brought with him to the consultation a map, in drawing up which, as it later proved, certain false and unfounded information had been used. This map showed the so-called Juan de Gama's land as lying to the SE. by E. of Avacha on latitude 47, 46 and 45 degrees north and south of that again, and the altered longitude[30] east was about 13 degrees. On the basis of the new information given by this map we agreed that we ought to touch at that Juan de Gama's land. So we all approved a course SE. by E. as far as latitude 46 degrees north and longitude 13 degrees east. To this we all put our signature.[31]

The other participant is Chirikov, whose report of 7 December 1741 to the Admiralty College on the voyage of his vessel, the *Sviatoi Pavel*, contains this passage:

> [We] all agreed, according to the articles [in the instructions of the Senate and Admiralty College], that the course for the search from this harbor for the American shores should be: first southeast by east by true compass, and to continue along this rhumb if we do not find land before 46° N. latitude, because according to the map of Professor Delisle de la Croyère there lies on that rhumb from this harbor at 47° N. latitude a land called Juan de Gama, which we expect is part of America. On the general maps[32] there is an outline of land from California to the place where Juan de Gama Land is shown, and the outline is represented also on the map of Professor Delisle de la Croyère. For this reason we proposed to take this route, reasoning that Juan de Gama Land, though [on the maps] it is not joined with America and lies as a special island, ought to be explored, in keeping with the isntructions, as one of the islands situated on the route to America.

Chirikov goes on to explain that if no land is found at the latitudes mentioned, the expedition would sail northeast until it struck land and then try to

29. It was first mentioned by a Russian zoologist who used the manuscript then in the tsar's library. Lev S. Berg seems to have used it in 1922 when it was in the possession of a private party. In 1938 it appeared in a Leningrad bookstore and was acquired by the Leningrad Saltykov–Shchedrin Public Library (Waxell 1940, pp. 5–6; 1952, p. 29).

30. The English translation reads "latitude," probably a printing error; the Russian reads "longitude."

31. Waxell 1940, p. 43; 1952, p. 100–1. The first citation is to a Russian translation of the German original, edited and annotated by Andreev. Waxell's account in his report of November 1742 to the Admiralty College (Golder 1922, p. 270) and the journal of Fleet Master Safron Khitrov, Bering's third-in-command and a participant in the sea-council (Waxell 1940, p. 161, n. 40), add nothing about the reasons for the decision reached; they record only the decision itself.

32. Evidently Chirikov refers to Homann's map of America (fig. 22), which he carried with him on the voyage (*EB*, p. 274).

work its way north and west to the 65th parallel, weather permitting, thence west to the Chukotsk Peninsula and back to Kamchatka by September.[33] He then concludes his explanation of the decision with this statement:

> Though we considered at this time that it might be easier, in the hope of a shorter distance, for us to go first to the Chukotsk land and then look for the American coast, as I had proposed to the Admiralty College before our departure from St. Petersburg, this view was not accepted for fear that the ice in the vicinity of the Chukotsk land, since it lies in the north near the 65th parallel, would hinder our course in the early summer. . . [EB, p. 274].

There is little or nothing in these passages to suggest that the members of the sea-council assented to the selection of the route against their better judgment, even though they later became distressingly aware that they had made the wrong choice. Precious time was to be consumed in a fruitless search for nonexistent lands and in following the longest route to America, leaving insufficient time to explore America. Joseph Delisle, of course, was not present at the meeting, though his brother was, but neither Waxell nor Chirikov indicates that the latter pressed unduly for the de Gama Land route.[34] The decision does not appear to have been forced upon the participants; it seems to have been one of consensus, agreed to by all in a signed statement.[35]

Not that Joseph Delisle's influence was not strong; it was. The Senate and Admiralty College had instructed Bering to give Delisle's views serious consideration, in keeping with his reputation and authority as an astronomer-

---

33. EB, pp. 273–74, Another, less literal, translation is in Golder 1922, pp. 312–13. Much the same description of the proposed course is given in Khitrov's journal (Waxell 1940, p. 161, n. 40) and in the journals of the Sviatoi Petr (4 May 1741) and the Sviatoi Pavel (5 May 1741) (Golder 1922, pp. 38, 284).

34. Stejneger (1936, p. 249) asserts the contrary to be true, but adduces no evidence in support of his assertion.

35. Sokolov (1851b, p. 374) states that according to official testimony the decision was "unanimous," but that according to the testimony of others, notably Müller (but not in his Nachrichten or "Lettre"), the participants in the sea-council were "not of one mind." Sokolov (1851b, p. 375), following Müller (1758a, p. 194; 1758b, 8:126–27), attributes much influence in the decision to the fact that Delisle's map did not show any part of the American coast east of the Chukotsk Peninsula and Kamchatka, only islands or lands southeast of Kamchatka. This view, it seems to me, overlooks the fact that although on the map no land is shown east of the Siberian coast—contrary to the signs of such land observed by or reported to Bering and his officers—Delisle does state in his memoir a belief that America lay to the east in the north and closest of all in the latitudes of the Chukotsk Peninsula.

Though Chirikov's report of the sea-council indicates that he acquiesced in the decision, one cannot help but think that he gave his assent reluctantly. He had proposed to the Admiralty College in 1733 that the expedition sail north to the Chukotsk Peninsula and thence east. In April 1740 he had proposed to Bering that since their vessels were not yet ready, he be permitted to take another vessel and make a preliminary survey by sailing north and then east, but he was refused on the ground that it would violate instructions (EB, p. 325; Grekov 1960, p. 110; Lebedev 1951, p. 24). And no doubt it was he who brought up the proposal again in the sea-council, only again to be refused acceptance.

geographer. Delisle displayed such certainty about the existence and location of de Gama Land and the other islands and only a measure of uncertainty about the conjectured lands east and northeast of Kamchatka, that his confidence was bound to affect the decision reached in the sea-council. His information was new to most of the members of the council and had to be taken into consideration. Müller writes that they had confidence in Delisle's map, believing that had his information been untrustworthy, he would not have put it on the map (1758a, p. 194; 1758b, 8:127). Their decision was based on the belief that these islands very likely existed.

Unless the members of the sea-council failed to mention that there were other factors affecting their decision, we may conclude that Delisle did only what he was asked to do—provide information; that he did not try to inject into the expedition's program a scientific project of his own—the settlement of the question whether de Gama Land and the others existed. He was already convinced that these lands existed and that it was largely a matter of sailing south and finding them.[36] Once his information had been provided and accepted, the instructions to the expedition and the rationale behind them became operative.

As Chirikov points out, de Gama Land was an island between Kamchatka and America, and it was such islands as this that the instructions required the expedition to explore—for their tribute-potential and mineral resources, we might add.[37] Müller notes another consideration: the fact that Juan de Gama Land had been seen only on its southern side and thus might extend northward, which would make it easier to find (1758a, p. 194; 1758b, 8:127). Presumably a third consideration that influenced the council was Delisle's observation that de Gama Land was not possessed by any other power. Moreover, at least one other route was considered, the one proposed by Chirikov to the Admiralty College, and that route was rejected on the reasonable ground that to sail north to the Chukotsk Peninsula and thence east so early in the navigation season risked danger or delay because of sea ice. All these were valid reasons for deciding on de Gama Land as the initial destination of the expedition. Parenthetically, we might add that although Esso Land, Company Land, State Island, and Juan de Gama Land up to this point are mentioned only once in the documents, one cannot but believe that wherever the documents refer to islands between Asia and America, the authors had in mind these mythical or misconstrued islands along with the ones mentioned in Mel'nikov's report. Meanwhile, what is usually lost sight of is that the itinerary finally agreed upon, did in fact incorporate most of

36. Cf. Golder's similar view of Delisle (1914, p. 183, n. 382), with which Andreev agrees (1965, p. 69).

37. Golder (1914, pp. 183–84, n. 382) is wrong when he writes that the Senate had not urged that a search be made for them.

Chirikov's proposed route except in reverse order. The route adopted would permit exploration of the American coast north of the 50th parallel and exploration of the islands opposite the Chukotsk Peninsula mentioned in article 6 of the Senate's report of 28 December. Thus the decision, which was at the root of much of the American expedition's failure to accomplish all it had been charged with doing, was in fact made in conformance with the official orders and in the expectation that this choice would best enable it to fulfill these orders.

IV

In chapters 3 and 4 of this study, we have insisted that the discovery of the route to America was the objective of Bering's first voyage, not the establishment of the presence of a land connection or strait between Asia and America. Yet, in the first of the ukazes of 2 May 1732, later in the Senate's report of 28 December (and instructions to the Admiralty College three days later), and finally in the college's instructions of 28 February 1733 there was provision for an expedition from the Lena River to Kamchatka to determine once and for all whether Asia and America are separate.[38] Does this fact undermine our contention or at least call for a qualification of it?

To find our answer we turn to the first half of article 2 of the Senate report:

> 2. The Admiralty College presented its view: in accordance with the instructions in his own hand which the Emperor Peter the Great of blessed and everlasting memory gave to Captain Commander Bering there was in the course of his expedition [to be] a search for where the Kamchatka land joined America, but as Bering reports, by force of his instructions he sailed from Kamchatka along the land between north and east as far as 67° latitude, and as is shown on his map of this expedition there is no connection with the American coast up to the point of the degree mentioned. [The area] above this latitude from this place between north and west to the mouth of the Kolyma River is shown on Bering's map. He placed this on the map on the basis of previous maps and reports.[39] Thus to assert the separation as certain is doubtful and not trustworthy. As for the sea route along the coast from the Ob River to the Lena and farther apparently it is possible[40] to go partly along the coast, but nothing is known about several places and accordingly it is not possible to speak definitely about it for there are no reliable maps or reports. Therefore, in accordance with the opinion of the College, for authentic information whether or not Kamchatka is connected with America and also whether there exists a north sea passage, there are to be built 24-oar sloops. . . [PSZ, vol. 8, no. 6291, pp. 1004–5].

38. The firm Senate decision to do this was made 12 September 1732 (PSZ, vol. 8, no. 6291, p. 1003).

39. In an earlier Admiralty College document quoted by Grekov (1956, p. 110, citing TsGADA, f. 206, op. 1, d. 1, l. 90 i ob.) this statement is expanded somewhat: ". . . and thus although according to this map some basis is shown for the information from Bering [that] supposedly there is no connection between the lands mentioned, nevertheless. . . ."

40. In the instructions of the Senate to the Admiralty College of 31December 1732 Pokrovskii saw fit to supply "not" before "possible" (EB, p. 91).

Nothing in this article contradicts or modifies our explanation of the provenance of Bering's first voyage. The statement that there was to be "a search for where the Kamchatka land joined America" embodies in compressed form the notions that America was the destination of the voyage and that Asia was connected with America, that is, that the Siberian littoral north of Kamchatka was joined to America, the conclusion that Bering and his officers reached before embarking on the voyage. The article makes no reference to his having searched for a strait or having been directed to answer the question of the geographical relation of Asia and America. Like Peter's instructions the statement takes for granted a particular concept of the geography of the North Pacific, though not the same one that Peter's instructions reveal. Our conclusions, then, about the purpose and destination of the voyage remain undisturbed.

On the other hand, it is true that the Lena-Kamchatka expedition was a response to Bering's failure to provide a conclusive answer to the geographical question in which he had become involved. According to his understanding of his instructions, he sailed northeast to 67° north latitude and found no connection between Kamchatka and America. He drew the conclusion also, on the basis of previous reports and maps, that there was no land connection between Asia and America in the area from the point of his turning back to the mouth of the Kolyma River. But the admiralty officials were not willing to accept this latter conclusion because of the hearsay character of Bering's evidence. There were still those in the Admiralty College, according to the news item in the *Sanktpeterburgskiia Vedomosti* of 16 March 1730, who believed Asia and America to be joined. Hence, the Admiralty and Senate officials decided to extend Bering's proposal to explore the Arctic coast between the Ob and Lena rivers to include the sector between the Lena and Kamchatka, to carry out firsthand the investigation that Bering had not. Recognizing all this, one needs, however, to remember that the Lena–Kamchatka expedition was the response to an incidental result of Bering's first voyage, not to the failure to accomplish its main purpose, that of discovering the route to America; and it was admiralty officials, not Bering, who proposed the expedition. One is reminded that Columbus did not set out to find a new world, but another route to Asia. Both men's discoveries raised other questions calling for further investigation.

A commonly ignored but relevant sidelight on the Lena–Kamchatka expedition is the fact that the Senate and admiralty officials foresaw the possibility that the expedition might become involved in the exploration of America. Earlier we quoted the first part of article 4 of the Senate report of 28 December, which deals with the treatment of natives by the Lena–Kamchatka expedition. The article continues:

Should they [the members of the expedition] reach a place where the Siberian coast joins the American coast, and it would therefore be impossible to reach Kamchatka, they are to follow the coast which leads to the northern country as far as possible, and en route are to treat the natives as stated above. Meanwhile, they are to find out how far across the land the Southern or Eastern Sea [Pacific Ocean] is located and then return to the mouth of the Lena and to Iakutsk as before, not delaying until such time as the ice forms there. If unexpectedly they reach some European possession while sailing along the northern coast, they are to act according to the instructions which will be given to Bering and Chirikov.[41] If no such connection with the American land is found, they are by no means to return, but are to proceed around the corner and reach Kamchatka as directed above [*PSZ*, vol. 8, no. 6291, p. 1006].

The contingency of two routes to America, neither of which could join the other was thus foreseen. If such proved to be the case, the Russians intended to exploit America along the northern route as well as along the southern. Once again the pragmatic goals of the planners of the Second Kamchatka Expedition and the important role of America in their plans are revealed.

V

Our final bit of evidence of the primacy of pragmatic rather than scientific purposes and objectives of Bering's second voyage is to be found in the requirement that the participants in the voyage, as well as those in the Lena–Kamchatka and Japan voyages, keep their instructions and activities secret. The injunction was laid down early in the planning of the Second Kamchatka Expedition. The first of the Senate ukazes dealing with the plans for the American and Japanese expeditions, that of 2 May 1732, concludes with the stricture that its contents were to be kept secret, even, apparently, from other state agencies except one, for it adds that the Foreign College would be informed about it. Since Russia had concluded the Treaty of Kiakhta with China only a few years before, the Foreign College was to be assured that there was no intention of disturbing relations with that country (*PSZ*, vol. 8, no. 6042, p. 775). The requirement of secrecy was spelled out in much more detail, however, in the Senate's report of 28 December 1732.

In the first part of article 13 of that report Bering and the commanders of the expeditions to Japan and from the Lena River to Kamchatka were enjoined to secrecy:

13. How Captain Commander Bering and the other commanders of the vessels mentioned are to act at sea while on these voyages: The Admiralty College will give instructions to each one specially, the same as those drafted in the College and sent to the Senate with any additions ordered by it. They are to keep them secret and in safekeeping, especially on the voyages. The College is to issue special instructions for public display to Bering and Chirikov, who are going to America, to Spanberg,

41. Those mentioned in article 13, which will be discussed later.

[who is going] to Japan, and to the sloop which is to proceed from the Lena east to Kamchatka. In them it will be declared that upon the wish and request of the academies at St. Petersburg and Paris and elsewhere the emperor Peter the Great of blessed and eternal memory, out of curiosity sent [an expedition] from his shores to determine whether the American coast joined the Asiatic coast, but this was not settled. For the satisfaction of these academies, Your Imperial Majesty, has ordered [the three expeditions] sent out, and upon obtaining the information, to return. If they reach the possessions of European or Asiatic powers on these voyages or meet their ships at sea, they are to request friendly information and a statement about the foregoing matters, and then on the proper occasion to declare orally and, if required, to show to the foreigners the instructions given to them, for there is nothing harmful in them to anyone. The European powers themselves have sent out maritime [expeditions] for such exploration, but no real investigation has yet been made whether or not the American coast is joined with Asia. . . .[42]

The requirement of secrecy was imposed also on the members of the academic contingent of the Second Kamchatka Expedition. Article 16 of the Senate's report stipulated that all reports and letters from the members to the academy at St. Petersburg and all correspondence of the academy to members of the expedition had to be routed through the Senate. They were to publish nothing openly or secretly about any discoveries made, lest these discoveries became known abroad before they were known in St. Petersburg. Violators of the prohibition were subject to fines (*PSZ*, vol. 8, no. 6291, pp. 1012–13). This censorship continued for the duration of the Second Kamchatka Expedition (cf. *EB*, p. 401, n. 14), which, though officially terminated in September 1743, was not finally phased out until 1748–49, and for some time after that Senate or imperial approval had to be obtained before anything about the discoveries of the expedition could be published.[43] When, in 1758, Müller published his account of Russian voyages in the Arctic and Pacific, he was not, he later wrote, allowed to tell all he knew about the Second Kamchatka Expedition (1890, pp. 252–53).

It is to be noted that only in article 13, of all the instructions issued to Bering, is there reference to the satisfaction of scientific curiosity as an explanation of the proposed maritime activity in the North Pacific and Arctic. That reference occurs as part of a deliberate effort to conceal from foreigners the true objectives of the American and Arctic expeditions, objectives which

42. *PSZ*, vol. 8, no. 6291, pp. 1010–11; *EB*, pp. 97, 376, n. 16, 378. This instruction was reviewed in a meeting of the Admiralty College on 5 January 1733 and repeated in shortened form in the Admiralty College's instructions of 28 February 1733 (*EB*, pp. 171, 389, art. 6).

43. Andreev 1959, p. 3; *EB*, pp. 7–8. Once beyond the grasp of Russian authority, Gmelin, who published his *Reise durch Sibirien* (1751–52), and Delisle, who published his *Explication de la carte* (1752), could do so with impunity. Delisle's pamphlet reinvigorated a controversy over the northeast passage that became lively and at times acrimonious and was not eased by the unwillingness of the Russian government to release all the information it had about the recent Arctic and Pacific explorations (Andreev 1959, pp. 5–7; Breitfuss 1939, pp. 87–99; Wroth 1944, pp. 223–27).

might arouse apprehension or jealousy, and therefore countervailing actions, on the part of the European colonial powers, as Spain's reactions to Russia's advances in the Pacific in the second half of the eighteenth century attest (Cook 1973, ch. 3). The readiness of the Senate officials to resort to this subterfuge, on the one hand, reaffirms the primacy of pragmatic as against purely scientific goals of the American expedition, and, on the other, makes more credible Polevoi's contention that Peter's statement to Nartov about the objective of Bering's first voyage was a smoke screen to conceal his real intentions.

VI

Because the Bering voyages did provide a tentative answer to the question of a strait between Asia and America and did give the world its first glimpse of America in the higher latitudes of the Pacific, it has long been taken for granted that these results fulfilled the primary purpose of the voyages—to establish a body of reliable geographical knowledge about the northeastern corner of Asia and the northwestern coast of America. The fact that most of the information the Russian government allowed to be released was geographical and scientific served only to reinforce this conclusion, hardly to challenge it (cf. *EB*, pp. 7–8). That both of Bering's voyages were failures so far as their primary objectives were concerned was not something leaders conscious of national prestige were prepared to admit. It was much better to let savants and others avid for more knowledge about the surface of the globe believe what they would and accept plaudits for having added to that knowledge.

In the case of Bering's second voyage we have seen that two main views of its purpose emerged, though neither has been coherently or extensively formulated. One view has it that Bering, aware of his failure to demonstrate without a doubt the existence of a strait between Asia and America, proposed a second voyage to settle the question—though how a voyage to America would do this is not said. The other is that Bering's second voyage was intended to clarify the relationship of America to Asia. Both views presume scientific goals.

We have found both of these views to be wanting and based on a less than careful reading of the evidence, even that evidence available before the disclosures of recent Soviet scholarship. To be sure, Bering proposed his second voyage because he was aware he had not achieved the goal of the first voyage, but that failure was not, however, the inconclusiveness of his proof of the separation of Asia and America; rather it was the failure to find America. Both his voyage to the east in June 1729 and his proposal the next year for a voyage to America indicate this.

In the hands of the officials of the Admiralty College and Senate Bering's proposal for a voyage to America became a more ambitious project, one designed to derive economic and political advantages from America. The imperial ukaz of 17 April 1732, commissioning Bering's second voyage, and the first Senate ukaz of 2 May 1732, containing the earliest detailed instructions for the Second Kamchatka Expedition, make this explicit, both stating that these enterprises were "for the profit of the state and the enhancement of our interests" (*PSZ*, vol. 8, no. 6023, p. 749; no. 6042, p. 774). The Senate's report of 28 December 1732 repeats the first half of the statement and later mentions "profit for the state" (*PSZ*, vol. 8, no. 6291, p. 1002) at the outset and in later paragraphs indicates the state's "interests," namely, . . . the fur-bearing animals that might be obtained as tribute from the inhabitants of the lands across the sea reported by the Chukchi, and minerals and precious metals. Golovin and Kirilov were mindful of the wealth in precious metals uncovered by the Spanish in Mexico and Peru. If Spanish America possessed such metals, then unknown America might too. But to obtain this natural wealth Russia had to possess or annex unknown America, and this, we have seen, was contemplated in the instructions to Bering, Chirikov, and the commander of the Lena–Kamchatka expedition. Still more, since its location was unknown, the part of America contrapositioned to Siberia would have to be found, and so the voyage was necessarily to be one of discovery as well—to find out where northwest America is in relation to Asia. Discovery was to be the means to an end. Thus two phases were contemplated for the voyage: to gather information and to take the first steps of acquisition.

As events worked out, the American expedition never really got into the phase of gathering information, let alone acquiring America. It did discover some islands adjacent to mainland America and a few of the Aleutian Islands, but these discoveries were made too late in the season to carry out the assignments ashore in any significant way. The reason for this unfortunate turn of events is traceable particularly to the search for the nonexistent Juan de Gama Land, but to other factors as well.

Bering and the others had hoped to begin the voyage in May, but it was not until 4 June 1741 that the expedition set sail, Bering commanding the *Sviatoi Petr*, and Chirikov, the *Sviatoi Pavel*. Proceeding southeast, the vessels reached 46° 5′ north latitude on 13 June. Finding no evidence of land, Bering and Chirikov agreed that they should turn north. The new course, had they maintained it, would have taken them to the Andreanov Islands in the Aleutian chain, but on 18 June Bering expressed doubt that the expedition had made as thorough a search for de Gama Land as had been contemplated in the instructions. Chirikov was in favor of continuing north to take advantage of a favorable wind, but that wind changed on 20 June, and in the strong winds that followed the two vessels became separated. Each commander spent a couple of days in an unsuccessful search for the other and then decided to proceed on his own. Chirikov assumed an easterly course on 22 June; Bering also sailed east on 25 June after returning to 45° north latitude. Chirikov was the first to sight land, on 15 July, north of the 56th parallel near the southern end of the Alaskan panhandle. Bering sighted land the next day between the 58th and 59th parallels at the northern end of the panhandle.[44]

The vain search for Juan de Gama Land had taken several days, which, in Bering's case, in light of his nautical position at the end of the navigation season, proved to be precious days. Too, the separation of the two vessels meant that when the *Sviatoi Pavel* later could have used the assistance of the *Sviatoi Petr*, the latter was not available. But most important was the fact that the search for Juan de Gama Land took the expedition south of the Aleutian Islands into the open Pacific so that the islands nearest Kamchatka were not discovered until the end of the two voyages. That part of northwest America discovered first was the part farthest from Kamchatka, much farther than Bering had expected,[45] and so the expedition was left with less time than anticipated to carry out its assignments. These misfortunes were compounded by subsequent developments.[46]

In less than a fortnight after his landfall, Chirikov suffered an irreparable calamity: he lost his two shore boats with their crews. The first one, a long boat, was sent into a bay with ten men under the command of fleet master Avraam Dementiev in Chirikov's first effort to carry out the instructions from the Senate and Admiralty College. According to the instructions that Chirikov handed to him, Dementiev was to go ashore, look for natives, and if found, to treat them kindly, offer them gifts, and ask them about their country and government. He was to ask them in what direction the land extended and whether there were any rivers. He was to see if there were a safe harbor and was to make a sketch of it if there were. He was to note the kind of trees and grass and "to look for any distinctive rocks and earth in which one might expect rich ores." If such were found, samples were to be brought on board. To assist him he was given a piece of silver ore for comparison. It is worth noting too that before Dementiev's departure Chirikov had him study carefully the instructions that could be made public.[47] The boat was seen to approach the bay and disappear from view. Thereafter no sign of it was seen, nor was the prearranged signal from it heard. After five days, thinking that the boat may have been damaged, Chirikov sent in the small boat with a carpenter and caulker. It too disappeared, and neither party was

44. Golder 1922, pp. 58, 65, 71, 93, 286, 287, 288, 290; Lebedev 1951, pp. 34–37, 40.
45. Cf. Steller's observation (Golder 1925, p. 26).
46. Grekov 1960, pp. 110–11. It perhaps should be kept in mind that in the eighteenth century the Russian calendar lagged eleven days behind the western calendar.
47. *EB*, pp. 275–76; Golder 1922, pp. 315–16; Lebedev 1951, pp. 51–52. There was no official assayer or mineralogist on the *Sviatoi Pavel*.

ever heard of again. Without these boats Chirikov had no means of carrying out the assigned investigations and negotiations with the natives or of obtaining fresh water. There was little he could do but return to Kamchatka as soon as possible, noting such lands as were sighted on the way back—a course agreed to by his fellow officers.[48]

Two months after his return to Kamchatka, Chirikov wrote a report to the admiralty on his voyage; and two days later, a supplementary report dated 9 December 1741. In the latter he proposed a follow-up voyage. One of the objectives of this proposed voyage, that of continuing the exploration, has been noted by a few scholars, but the other has been ignored. In the report Chirikov writes: "Should it be the wish of Her Imperial Majesty for us to explore the newly discovered land as well as that part which is supposed to lie opposite the Chukchi country and (according to the instructions to Captain Commander Bering) *to bring the inhabitants into submission under Her Majesty* [emphasis added], it would be necessary to increase the number of men on the ship. . . " (Golder 1922, p. 325). Further on in the report Chirikov writes the following in the same vein:

> According to the instructions of the Admiralty College we were required to bring to St. Petersburg a few inhabitants of the newly discovered land, or of land we might discover in the future [*sic*]. We could not persuade them to come, and to force them against their will without special instructions was dangerous. . . . It is not likely that they will come on board willingly, and I do not suppose Her Imperial Majesty would have us use force. . . .[49]

He did try in fact to continue the exploration, specifically of the island of Attu, which he had seen on the return voyage. In June 1742 he sailed to the island, but was forced to turn back because of bad weather and the physical condition of his crew members, who had not yet recovered from the scurvy incurred on the preceding voyage.[50] However much this and the rest of the evidence about the political and economic objectives of the American expedition have been unknown to or ignored by subsequent generations of scholars, it is clear that Chirikov knew his orders well and sought conscientiously to carry them out.

Bering's situation after his first landfall was not much better than Chirikov's. Weary and depressed after ten years of preparing the several Arctic and Pacific expeditions and hassles with Siberian authorities, Bering

48. *EB*, pp. 278, 295; Golder 1922, pp. 297, 317; Sokolov 1851b, pp. 399–402; Lebedev 1951, p. 63. Beaglehole (Cook 1967, p. lix) and Golder (1914, pp. 186–87, n.) advance the same explanation for the disappearance of the two boats.

49. Golder 1922, pp. 325–26. Chirikov's only meeting with natives was in a bay of Adak Island on 9 September (Golder 1922, pp. 302–5; Lebedev 1951:306–14).

50. Grekov 1960, pp. 128–29; *EB*, pp. 290–94. Grekov notes Chirikov's point about the unfulfilled task of exploring the land east of the Chukchi country, but not the point about the subjugation of the natives.

became concerned, after reaching America, mainly about the lateness of the season, the storms and fog that were encountered in the strange waters, the uncertainties and dangers that lurked near the shore, and the possibility of a shift of wind from easterly to westerly (Golder 1925, p. 34). As a consequence, he and his officers, who shared his concerns, made only two landings: one on 20 July on St. Elias (now Kayak) Island, and the other at the end of August on one of the Shumagin Islands, to take on water. For the rest they settled for observation of the coast from the sea when the weather permitted or chance dictated. In the course of both landings, brief efforts were made to establish contact with the natives, but those on St. Elias Island fled to the woods, and at the Shumagin Islands the language barrier only sustained mutual distrust. Steller did search for ore-bearing rock during his six to ten hours on St. Elias Island, without success (Grekov 1960, p. 357, n. 88), and the Russians did leave or offer gifts while on each island (Golder 1922, pp. 272, 274), but beyond these gestures none of the activities that were to be carried out by the expedition upon reaching America was undertaken by Bering and his command. On 10 August, Bering and his officers decided the time had come to begin the return journey to Kamchatka. Storms, a scurvy-ridden crew, and a shortage of fresh water led Bering and his officers finally to seek refuge on 6 November on Bering Island, some four hundred miles from Avacha Bay. Here Bering and several others later died. The following summer, the forty-six survivors of the original complement of seventy-six men rebuilt the stranded and damaged *Sviatoi Petr* and returned to Avacha Bay (Golder 1922, pp. 96–99, 120, 141–48, 209–10; 1925, pp. 34, 40, 57). With them they brought some six hundred or more pelts of sea otter, fur seal, and fox acquired during their months on the island—a catch that was to prove as consequential as any other single event in the course of the expedition (see chap. 7, n. 89).

Thus the several tasks that the American expedition had been commissioned to perform once it reached America were scarcely performed at all. Yet it was these tasks toward which the whole expedition had been directed, its *raison d'être*, and it has been these tasks that, until rather recently, scholars have overlooked. Certainly their meaning and significance have not been understood as they should be.

Moreover, except for Chirikov's tentative effort, there was no follow-up of the American expedition. The Second Kamchatka Expedition had been an exceedingly costly venture—more than two million rubles—far beyond initial expectations.[51] At the end of 1741 a palace revolution put the Empress Elizabeth on the throne, and a different regime took over. Kirilov was dead. Osterman was sent into exile. Several exiles in Siberia, some of them hostile to Bering, were returned to St. Petersburg and high office. Golovin re-

51. Makarova 1968, p. 42, n. 18; 1975, p. 233, n. 18; cf. Gorin, ed. 1935, p. 137.

mained president of the Admiralty College, but had lost influence (*EB*, pp. 51–57; Grekov 1960, pp. 160–61). Too, preoccupation with European diplomatic affairs, the war with Sweden (1741–43), and awareness of the struggle between Austria and Prussia in the War of the Austrian Succession could well have lessened interest in following up the discoveries of Bering and Chirikov. In these circumstances, no efforts were made to complete the unfinished business of the American expedition. Instead it was officially ended in September 1743 (*EB*, pp. 57, 372; Divin 1953, pp. 187–89). Thus the gathering of information remained the only accomplishment of Bering's second voyage. The pragmatic objectives would ultimately be realized, but in an unanticipated and unplanned way.

It should not surprise us, meanwhile, that practical goals gave rise to Bering's voyages. The search for readily acquired wealth and the pursuit of trade lay behind much of modern European geographical discovery, from the time of Prince Henry the Navigator and Columbus down to recent times, and before their time too. It was the pursuit of furs, which they found, and of gold and silver, which they did not, that had resulted in the Russians' exploration and conquest of Siberia. Bering's voyages were an extension of that process, as we shall see in the following chapter.

7

The Purposes of the Voyages

THE PURPOSE OF Bering's first voyage, as we have seen, was not the commonly accepted one of settling the geographical question of the existence or nonexistence of a land connection between Asia and America—a strictly scientific venture—but rather, it was to go from Kamchatka to America and reconnoiter the coast. The purpose of his second voyage was not just a matter of exploring the North Pacific to establish the geographical relationship of Asia and America, but to establish Russian sovereignty in northwest America to the end of exploiting its fur and mineral resources. These conclusions do not, however, exhaust the question of purposes.

Peter set for Bering a specific and limited objective, the gathering of information only. As long as it was thought that the information Bering was to obtain related to an Arctic–Pacific passage, the purpose of this information-gathering enterprise seemed clear. But since we understand that the information to be gathered related to the route to America, the matter of Peter's ultimate purpose requires a new answer. Unfortunately the data for an assured or definitive answer are not at hand.[1] Our efforts to find at least *an* answer will take us into areas for which materials have not been made available, if they do exist, and about which much still remains to be learned. Thus, we will have to depend considerably upon conjecture and educated guesses in considering the ultimate purpose of Bering's first voyage. Fortunately this is far less true for the second voyage, as we have seen.

I

Several Soviet scholars have advanced answers to the question of Peter's ultimate objective, but not on the basis of the kind of detailed and intensive

1. *EB*, p. 11. Pokrovskii was unable to uncover any documents in the archives that would answer this question, and Andreev apparently encountered none (1965, chap. II). One can hope that some other scholar with access to the Soviet archives will find such documents, if indeed any have survived.

research that has been given to the preparation for the voyage and the voyage itself. The first scholar to attempt an answer to the question in more than a passing or cursory examination is Pokrovskii, as we noted in chapter 2, section VI.[2] Pokrovskii did not abandon the traditional view of the search for a strait, but he did acknowledge that the intended destination for Bering was a city in America of European possession. Pokrovskii held that Bering had two tasks: (1) to determine where the two continents are separated, and (2) to sail along the American coast to a European settlement. In the first year of his voyage, in 1728, Bering more or less successfully fulfilled the first task. In the second year, in 1729, he made a brief attempt at fulfilling the second task and failed. Pokrovskii had no doubt that the second task was the major task of the expedition, and this explains why on the return of Bering and his officers to St. Petersburg the expedition was declared almost totally "fruitless." The nearest European possessions in western America, Pokrovskii noted, were Spanish, notably Mexico and Peru. Accordingly he took Mexico, the nearer to Russia of the two, to have been Bering's intended destination; and the purpose of Bering's visit he regarded as the first step in the establishment of trade with Spain's colonies. From approximately 1718, he explained, diplomatic relations between Spain and Russia had begun to improve, and in 1723 discussions regarding trade were undertaken and continued for a couple of years, both sides showing interest. The Russians wanted both Spanish and American goods, such as gold from Mexico and Peru, silver from India and Mexico, pearls, emeralds, cocoa, and vanilla. The list of goods desired suggests that Spain was to become an intermediary between Russia and other parts of the world. This interest in trade with Spain reflected Peter's desire, at the time he wrote the instructions for Bering, to improve trade relations with other countries, including France and Germany. A first step toward establishing trade with Spain was an expedition of three vessels, carrying a variety of goods, which sailed from Reval in March 1725 and reached Cadiz in August, where it remained several weeks and then went to Portugal. Thus, in that year Peter sent two expeditions to Spanish dominions, one to the mother country and the other to one of its American colonies. Pokrovskii was convinced that Bering's first expedition took shape under the influence of this thinking within the ruling circles of Russia, that it was one of the segments in Peter's broad plan to establish trade with Russia's neighbors, to push rapid commercial growth. In light of this aspiration the fact that Bering sailed to the East Indies before joining the Russian service recommended him to the authorities as one with experience in setting up new commercial connections (*EB*, pp. 21–25).

Pokrovskii then shifted from Bering's first voyage to his second, to the American expedition, and maintained that the men who planned that expe-

2. Pokrovskii's statement is in *EB*, pp. 20–31.

dition likewise had trade with Spain's colonies in mind. In his second proposal in 1730 to the Senate, Bering noted that by finding the way to America it would become possible to open trade with the lands discovered there. The second of the Senate's ukazes issued on 2 May 1732 and authorizing the Second Kamchatka Expedition repeats this statement. In the Senate's final report of 28 December 1732 Mexico appears as the ultimate destination.[3] Pokrovskii believed that the thinking of the planners of the American expedition reflected Peter's thinking, and that the planners were seeking to fulfill Peter's purposes, the realization of which had been cut short by his death.

But Pokrovskii was faced with the facts that no document related to the American expedition after the ukaz of 2 May 1732 mentions trade as the objective and that early in 1733 Mexico was eliminated as the destination of the expedition. This undercut his thesis of trade as the objective of the two Bering voyages so he tried to meet these facts with a somewhat involved explanation which argues that the deterioration of diplomatic relations between Spain and Russia made it impractical to pursue further the establishment of trade with Spain's colonies. The deterioration resulted from the conflict between Russia and France, with which Spain was allied, over the succession to the Polish throne late in 1732 and early in 1733 following the death of Augustus II of Poland. Nothing of this is mentioned in the documents, Pokrovskii noted. Nevertheless, these real reasons for abandoning Mexico as the ultimate destination were papered over, and instead the Russian officials gave as reasons those contained in the protocol of 16 February 1733 of the Admiralty College. That the American expedition could not carry out all its assignments in one navigation season and still go to Mexico, that the American coast below Cape Mendocino was already known, and that the efforts to invade Spain's monopoly of its colonies' trade risked conflict. This new development—the growing friction between Spain and Russia— explained too why secrecy was imposed on the expedition. By thus substituting alleged reasons for stated reasons, Pokrovskii tried to preserve trade as the original, even though discarded, objective of the second voyage and so reinforce his argument that trade had likewise been the objective of the first voyage.

A decade after Pokrovskii, Efimov addressed himself to the question of the purpose behind the Bering voyages in his study of Russian discoveries in the Arctic and Pacific oceans in the seventeenth and first half of the eighteenth centuries (1950, pp. 23–26, 230–36). Like Pokrovskii's explanation, Efimov's discussion is not confined to the ultimate objective of Bering's first voyage, but goes as well into the objectives of the Second Kamchatka Expedition as a

3. In the report "city of European possession" is specified, not Mexico, but from other documents discussing this destination we know that the planners had Mexico in mind. Cf. *EB*, p. 207.

whole without always explicitly differentiating between the goals of Bering's two voyages or between the goals of the second voyage and those of the other component maritime ventures of the Second Kamchatka Expedition.

Efimov saw the two Bering expeditions as parts of Peter's geographical plans directed towards political objectives. He disagreed with Pokrovskii's conclusion that trade with America was one of the goals. He conceded that opening the way to trade with Japan, China, and the East Indies was an objective of the Second Kamchatka Expedition—the Arctic expeditions were to find a sea route for trade in the Pacific and the voyages to Japan were to open up trade with that country—but establishment of trade with America was not. He quoted Stepan P. Krasheninnikov, one of the academicians who participated in the Second Kamchatka Expedition and who wrote the first and still basic description of Kamchatka.[4] Krasheninnikov states: "In the extension of Russian power in the north and the establishment of settlements on the best known rivers which empty into the Arctic Ocean from the Lena eastward to the Anadyr increasingly the effort was made to explore the land beyond the Anadyr and to bring the natives living there under subjection." Regarding trade he writes: "Although traders went to Kamchatka with the [tribute] collectors even at the time of the conquest of Kamchatka, nevertheless it is impossible to think of them as merchants for they cared not so much about merchantry as about [state] service, and often the *prikazchiki* [local commandants] put a [military] command under them. . . ."[5]

In rejecting trade as an objective of the Bering voyages Efimov did not, however, reject other economic considerations. The great reduction in the supply of fur-bearing animals in Siberia by the end of the seventeenth century coincided with the tremendous strain put on Russia's financial resources by Peter's reforms and engagement in widespread military and diplomatic activities. "Collect as much money as possible for money is the artery of war," Peter ordered the new Administrative Senate.[6] Thus more exploration became necessary for acquiring new lands and islands with unexploited resources. As early as 1 November 1697, Peter ordered the voevoda at Tobolsk, the highest administrative official in Siberia, to push the conquest of new lands (Okun' 1935, pp. 10–11). Further, Efimov noted, no one has paid much attention to the remark in Kirilov's memorandum that, although the Siberian and Kamchatka expedition was already known to everyone, what was not known was the expectation of great profit from it (Efimov 1950, pp. 25, 289).

Efimov did not reject geographical exploration as an objective either, but

4. See bibliographical entry.

5. Krasheninnikov 1949, pp. 473, 514. The English translation contains an error in the latter passage (1972, p. 338).

6. *PSZ*, vol. 4, no. 2330, p. 643. The Senate was established in February 1711.

like trade, it was not a self-sufficient reason for the Bering expeditions, as the participants in the second expedition knew by virtue of the official secrecy imposed on them and the preparation of a public version of their instructions for display during the voyage. As Polevoi did later, Efimov saw Peter's remarks on the objective of Bering's first voyage as recorded by Nartov to have been a deliberate effort to mislead outsiders about the real objective.

Matters of geography, of trade, of the discovery of unknown lands rich in furs and gold were important, but they were, however, subordinate to another far more important task of state, which Efimov saw as the major consideration behind Bering's voyages. To explain his point he related the episode told by Kirilov in his memorandum when in a discussion in the Senate in December 1724 he informed a disbelieving Peter that there was no satisfactory map of Siberia and that Kamchatka was farther away than Japan, whereupon Peter requested him to draft a map of Siberia, which he did that same night. "If we juxtapose," Efimov writes, "the facts that the conversation between Peter and Kirilov occurred in December 1724, that Kirilov completed the map in one night, and that in January 1725, in the presence of Nartov, Peter talked with General-Admiral Apraksin about commissioning the expedition, it must be recognized that among the circumstances which called forth the commissioning of Bering's first Kamchatka Expedition was the question of a collision on the eastern frontier" (1950, pp. 25, 289).

After the War of the Spanish Succession, Great Britain had become the dominant power in the west, replacing France. After Russia's victory over Sweden, Russia had become a mighty naval power and had gained a strong position in the Baltic, having annexed Baltic coastal lands that "made a firm cushion for Petersburg." Meanwhile, "at the beginning of the eighteenth century the stormy colonial colonization of North America from the side of Europe was getting under way," and in 1700–2 Russia had obtained definite and sufficiently detailed information about Japan. These developments, Efimov concluded, combined to pose the question of the security of Russia's eastern frontier in great sharpness (1950, p. 26).

Elsewhere, in support of his contention that the Russian leaders saw a security problem on their Pacific sea frontier, Efimov called attention to the ukaz of 2 May 1732. This contains the warning to Bering and the other commanders that in their search for lands in the Pacific they were not to visit any place belonging to China, Japan, or a European power so as not to cause suspicion or by their arrival to reveal the route to Kamchatka, of which the foreigners were then ignorant. Because of the sparseness of population there, the Russian officials feared foreigners might be tempted to seize "the needed docks" there (PSZ, vol. 8, no. 6042, p. 774). Further, Efimov noted, in abandoning Mexico as the final destination of Bering's second voyage one of the reasons given was the desire not to cause conflict with Spain (1950, p. 232).

A decade or so later Polevoi offered a third view. Referring to Peter's instruction to Bering "to go to a city of European possession," Polevoi agreed with Pokrovskii that Peter had in mind the Spanish settlements on the west coast of North America, a point confirmed in Chirikov's memorandum of 12 February 1733 to the Admiralty College in which he writes that Peter had ordered Bering to go to the Mexican provinces of Spain (*EB*, pp. 206, 207). Unlike Pokrovskii, however, Polevoi argued that while Peter was not opposed to trade with America as such, it is difficult to believe he was unaware that Spain did not allow direct trade between its colonies and other countries. Also it must be remembered that Peter did not order Bering to sail without fail to a city of European possession. He could limit himself simply to meeting a European vessel. Thus it is evident that Peter was interested not in trade, but only in establishing contact with Europeans so that the Spanish themselves or other Europeans could testify that the Russians had been the first to pass along the shores of the still unknown part of North America.

This was to be the first step toward increasing Russia's fur income. That income was declining because of a significant reduction in the number of fur-bearing animals in Siberia. This reduction could be reversed by the discovery and annexation of new rich hunting regions in North America.

Peter, aware of the colonial struggle of France, England, and Spain in eastern North America going on as part of the War of the Spanish Succession understood that in time the western colonial powers would want to extend their control to the northwestern part, which faced Russia across the Pacific. Possibly too, Peter knew that the western powers, when appropriating territory in eastern North America, claimed the land "from sea to sea" without knowing where the second sea was. Meanwhile, urged by western scholars to send an expedition to determine the presence of a strait between the two continents—something the western powers were not in a position to do— Peter decided that sending a vessel to the northwest coast of America could be of practical value to Russia. It was important to be able to claim the right of first discovery. The sooner Russians appeared on these shores, the more land Russia would obtain. Peter understood that it was here in northwestern North America that the limits on Russia's eastward expansion, so beneficial to the state, might be placed.

At the same time Peter was aware of the uninterrupted expansion of the western powers in North America and knew that he would have to avoid their suspicions lest they block the Russians. Hence he gave out the official word, for consumption by foreign scholars, that the purpose of Bering's voyage was to settle the geographical question, under the guise of which the acquisition of territory by right of first discovery could be carried on. The expedition was organized without publicity. The number of foreigners in the expedition was kept to a minimum, and no foreigners from states with territorial ambitions in America were included. The further precaution was taken of keeping the participants in ignorance of the political objective of the expedition. That is why both in St. Petersburg and among the participants the impression existed that Peter had only discovery of a strait in mind. Even Bering himself believed this.[7] Meanwhile, there was no doubt that Peter looked upon the annexation of the unknown lands of the northwest coast of North America as a continuation of the colonization of Siberia, of the Russian eastward movement (1964a, pp. 92–94).

II

Pokrovskii saw trade with New Spain as Peter's ultimate goal; Polevoi thought that Peter wanted more territory like Siberia to increase the income from furs; Efimov stressed the security of Russia's eastern frontier as Peter's foremost concern, though he admitted scientific, economic, and other political objectives as secondary concerns. Where does the truth lie? No final or assured answer is possible given our present state of knowledge, and whatever the real answer may turn out to be, it probably will not be simple. Such information as we have, however, suggests that Polevoi comes nearer to the right answer than the other two.

On first reading, Pokrovskii's thesis of trade with New Spain seems to have a strong argument in its favor in the well-known interest of Peter in expanding Russia's foreign trade and extending it to countries with which Russia then had no direct commercial relations. During the last decade or so of his reign, Peter sent out several expeditions. Some of these had the establishment of trade with neighboring countries as their objective. In May 1714 an ukaz of the sovereign announced an expedition to Bukhara headed by Prince Aleksandr Bekovich-Cherkasskii in the course of which its khan was to be approached and matters of trade discussed (*PSZ*, vol. 5, no. 2809, p. 105; no. 2815, pp. 108–10; Lebedev 1950, p. 109). The expedition failed, however, to reach its objective. Two years later Peter ordered Bekovich-Cherkasskii on a second expedition; part of his assignment was to explore the course of the Amu-Dariia River in the hope that it might provide a route for trade with India. In 1715–17 Colonel Ivan D. Bucholtz and in 1719 General I. M. Likharev on Peter's orders undertook to explore the upper Irtysh and to find the alleged gold sands of Iarkand, though without success. Even if gold were not found, these rivers, Peter reasoned, might enable Russia to trade with India (Lebedev 1950, pp. 109–19; Grekov 1960, pp. 215–16; Donnelly 1968, pp. 40–41). In 1723 Vice-Admiral Daniel Wilster, a Swedish naval officer in the Russian navy, was ordered to take two frigates to East India, specifically

7. This view of Polevoi's was noted and rejected in chapter 4.

to Bengal, and there to try to persuade the Great Mogul to permit trade between the two countries (Lebedev 1950, pp. 133–34; Andreev 1965, p. 27). We know too from Pokrovskii that an expedition was sent to Spain in an effort to open up trade with that country, and we noted early in this study, in chapter 2, Peter's statement to John Perry regarding the desirability of opening a northern sea route to the Pacific whereby Russia might trade with Japan and China.

There are, however, some aspects of these examples that weaken their support of Pokrovskii's thesis. For one, if trade was an objective of an expedition, the official orders said so even though the members of the expedition might have been asked to maintain secrecy about the objective. Too, the orders directed the commander to deal with the ruler or highest officials of the country to which the expedition was being sent. Both of these features are missing in Peter's instructions to Bering. For another, as Polevoi points out, Peter gave Bering the alternative of obtaining the desired information from a European vessel. This was a reasonable alternative to visiting a city for obtaining geographical information, but it was hardly the proper way to open negotiations regarding trade. Moreover, Peter's language gives rise to the question whether he had only New Spain or a Spanish vessel in mind. He did not write "go to a Spanish settlement," but to a European one. If his choice of words was deliberate, then given the activity and conflict in America of the British and French, could not Peter have had in mind the possibility that either of these people could have penetrated to the northwest coast of America and establish a claim or jurisdiction there or that one of their vessels might be cruising in the adjacent waters? Most to the point, however, is the difficulty noted by Efimov and Polevoi in believing that Peter did not know of Spain's monopoly of its colonies' trade and that he would run the risk of provoking Spain into a conflict by seeking to violate the orders to Spanish colonial officials not to engage in trade with foreigners. The planners of Bering's second voyage knew of the monopoly, and if, as Pokrovskii himself argued, these men reflected Peter's thinking, then one is again led to the conclusion that Peter's purpose in sending Bering to Kamchatka and the North Pacific was not to open trade with Spain's colonies. Moreover, if we assume that Peter did hope to penetrate the monopoly legally, he would not have done so by approaching or negotiating with the colonial authorities or a ship captain at sea, but would have dealt directly with the royal authorities in Spain.[8] It took a war for Great Britain to penetrade that monopoly.

8. Though the available evidence does little or nothing to support Pokrovskii's thesis about establishing trade with Spain's American colonies, it is conceivable that Peter hoped he could negotiate such an arrangement at Madrid, in which case it would have been worth knowing where those colonies were situated relative to Siberia or Kamchatka.

As a final observation, we may note that in Peter's musings and activities for expanding Russia's trade, much may be found about developing trade with Asia, the Central Asian khanates, India, China, and Japan, but almost nothing about trade with America. The former were countries known to the Russians by report and sometimes by actual contact. They were civilized or advanced societies reputed or known to be sources of valuable metals like gold and silver, of precious stones, of fine textiles, especially silk, and of many other exotic or useful goods. If the Russians could find a northern sea route to these countries, or an overland route, particularly to India, then, as Peter observed, Russia's geographical position would give her an advantage as middleman between western Europe and Asia (cf. Campredon's report in chap. 2, sec. I, and Perry 1716, p. 61). On the other hand, Russia's geographical position seems to have been much less advantageous for the role of middleman between Europe and America, certainly not advantageous enough to offset the difficulties or risks of collision with Spain's monopoly of its colonies' trade.

Yet, if a remark made by Peter in 1722 is to be taken seriously, one can not rule out categorically the possibility that he may have had in mind trade with America via Siberia and the Pacific. Fedor I. Soimonov, the naval officer and cartographer of the Caspian Sea, reports a conversation in 1722 with Peter while on the naval expedition against Persia on the Caspian Sea. The subject under discussion was geographical discovery. Soimonov writes:

> Then I decided to recall or mention what had been on my mind for a long time, particularly about the east Siberian maritime places, Kamchatka and others. So after His Majesty had finished talking to Pospelov about searching for new places, I began speaking thus: "Just as there were much work and danger for Christopher Columbus and Amerigo Vespucci in searching for America, no less than that did the Dutch and others in their commercial voyages around the Cape of Good Hope to the East Indies undergo in their time, both hardship and long passages of time. As is known to Your Majesty the east Siberian places and especially Kamchatka may, it is to be hoped, be found not to be at a great distance from all those places, from the Japanese and Philippine Islands, from Kamchatka to America itself along the west coast of the island of California. Accordingly it should be possible much more readily and with less loss for Russian mariners to go [to those places] as against the fact that the Europeans have to go almost a whole half-globe." . . . as soon as I had finished talking, just as quickly he deigned to say to me: "Listen, I know all this, but not now, in the future" [Andreev 1946, p. 198(18)].

The full meaning of Peter's response remains enigmatic. Did "all this" include America? Did it envisage trade with Spain's colonies (the Philippines were a Spanish colony)? Unfortunately Peter's remark reveals little as to what Peter saw the value of America to be for Russia. So one has to turn to circumstantial evidence again, and that evidence indicates that America lured the Russians in the eighteenth century as Siberia had lured them in the seventeenth as an elaboration of Polevoi's view will show.[9]

III

A stronger case can be made for Polevoi's thesis of territorial aggrandizement in the manner of the conquest of Siberia, and for similar reasons.

It is well established that from the onset of the conquest of Siberia the profusion of fur-bearing animals was the lure that drew the Russians ever eastward toward the Pacific and that their pelts became a major source of revenue for the Russian state. Just what proportion of the state's revenue was accounted for by the furs sent across the Urals and how much it amounted to in volume and value are matters that cannot be measured with exactness or certainty.[10] Nevertheless, the fur income, from the tribute imposed on the natives and the 10 percent first fruits tax collected from Russian promyshlenniki and traders, more than paid the costs of the conquest and administration of Siberia and left a considerable surplus. Furs were the *raison d'être* of the Russian conquest and presence in Siberia (Lantzeff 1943, pp. 85, 115, 123, 151–54, 200). It was, however, characteristic of the fur trade in Siberia, as elsewhere, that it was predatory and extractive; the supply of fur-bearing animals was depleted with little or no effort at replenishment. The initial high yields did not last long, and the pressure to find new untapped regions was continuous (Fisher 1943, chap. VI). By the end of the seventeenth century, the fur yields in the area under effective Russian control were experiencing a notable decline. At the same time, at the opening of the new century, Peter embarked on his military ventures, which demanded more and more money, leading to reforms that in themselves cost money.

9. Kushnarev rejects Pokrovskii's trade thesis, though for some wrong reasons (1964, pp. 7–9; 1976, pp. 9–11). Kushnarev contends that Bering's primary goal was to explore the northeastern limits of Siberia, not to go to America. America, he insists, was an optional and secondary goal at best. To support his contention he states that Chirikov and the Admiralty College so regarded it. This view ignores Chirikov's remark in his statement to Bering on 13 August 1728 about the necessity of going to the places indicated in Peter's ukaz, his memorandum of 12 February 1733 to the Admiralty College regarding the difficulties posed by the order to go to Mexico, and his inquiry to the College of 9 December 1741 about returning to America to subjugate the natives. It also does not explain why, if America was a minor and not a required objective, the Admiralty College originally made a city in America belonging to a European sovereign the objective of Bering's second voyage. Kushnarev further states that at no time on his voyage in 1728 did Bering deviate from his course and sail toward America. This is true, but he overlooks Bering's brief voyage to the east in June 1729. To be sure, in arguing that Bering's vessel carried provisions for only one navigation season and that he could not have sailed north and then south along the American coast to Mexico in one season he makes a stronger point. But he overlooks Chirikov's recommendation to winter in the vicinity of the Big Land and continue on to cities of European possession next year.

10. Fisher 1943, chap. VII; Vernadsky 1969, pp. 304–6, 546–48; Miliukov 1905, p. 113.

Under this pressure Peter resorted to all sorts of measures and arrangements for increasing the state's revenue.[11] In these circumstances it is not unexpected that the central government should try to increase the income in furs from Siberia and do it not so much by "mining" the older hunted-out areas as by conquering new lands and strengthening control over weakly held ones (cf. Okun' 1935, pp. 8–12).

At the time Peter took over personal rule as tsar, just before the turn of the century, much of the easternmost part of Siberia had yet to be conquered or had not come under effective Russian control or was being neglected for want of manpower. Contact between Iakutsk and the rivers to the northeast had lessened. The land of the Chukchi lay outside Russian rule. Russian control of the territory south of the Anadyr River to the mouths of the Oliutora and Penzhina rivers, the approaches by land to Kamchatka, was tenuous. The conquest of Kamchatka was only beginning. And the seaboard along the western edge of the Sea of Okhotsk, except the area around Okhotsk itself and the mouth of the Uda River farther south, lay outside Russian jurisdiction.

Heretofore the initiative in looking for new lands had often come from the commandants (*prikazchiki*) in the outlying posts like Nizhne-Kolymsk and Anadyrsk (Fisher 1943, 38–42). The conquest of Kamchatka by Atlasov in 1697–99 was organized and carried out from Anadyrsk (Lantzeff and Pierce 1973, pp. 195–200). But after the turn of the century the central authorities at Moscow, and later St. Petersburg, showed increasing interest in pushing exploration, conquest, and pacification (Belov 1956, pp. 183, 244). At the end of the first decade an intensification of activity in northeast Siberia occurred, instigated on orders that went back to Moscow or St. Petersburg. In 1710 orders were received from the central authorities by Prince Matvei P. Gagarin, the governor of Siberia, at Tobolsk, who in turn sent his nephew to Iakutsk to give orders to Dorofei Traurnikht, the voevoda there, to investigate the islands in the vicinity of the mouths of the Iana and Kolyma rivers and off the coast of Kamchatka (Müller 1758a, pp. 33–34; 1758b, 7:104–6). In the same year Ivan L'vov, the alleged author of a map previously discussed and commandant at the outpost near the mouth of the Iana River, was ordered to investigate the island reported opposite the mouth of that river (*PSI*, 2:504), and such an attempt was made two years later. Too, a party was sent that same year to explore the islands seen off the mouth of the Kolyma River (*PSI*, 2:504–6), and another party was sent in 1714 (Belov 1956, p. 246). In 1711, as we have noted elsewhere, Petr Popov was sent from Anadyrsk to the Chukchi in another unsuccessful attempt to persuade the

11. Miliukov, Seignobos, and Eisenmann 1968, 1:256–59, 294–97; Kliuchevskii 1961, chap. 7.

Chukchi to accept Russian rule and pay tribute (*PSI*, 1:455–59). Two years previously the commandant at Anadyrsk was ordered to build an outpost on the Penzhina River as a base for subjugation of the hostile Koriak natives of that area (*PSI*, 2:507–15). Efforts to pacify the Koriaks, as well as the Iukagirs, followed (*PSI*, 2:475–93). Between 1709 and 1712 several orders in the tsar's name were issued to cossack leaders at the outpost near the mouth of the Uda River to investigate the islands (Shantarskie) situated off the mouth of that river (*PSI*, 2:493–99). The next year Traurnikht was ordered to find a route to Kamchatka across the Sea of Okhotsk and to look for islands believed to lie off the coast from the Kamchatka River (*PSI*, 2:522). This was followed in 1713 by an order from Peter to build a vessel at Okhotsk to find that sea route, and in 1716 one Ivan Treska and a small crew did cross the Sea of Okhotsk to the Tigil River in an open boat. This discovery eliminated the need to take the long and round-about route from Iakutsk to Kamchatka via Anadyrsk (Lantzeff and Pierce 1973, pp. 196–208). Meanwhile, on orders issued in Peter's name, the cossack ataman, Danilo Antsiferov, accompanied by Ivan Kozyrevskii, in 1711 crossed to the northern Kurile Islands from the southern tip of Kamchatka (Ogryzko 1953, p. 177). They were the first Europeans to explore these islands, which were long to hold great interest for the Russians.

In the directives ordering these activities nothing is said by way of admission that their intensification was due to the demands of war. Yet that such was the case is suggested in an instruction written by Peter himself to the Siberian Department. On 31 [*sic*] June, 1711 he ordered that department to have sent from Siberia during that year or by the end of the first months of 1712, 50,000 r. in money, 70,000 r. in silk cloth, and 80,000 r. in furs. specifically, sables, foxes, arctic foxes, squirrels, and, most necessary of all, ermines, over and above the amount of income already set for such sources, to help pay the expenses of the army. A department official was to proceed from Moscow to Irkutsk with all speed, day and night, to present the order to the voevodas in all the towns (*PSI*, 1:454).

The next step in the efforts of the central government to stabilize and expand Russian control in the easternmost regions was the Great Kamchatka Command, mentioned in chapter 3. In 1716 or earlier Iakov A. Elchin, voevoda at Iakutsk, was called to Moscow by the Siberian Department to furnish information about newly acquired lands. It turned out that from the fragmentary and confusing reports of cossacks he could not assemble enough definite information, so the Siberian Department decided that an expedition was necessary and requested highest approval for one in eastern Siberia with Elchin in command. In instructions issued through Governor Gagarin at Tobolsk, under date of 19 December 1716, Elchin was ordered to explore

Kamchatka and the lands of the Chukchi, Koriaks, Iukagirs, and other natives, and to engage in trade with the Christianized natives;[12] to send out expeditions and to establish outposts on the Arctic and Pacific coasts and the Kolyma, Kamchatka, Penzhina, Okhota, Uda, Tugur, and other rivers; and to conquer the unknown lands reported to lie opposite the mouths of these rivers (Sgibnev 1868, p. 131; Lebedev 1950, p. 37). Gagarin also ordered Elchin to investigate the report that ores were transported to Japan from the sixth Kurile island (Müller 1758a, pp. 105–6; 1758b, 7:320–21). Elchin was made in effect supreme military commander in the vast area between the Arctic Ocean and the mouth of the Amur River. Preparations were begun at Iakutsk, Okhotsk, and Nizhne–Kamchatsk for the construction of vessels, supplies were assembled, and men were assigned to carry out the several tasks ordered. But Elchin became involved in a quarrel with the voevoda at Iakutsk and in 1718 was sent to St. Petersburg. Subsequently the enterprise was found to be beyond the resources then available in Siberia, and the Siberian Department ordered it discontinued, though not in time to forestall a force that went from Okhotsk to the Shantarskie Islands and brought back a large quantity of furs. Earlier Elchin had sent expeditions down the northern rivers to find the islands opposite their mouths, but they were unable to do so.[13]

Ten years later, not long after Peter's death, a second large-scale undertaking was organized, while Bering and his men were making their way arduously across Siberia to Kamchatka. This was the expedition of Shestakov and Pavlutskii, authorized by the Senate and the newly created Supreme Privy Council. Its tasks were much the same as those given the Great Kamchatka Command, but with more manpower and other resources authorized.

Afanasii F. Shestakov was a cossack leader in eastern Siberia, based at Iakutsk. As a consequence of his protest against the detachment from his command of 105 men and their despatch to Tobolsk and his offer to undertake instead the conquest of native lands, he was sent to St. Petersburg, where he arrived at the time of Peter's final illness and death. Here, though some thought him to be a fraud, he succeeded in impressing leading officials in the Admiralty College, Senate, and Supreme Privy Council with his knowledge of the lands along the Chinese border, of Kamchatka, of the Japanese Islands, and of the Kurile Islands. The Kurile Islands, he assured his listeners, had "underground treasurers," that is, rich ores.[14] The interest

12. This last and unusual provision points to the desire of the state officials to tap every possible source of furs. Tribute could not be imposed on baptized natives. Their furs would have to be obtained through trade.

13. The earliest and most detailed account of the Great Kamchatka Command is in Sgibnev 1868, pp. 131–39. Efimov (1950, pp. 145–46) and Grekov (1960, pp. 10–11) provide short accounts incorporating some new information.

14. Divin 1971, p. 71, citing TsGADA, f. Senata, d. 664, l. 88.

he aroused was heightened by a map he had made for him, probably in St. Petersburg, which shows northeastern Siberia from the Lena River on the west and the Amur River on the south to the Pacific and Arctic oceans.[15] On it are shown an island and a Big Land in the Arctic Ocean north from the Kolyma River, with an inscription stating that on that land are many natives, fur-bearing animals, and forests. Southeast of the Chukotsk Peninsula are placed two other islands with inscriptions that they abound with sables and other fur-bearing animals. The same is said about Karaginskii Island. Other inscriptions indicate several areas with natives—Iukagirs, Chukchi, and Koriaks—not yet conquered by the Russians. The interest Shestakov aroused is revealed in a letter of July 1725, which Admiral Petr I. Sivers, later vice-president of the Admiralty College, wrote from the Kronshtadt naval base to Prince Aleksandr D. Menshikov, head of the Supreme Privy Council:

> At the time of the passing of His Imperial Majesty there appeared here from Siberia cossack head Shestakov, who in talks with me spoke of many irregularities about local [i.e., Siberian] affairs. I decided that day to recommend him to Y[our] S[erenity] for Y[our] S[erenity] maintains an interest in the preservation of the glory of our state. This Shestakov will report to Y[our] S[erenity] about local conditions in the lands next to the Chinese border and about Kamchatka and the Japanese Islands, for, as I have heard from him, he knows these places quite well and has a special map of them, and he can say something regarding the expedition on which Captain Bering has been ordered for the best fulfillment of the expedition.[16]

Sometime in 1725 Shestakov did in fact present a report, to the Senate, along with his map and requested that "service-men be despatched for the pacification of defectors . . . and the conquest of other [natives] who up to this time have not been under subjection."[17]

The kinds of reports about islands in the Arctic and Pacific oceans that helped inspire the Great Kamchatka Command persisted, and quite likely they helped prepare the Senate and Admiralty College officials to look favorably on Shestakov's request. In 1722 the Siberian governor, Prince A. Bekovich-Cherkasskii informed the Senate that service-men who had sailed

15. This map has circulated in more than one version. See Golder 1914, p. 111; Perevalov 1949, p. 133; Bagrow 1975, p. 160; and Breitfuss 1939, insert, for three examples. It is a primitive kind of map and badly distorts Siberia west from the Sea of Okhotsk (Divin 1971, pp. 70–71; Fel' 1960, pp. 144–46, 151–52). It is worth noting that it too, like the Anadyrsk Map (fig. 17), Strahlenberg's map (fig. 18), the Homann map (fig. 25), and several others discussed in chapter 3, section II, shows a northward extending peninsula on the Arctic coast west of the Chukotsk Peninsula, i.e., our Shalatskii promontory.

16. Belov 1956, p. 258, n. 3, citing TsGA VMF, *f.* 315, *d.* 334, *l.* 4. Beginning with Müller, scholars have usually dated Shestakov's arrival in St. Petersburg in 1726. The evidence in the passage quoted here indicates an earlier date and is reinforced by Fel' (1960, pp. 145–46) who puts it as early as late 1724.

17. Fel' 1960, p. 146, citing TsGADA, *f.* Senata, 1723–33, *d.* 666, *ll.* 6–17.

on the Arctic and Pacific oceans reported "many islands," at the Anadyrskoi Nos and other capes, some uninhabited, others inhabited by natives still free of Russian authority. Many of these service-men requested permission to search for new lands and islands so as to bring them under Russian rule.[18]

Kirilov, senior secretary of the Senate, gave Shestakov his support and pushed the proposed enterprise (Andreev 1943a, p. 35; Efimov 1950, p. 290). On 18 January 1727 the Senate sent a report to the Empress Catherine that better indicates the thinking of the top officials than do the later imperial and Senate ukazes authorizing the expedition. After mentioning the increase in the Russian population at Iakutsk, Irkutsk, Nerchinsk, and other places, despite their great distance to the east, the report noted that beyond Iakutsk there had recently been discovered lands "which lie in the direction of the Arctic and Pacific oceans and Kamchatka, where there are many outposts already built and the natives have been conquered and subjected to payment of tribute, as indicated on the map. However, because of the shortage of men from Iakutsk conquered natives betray the service-men sent out and kill them. . . ." The report went on to say that there were lands adjacent to Russia's far eastern possessions not belonging to any foreign power and easily brought under Russian dominion. It emphasized the importance of acquiring such new lands by noting that in them "sables and other animals breed and are exported." Also it advanced the idea that direct trade with Japan could bring great profit to the treasury.[19]

The report recommended several measures for strengthening Russian control in the far east, the most important being the building of additional outposts from which to force defecting natives back under Russian rule and to add new natives as payers of tribute, and the reinforcement of the forces stationed in the far east with some four hundred men from western Siberia. However, with an eye to relations with other powers, particularly, one suspects, those seen as potential trading partners, the Senate advised a cautious procedure whereby an island was to be explored at first-hand to find out what kind of people lived on it, who ruled them, and with whom they traded. There was to be no rush to conquest. If the inhabitants submitted voluntarily and agreed to pay tribute, then well and good. The Senate also recommended that Shestakov be furnished with goods—cloth, tinware, needles, beads—to be exchanged for sables "with value in excess" of the goods (Divin 1971, pp. 72–73).

By an ukaz of the Supreme Privy Council dated 11 April 1727,[20] which confirmed the recommendations of the Senate and Siberian Department,

18. Divin 1971, p. 69, citing TsGADA, f. Senata, d. 666, l. 6.

19. Divin 1971, pp. 71–72, citing TsGADA, f. Senata, d. 666, l. 7; Kushnarev 1964, p. 14.

20. The Supreme Privy Council discussed the report of the Senate on 1 February, and on 9 February it agreed to provide Shestakov with soldiers and officers (*Materialy dlia istorii russkago flota*, 5:443).

Shestakov was directed to take over supreme military authority in the Iakutsk jurisdiction for the purpose of forcing "traitorous" natives back to paying tribute and of seeking out new lands and bringing their inhabitants under payment of tribute. He was to build up a force of 1500 service-men drawn from various social categories and was to distribute them in the several outposts, particularly those near the "hostile" natives in the Uda, Okhotsk, Tauisk, Kamchatka, and Anadyr areas. In addition, an expert officer was to be selected from among the senior army officers in Siberia, and 400 of the 1500 men were to be assigned to him to enable him to conquer new lands. Dmitrii I. Pavlutskii, captain of dragoons in Tobolsk, was selected by the governor of Siberia for this responsibility and given separate authority. In addition there were assigned to the expedition navigator Ia. Ia. Gens, assistant navigator Ivan Fedorov, geodesist Mikhail Gvozdev, metallurgist Simon Gardebol', as well as shipwright Speshnev, three or four other geodesists, and ten sailors. In particular, Shestakov was to send a detachment, including native hunters, to the Shantarskie Islands, not for conquest, but to learn what natives lived there, what animals they hunted, whether they paid tribute to China, and how close to the Uda River the islands are; as well as to establish a fort on the Oliutora River from which to subjugate the Oliutora and Koriak natives and to advance from there toward the Anadyr.[21] Though no other islands were specified as objects of search, the despatch of navigators, sailors, and a shipwright points to a search for islands—a search that in fact was made. The geodesists were to make maps of the areas visited.

It is relevant at this point to note a comment by Osterman, then serving as tutor to the young Peter II. In a manual he wrote for his charge, which was published in 1728, he remarked: "Finally, because in addition there are many bordering lands unknown to the Russian state, especially in the Arctic and Pacific oceans, His Imperial Majesty himself will know from this where it is necessary to continue the investigation begun by Peter and what means and routes may be used for this."[22]

Unfortunately the results of the Shestakov–Pavlutskii expedition were not commensurate with the efforts expended. Quarreling between Shestakov, who as an illiterate was jealous of his literate associates, and Pavlutskii, who claimed equal authority with Shestakov, hindered the efforts of the expedition. Shestakov left St. Petersburg in June 1727 and arrived in Okhotsk two years later. His attempts to pacify the natives along the Oliutora River ended in disaster when he was killed in a battle in March 1730, and a contingent coming to his support was subsequently wiped out. Another contingent sailed south in 1730 to the Uda River and inspected the Shantarskie Islands

21. *PSZ*, vol. 7, no. 5049, 770–72; *Materialy dlia istorii russkago flota*, 5:471, 489.
22. Grekov 1960, p. 348, n. 3, quoting Andrei I. Osterman, *Raspolozhenie uchenii gosudaria imperatora Petra II* (Sanktpeterburg, 1728), p. 47.

before returning to Okhotsk, but the new and more accurate geographical information it obtained seems to have scarcely been used. The same was true of another maritime contingent that explored the four northernmost Kurile Islands. Pavlutskii and his men left Iakutsk in 1729 for Anadyrsk, from which he departed on an expedition in 1731 to conquer the Chukchi on the Chukotsk Peninsula. The Russians defeated the Chukchi in several battles, but could not subdue them. On his third appearance in Chukotka, in 1747, Pavlutskii was killed, and the Russians gave up for the time being their attempts to impose their rule on these most formidable natives (Vdovin 1965, pp. 117–23). Before embarking on his first Chukchi campaign, Pavlutskii learned of the death of Shestakov, in April 1730, whereupon he ordered navigator Gens, assistant navigator Fedorov, geodesist Gvozdev, and the others to come to the mouth of the Anadyr River so as to consolidate what was now his command alone and to explore the Big Land to the east. Gens and the others arrived at the mouth of the Kamchatka River in the spring of 1731. Because of a native rebellion and his own illness Gens had to stay at Nizhne–Kamchatsk, so Pavlutskii ordered Fedorov and Gvozdev to go on in Bering's ship, the *Sviatoi Gavriil*, to look for the Big Land.[23]

Then followed the most noteworthy part of the Shestakov–Pavlutskii expedition. Fedorov and Gvozdev with a crew of thirty-nine left the mouth of the Kamchatka River late in July 1732, sailed to a point on the eastern face of the Chukotsk Peninsula from which they turned eastward to look for the Diomede island sighted by Bering in 1728 and for the Big Land. They found both of the Diomede Islands, landing on probably the larger one, and then sailed east to the Big Land. The vessel anchored off the coast of the Prince of Wales Peninsula at a distance of about three miles, but the Russians did not go ashore to investigate the area first-hand. Later they coasted south along the land, then headed southwest, sighting King Island, and returned to the Kamchatka River late in September.[24]

The men on the *Sviatoi Gavriil* became the first Europeans to see northwestern America, but their discovery created almost no stir at the time, and it is open to question whether the participants and Siberian officials understood the significance of the discovery—that the Big Land was part of America—though later that was understood. Information about the discov-

23. The earliest and most detailed account of the Shestakov–Pavlutskii expedition is in Sgibnev 1869c. Golder gives an account in English in 1914, chap. VII. He erroneously gives 1742 as the date of Pavlutskii's death. More recent accounts are in Grekov 1960, chap. III; Divin 1971, chap. III; and Belov 1956, pp. 258–60.

24. For accounts of the voyage, see Polonskii 1850a, pp. 385–402; Sokolov 1851a; Sgibnev 1869c, pp. 25–27; Grekov 1960, pp. 49–53; Divin 1956; 1971, pp. 77–85; Belov 1956, pp. 260–62; Golder 1914, pp. 158–63. There are some primary materials concerning Fedorov and Gvozdev in *EB*, pp. 71–80. Efimov (1971, pp. 222–35), using new data, recently has presented the most detailed analysis of the voyage.

ery was slow in reaching St. Petersburg. Gvozdev filed a short report in Okhotsk, and shortly thereafter was jailed for three years on the complaint of a fellow member of the crew. Nine years later the Okhotsk chancery sent to the Irkutsk chancery a deposition about the voyage of one Il'ia Skurikhin, another member of the crew (Andreev, ed. 1948, pp. 104–6). Friction between Gvozdev and Fedorov, the joint commanders of the expedition, resulted in failure to collate their notes and to make an adequate map. Fedorov died early in 1733 from the illness that had nearly incapacitated him on the voyage (Divin 1971, pp. 83–84). It was not until ten years after the event that Gvozdev, at the request of Spanberg, Bering's successor in command of the Second Kamchatka Expedition, made an extended report (Efimov 1948, pp. 244–49). Though the voyage became known to the authorities at Okhotsk and Iakutsk, it does not appear to have become known in St. Petersburg before 1738. Thus the voyage had little or no influence on the plans for Bering's American expedition, and Gvozdev and Fedorov failed to obtain the kind of information about the Big Land wanted by the Senate.[25]

Our interest, however, is not in the successes and failures of the Shestakov–Pavlutskii expedition and its predecessors, but in the attitude and intentions of Peter the Great and his officials which the documents concerning them reveal. The undertaking of increasingly larger scale expeditions, culminating in the Shestakov–Pavlutskii expedition indicates a desire to bring all of easternmost Siberia under effective Russian control, and the reason most often advanced for such control is the extraction of tribute from the natives. That the Russians were not content to stop at the waterline in eastern Siberia is made evident by their interest in the offshore islands, again with an eye to the possibility of subjecting their inhabitants to tribute, though one can not exclude the possibility that some islands like the Kuriles might open the way to trade, in this instance with Japan. The natives of these neighboring islands, like the natives in Siberia, lacked the political structure or military power such as China, Japan, and India possessed. Exploitation could be direct and cheaper than by means of trade, which called for a *quid pro quo*. We have already made this point in connection with the American expedition of 1741, and it appears just as valid for these two previous expeditions.

The intent of this more than casual description of Russian activity in easternmost Siberia during Peter's reign should by now be clear: to advance the thesis that what Peter authorized for eastern Siberia he could well have

25. In the request that Chirikov submitted to Bering in April 1740 to make a preliminary voyage to the Chukotsk Peninsula, he refers to "other places on the west side of America" (see chap. 6, n. 35; *EB*, p. 325). The use of this phrase rather than "the Big Land" suggests that Bering and Chirikov had learned of the voyage of Fedorov and Gvozdev. Chirikov's request, however, makes no reference to it.

had in mind for northwestern America, the part of North America situated in the same latitudes as Siberia and believed not yet to be claimed by any western imperial power. Having become a naval power, Russia need no longer look on the ocean as a barrier to continued eastward expansion, an expansion that had been very profitable. Russia's geographical proximity to this part of America gave her an advantage, at least in Peter's mind. The Russians were already on the Pacific unlike the English, French, and Dutch, who had to sail halfway around the globe to reach the North Pacific. This thesis does not necessarily exclude the possibility that Peter also had trade in mind, but given Russian experience with aboriginal peoples, it has to be regarded as a secondary and minor factor in Peter's interest in North America. Meanwhile, before Peter could take overt steps toward establishing a foothold in North America, he had to know exactly where northwest America was situated in relation to Siberia and how close to Russia the possessions in America of the western imperial powers were. And so, as his first step, Peter sent Evreinov and Luzhin to find out if America was joined to Kamchatka. Learning that it was not, he then sent Bering to find America.

IV

The third explanation of ultimate objective, that of Efimov, does not exclude geographical inquiry and economic gain, but it does stress security of Russia's eastern frontier as the primary concern of Peter and his heirs. This thesis has the appeal of relating Bering's first voyage to a matter of high policy and enlarging its significance. Unfortunately Efimov's explanation consists largely of generalities and is lacking in specifics and documentary support, particularly of his major point. It may be heuristic, but it is not conclusive.

For our purpose Efimov's thesis, or rather his statement of it, is difficult to deal with because for the most part he refers to the expeditions to the east collectively in expounding it. He does not make clear, except in one instance, to what extent his thesis applies to Bering's first voyage as against the second and to the second voyage as against the Second Kamchatka Expedition as a whole. Nor does Efimov differentiate between Peter and his successors. Apparently, in his mind Peter and his successors thought and acted as one. That Kirilov, Golovin, and Osterman were strongly influenced by Peter and that in organizing the Second Kamchatka Expedition they pursued essentially a Petrine policy, we have already suggested, but this is not proof that Peter had the same ultimate purpose in sending Bering out the first time as Kirilov and the others in sending him the second time. Efimov's thesis raises more questions than it purports to answer.

In respect to the ultimate purpose of Bering's first voyage, our main concern here, Efimov does say explicitly that concern for the security of the eastern frontier was the reason for sending Bering to Kamchatka and the North Pacific, but he does not say how the First Kamchatka Expedition would advance the security of that frontier. The conclusion he draws from the juxtaposition in Kirilov's memorandum of Peter's conversation with Kirilov in late December 1724, the making of the map of Siberia, and Peter's remarks to Admiral Apraksin before Nartov is inferential at best and is not the only inference that can be drawn. The three data can just as well point to a desire on the part of Peter to open up trade in the Pacific basin, an alternative conclusion that seems to be supported by Peter's response to Soimonov's remarks in 1722. Moreover, it was a discussion of the Sino–Siberian boundary, not the Pacific frontier, that prompted Peter's conversation with Kirilov and his order to draft the map. The evidence adduced by Efimov is simply too inadequate for a firm or reliable conclusion.

He develops his thesis further by drawing on evidence related to the Second Kamchatka Expedition. Most striking is the statement in the ukaz of 2 May 1732 warning Bering against visiting any American or Asiatic territory belonging to a European power or China or Japan "so as not to cause suspicion or by his arrival to open the routes to Kamchatka, of which as of now they are ignorant and so that particularly in the present sparseness of population there they do not seize the needed docks for that reason" (*PSZ*, vol. 8, no. 6042, p. 774; cf. no. 6291, p. 1007). This quotation does indicate an apprehension of the planners of the Second Kamchatka Expedition, but it does not assure us one way or the other that this was a specific concern of Peter. We can only guess.

Efimov felt justified in attributing to Peter concern over Russia's Pacific frontier because of "the stormy colonization from the side of Europe" which had begun at the opening of the eighteenth century, but he does not develop this point, leaving its meaning mostly to implication. We can note that in the settlement at Utrecht in 1713, which ended the War of the Spanish Succession, France released to Great Britain its claims to Newfoundland, Nova Scotia, and the Hudson's Bay territory, and by the *asiento* Great Britain cracked Spain's monopoly of the trade with its colonies. The British with their strong navy appeared as a power capable of reaching into the North Pacific, and also perhaps of advancing westward overland from Hudson's Bay. The northern limits of Spain's colonies on the Pacific were fairly accurately known, but Spain might push farther north, as in fact it did in the 1770s when it advanced into Alta California. France had suffered setbacks in Canada at the hands of the British, but was continuing the struggle with them as well as the exploration of the interior; and Peter knew from his conversation with members of the Paris Academy that the French were interested in the northwest passage into the North Pacific.

Kushnarev, however, has examined Efimov's notion of a European menace to Russia in the North Pacific, and he rejects it. He does not see how the western European powers at that time could constitute any real threat to Russia in the east. Much of northwestern America had not only remained unconquered by Europeans, it had not even been discovered. The limitless expanses of the Pacific Ocean lay between Russia and America, and they had not been penetrated in their northern latitudes by anyone. The coast from Cape Lopatka to the Chukotsk Peninsula had not yet been explored and put accurately on the map. How could enemies attack the eastern frontiers of Russia and the Russians defend them if they were not known at all to the former and only indefinitely to the latter? The noted Mikhail V. Lomonosov, a student of the Arctic among his several interests, later pointed out the difficulties for European powers in attacking Russia from the east (1952, p. 498); and when armed attack did come, it was not until the Crimean War and was a minor affair mounted with no intention of seizing territory.[26] We agree with Kushnarev's conclusions and arguments, but they say only that Peter had no need to worry, not that he did not worry. We can only conclude that in view of the sparseness of data either Kushnarev or Efimov could be right—and that is concluding that we do not know.

There is one datum that might enlighten us a bit in this matter: Peter's use in his instructions to Bering of the phrase "city of European possession." Chirikov and the planners of the Second Kamchatka Expedition understood Peter to have meant a Spanish possession (*EB*, pp. 206, 207), but did he? If he did, why did he not use the word "Spanish"? His use of "European" suggests uncertainty in his mind as to the western limits of the possessions of the European powers in America, at least of France and Great Britain (their territorial claims were often from the Atlantic to the Pacific). If such were the case, it does not seem as likely that in his ignorance of the political status of northwest America Peter had developed an apprehension over the security of his eastern frontier as that he had developed a curiosity about the limits of the possessions of the western colonial powers in northwestern America. And if the views of Kirilov and his colleagues are a clue to Peter's thinking, then their proposed intrusion into northwestern America hardly indicates an apprehension inherited from Peter despite their precautions of secrecy. Their offensive attitude does not confirm the defensive implications of Efimov's thesis. Rather, it indicates that Polevoi's thesis is the more plausible of the two. In short then, our response to Pokrovskii's explanation having been "no" and to Polevoi's "probably yes," our response to Efimov's at the most can only be "maybe."[27]

26. Kushnarev 1964, pp. 10–11. See Efimov (1971, pp. 164–65) for a brief response to Kushnarev.

27. It is of interest to note that in June 1746 in response to a request of the Admiralty College

It is perhaps characteristic of Peter's autocratic manner that we know less about the two enterprises he initiated, those of Evreinov–Luzhin and Bering, than we do of the three generated through the bureaucratic apparatus of the Senate, Siberian Department, and Admiralty College—the Great Kamchatka Command, the Shestakov–Pavlutskii expedition, and the Second Kamchatka Expedition. The autocrat did not have to give his reasons; his subordinates did. We are left in the dark, consequently, as to his ultimate interest in America. The most we can claim with assurance about his reasons for sending Bering on his first voyage is that, as Grekov states, he wanted to learn who and where his nearest neighbors in America were (1960, p. 21). Why, we do not really know.

V

In the case of Bering's second voyage, the expedition to America, it has not been necessary for us to resort to conjecture to ascertain the purpose behind it. The Senate's report to the empress and instructions to Bering and his commanders contain the information that has enabled us to determine its purpose; and the statements by Golovin and Kirilov make the larger purpose quite explicit: the expedition was the first step toward territorial aggrandizement in northwest America. Consequently there is little to add to the explication of purpose given in the preceding chapter, but that little should be said.

It is to be noted that the American expedition in particular and the Second Kamchatka Expedition as a whole constitute the climax of a development that began with the Great Kamchatka Command, if not earlier. In commissioning that expedition, the central authorities at Moscow and St. Petersburg, primarily the Siberian Department, took on the role theretofore usually performed by the Siberian authorities of initiating and organizing a comprehensive expedition of exploration and conquest in eastern Siberia, and they did so on a scale greater than that of previous expeditions there. The failure of the expedition left the task still to be carried out, and a second effort was organized in the form of the Shestakov–Pavlutskii expedition, this time by the Senate and Supreme Privy Council and on a scale greater than

to present recommendations for the economic development and protection of Eastern Siberia Chirikov proposed, among other measures, that Russia annex northwestern America by right of first discovery, that the natives be brought under Russian rule, and that a suitable place for a fortified stronghold be found because of the possibility of encroachment on Russian territory by foreigners. (Divin 1953, pp. 207–8, citing TsGA VMF, *f.* Golovina, *d.* 1, *l.* 53. Part of Chirikov's report is in Sokolov 1851b, pp. 453–67). This is the first bit of explicit evidence I have encountered that some Russians viewed northwest America as of strategic value for the defense of Russia's eastern seaboard; but from the very nature of the situation this was a development subsequent to Bering's second voyage and so does not tell us anything definite about attitudes toward territorial security before the voyage.

that of the Great Kamchatka Command. This expedition was to give more attention to exploration beyond the continental limits of Siberia, to nearby islands and lands; but it too met with little success. Meanwhile, two other expeditions, those of Evreinov and Luzhin and of Bering, were undertaken on the initiative of Peter himself, though on a small scale and with quite specific and limited objectives. The former two expeditions had conquest and tribute-paying natives as their objective. The latter two sought only geographical information—for what further purpose Peter did not say.

Given these four expeditions as background, as expressions of an attitude prevailing among the officials at the top, one can see why Bering's proposals of 1730 met with ready acceptance by the Senate and empress' Cabinet and were enlarged beyond the comparatively modest suggestions in his second set of proposals. The resulting Second Kamchatka Expedition combined the old with something new. The old was exploration, trade, and conquest—exploration of routes to America and Japan and along the Arctic coast, trade with Japan, and conquest in the new world and of the islands in between. The new was the shift in locus of activity from land to sea, from Siberia to the North Pacific, and the use of a new means, the maritime expedition manned by naval officers and sailors and directed from the capital. It is the new in the Second Kamchatka Expedition that has contributed to the common view of it as a singularity standing in near isolation and having come full blown into existence; whereas actually it was the consequence of the acceleration by Peter the Great of a process in Siberian history that went back more than a century.

The American expedition was a characteristic part of the Second Kamchatka Expedition. It was a continuation of exploration and conquest for economic gain as in Siberia, now directed overseas to northwestern America and the islands of the North Pacific and using the new means, the naval expedition. It went beyond the quest for information that Peter had had in mind in sending Bering on his first voyage, and it went beyond Bering's proposal that the route to America be found so as to open trade with its inhabitants. It was directed toward a careful exploration of the American coast, the search for minerals and compliant natives willing to accept Russian dominion and pay tribute. Viewed in this historical perspective, Bering's voyages appear not as unprecedented or isolated attempts by Peter and his successors to gain glory by solving certain geographical problems, but as parts of a long on-going process of Russian expansion to the east that was to reach its farthest limits on the shores of northwestern America rather than in Siberia. They must be looked at primarily as marking a new stage in Russian eastward expansion, not just as undertakings in scientific geographical inquiry or episodes in the exploration of the Pacific basin.

VI

We have reserved to the last the critique mentioned in chapter 1 and directed to the thesis about the purpose of Bering's voyages advanced in 1931 by the American scholar Robert J. Kerner (1931, pp. 111–14). Kerner held that Bering's voyages, especially the second, had as a secret objective the reacquisition of the Amur River basin. He was convinced that Peter was aware of the seriousness of the loss of the Amur in 1689 and wanted to get it back, for that basin held the prospect unequaled in eastern Siberia of access by river to the sea, of the development of foreign trade, and of a major source of food. As evidence of this awareness, Kerner referred to Peter's alleged statement that there were three points of capital importance to Russia—the mouths of the Don, the Neva, and the Amur—and to a statement by Sava Vladislavich about the advantages Russia would derive from possession of the Amur.[28]

To establish a connection between Bering's voyages and the question of the Amur, Kerner presented three points of evidence. First, under the guise of finding out the relationship between Asia and America, Bering or his associates were to try to reopen the Amur question, possibly in connection with an expedition by land, an expedition that Kerner believed to be revealed in the "Secret information" of Vladislavich, a document submitted to the Empress Anna in December 1731.[29] Kerner wrote: "In describing the various routes from Siberia to China Sava Vladislavich takes up the one from Nerchinsk down the Shilka and Amur to the sea and then by sea to the 'famous port' of Toundji (Tientsin?) seventy versts from Pekin. He adds, 'An attack is being prepared to seize this route. We shall need a strong fleet. That is the task of Bering.'" Second, Kerner referred to Bering's second set of proposals in 1730, to his statement, "it would not be without advantage to find a sea route from the Kamchatka or Okhota River to the Amur or Japan, since it is known that these regions are inhabited. . . ." Third, he finds in Article 13 of the Senate's report of 28 December 1732 indications that there were objectives other than those revealed in the report. That article in the translation by Golder, which Kerner used, states that Bering and his commanders "should keep secret the instructions from the Admiralty College" and that a different set of instructions, which could be shown, if necessary, to

28. Elchin, incidentally, recommended repossession of the Amur (Grekov 1960, p. 11), and Chirikov mentions the advantages of possession of the Amur in his report to the Admiralty College of 16 June 1746 (Divin 1953, p. 209).

29. Its full title is "Secret Information about the Strength and Condition of the Chinese Empire and Other Matters." It is a confidential report prepared by Vladislavich at the request of State Chancellor Gavriil I. Golovkin (Bartenev, ed. 1900, pp. 572–80). The Russian original was published under the title "Sekretnaia informatsiia o sile i sostoianii kitaiskago gosudarstva, i o protchem" (see bibliographical entry).

any foreigners encountered, would be provided. Kerner then ended the statement of his thesis with this passage:

> Evidently here is a splendid opportunity for the historical investigator to discover the secret instructions, written or oral, explaining all the motives of Peter the Great and his successors in regard to Bering's voyages. Enough has been shown here to indicate that the reacquisition of the Amur very probably was one of the most important among them. It would appear, also, that the founding of Russian America was more or less an accident, a by-product of this major purpose. . . .

It is not necessary to respond here in detail to Kerner's arguments, for I have done that elsewhere (1969, pp. 397–407). We will limit ourselves to the crucial parts of my refutation and to the corollary conclusion advanced by Kerner.

To substantiate his first point, Kerner depended on a faulty summary account in French by Gaston Cahen based on the Russian of Vladislavich (1912, p. lxxii), and Kerner compounded the error by his own mistranslation of the first of three sentences from French into English. About the route of China via the Amur and the sea Cahen wrote: "This route would lend itself to an attack. A strong fleet would be necessary. This is Bering's affair." Kerner translated it thus: "An attack is being prepared to seize this route. We shall need a strong fleet. That is the task of Bering." Kerner changed Cahen's conditional mood to the indicative and a potential route for an attack into the preparation of an attack. Vladislavich actually wrote (1842, pp. 304–5):

> If there is a passage by sea, and undoubtedly there is, then there should be a passage to the famous port called Tunzhii. This route might be the most suitable and certain one for the easy entry into and devastation of the Chinas because it is 70 Russian versts from this port to Pekin. But *because of such navigation it would be necessary to have a strong maritime fleet and above all to look for the route and to know the passage* [emphasis added].

In short, Vladislavich says nothing about an attack being planned. Even if he had, the vessels Bering later built at Okhotsk for the American and Japanese expeditions hardly constituted a strong striking fleet. Though armed, the vessels were intended primarily for exploration. At the most the search for the route to Japan might be viewed as a preliminary step toward an Amur venture. But Vladislavich's attitude is made clear at the end of his "Secret information" where he cautions the Russians against becoming involved in even a minor quarrel with China lest it become a major one (1842, pp. 322–23). What must be kept in mind is that his "Secret information" was an intelligence report presented to the empress, not an official declaration of policy or set of plans. It dealt only with possibilities. And finally, the reference to Bering at the end of Kerner's passage, as well as Cahen's, does not belong there at all. Inexplicably it was transposed in the French summary from the description of another route, the one through Kamchatka, where it is relevant, to the end of the description of the Amur route, where it is not.

In making his second point, Bering's reference to the advantages of finding a sea route to the Amur or Japan, Kerner took the statement out of context. In the original the context was Bering's proposal to find the way to Japan to open trade with that country, not a route of attack on China, as Kerner suggested. Apparently he did not know that in the ukaz of 2 May 1732 Bering and his commanders were warned explicitly not to encroach on Chinese territory or become involved with the Chinese (*PSZ*, vol. 8, no. 6042, p. 774).

Kerner's third point relates to secret instructions from the Admiralty College to Bering and his commanders. It is in these "secret instructions" that Kerner expected to find set forth the secret objectives of Bering's voyages. He based this idea of secret instructions on Article 13 of the Senate report of 28 December 1732, as translated by Golder. The first sentence of the translation reads: "Captain Bering and all the officers in command of the ships at sea should keep secret the instructions from the Admiralty College" (1922, p. 31). It was Kerner who gave them the identity of secret instructions, of a third set of instructions apart from the report in which Article 13 appears and the special set of instructions to be shown to foreigners. He assumed that the content of the supposed secret instructions would be different, revealing hitherto undisclosed objectives. He did not ask why such secret objectives should be revealed in the orders to the commanders at sea and not in the report to the empress, why they should be in instructions issued by an executive and subordinate agency, the Admiralty College, and not in an ukaz or set of instructions from the policy-formulating and superior body, the Administrative Senate.

Actually the sentence in the translation on which Kerner based his notion of secret instructions is an abridged translation. Golder's opening sentence of Article 13 is a reduction of the first three sentences of the article in the original: "Art. 13. How Captain Commander Bering and the other commanders of the vessels mentioned are to act at sea while on these voyages: The Admiralty College will give instructions to each one specially, the same as those drafted in the College and sent to the Senate with any additions ordered by it. They are to keep them secret and in safekeeping, especially on the voyages. . . ." These sentences tell a clearer story. The instructions drafted in the Admiralty College and sent to the Senate for revision and confirmation and then to be issued to each commander "specially," that is, individually, could hardly have been other than operating instructions, in each individual case tailored to the circumstances of the particular voyage. The Senate wanted to be certain that these instructions, which would reveal the objectives mentioned in its report to the empress, were not seen by foreigners. That they were to be kept concealed from outsiders is little indication and no proof of contents nowhere else disclosed. Those sets of instructions from the Admiralty College which have been published, those of 28 February 1733 to Bering and Spanberg, commander of the expedition to Japan, and those to the officers commanding the Arctic expeditions (*EB*, pp. 104–12, 151–86), disclose what might be expected; that is, they reveal nothing about objectives that is not found in the Senate's report of 28 December, least of all any statement or hint about regaining the Amur basin.[30] Using incorrect information and misreading the rest of his evidence, Kerner was wrong on all three of his points, and so his thesis collapses.

With the collapse of Kerner's thesis, his corollary conclusion becomes invalid, namely that the founding of Russian America was an accidental by-product of the Bering voyages. The thrust of this entire study has been a demonstration of just the opposite of that conclusion: the founding of Russian America was what the planners of the Second Kamchatka Expedition hoped to accomplish, and quite likely Peter the Great did too. To be sure, the founding did not come about in the way the planners intended, but they and Peter purposely set in motion the events that led to the discovery of Alaska, to be followed by the relentless advance of promyshlenniki along the Aleutian chain of islands and coastal Alaska,[31] the establishment there (and later in California) of Russian settlements, and then the creation of the Russian-American Company, which exploited and administered Russian America from 1799 to the time of Russia's departure from North America in 1867.

30. The so-called public instructions have not been published, but we know that Bering and Chirikov carried them on their voyages. Chirikov mentions giving a copy of them to Dementiev before the latter left the *Sviatoi Pavel* on his ill-fated trip ashore (Golder 1922, p. 315). Also Chirikov reported receiving from Waxell, who had received them from Bering, one set of instructions to him from the Senate, two from the Admiralty College (one public and one "secret") instructions from the Academy of Sciences, a copy of the Senate's instructions of 31 December 1732 to the Admiralty College, copies of the treaties of 1689 and 1728 with China, and "instruments" (i.e., documents) of the boundary commissions of both countries (*EB*, p. 297). Presumably these latter items were given to Bering because one expedition would approach the Amur River along the Siberian coast and explore the Shantarskie Islands, and another would try to reach the Pacific Ocean near the Uda River from Lake Baikal.

31. It was the furs which Steller and the survivors of Bering's crew brought back from Bering Island that alerted Russian merchants and traders to a new source of fur-bearing animals, especially the sea otter, to be found in abundance in the waters east of Kamchatka (Berkh 1823b, p. 143; 1974, p. 79). The subsequent fur rush accomplished what the government enterprise had been unable to achieve. The most recent and detailed account of this Russian advance along the Aleutian Islands and coastal Alaska is that of Makarova (1968, 1975). Following Berkh (1823b, pp. 1, 137; 1974, pp. 1, 76), she credits Chirikov's crew with bringing back 900 fur pelts (1968, p. 43, n. 22; 1975, p. 234, n. 22). But neither she nor Berkh explain how those pelts were obtained in the absence of small boats and with only one brief encounter with the natives on an Aleutian island on 9 September 1741. There is nothing in Chirikov's account of his second voyage, to Attu in the summer of 1742, to suggest that the pelts were obtained then.

Private initiative picked up where the central government at St. Petersburg was unwilling or unable to continue and carried through the conquest of Russian America. Ultimately, the aspirations of the planners were realized far more successfully than they could have believed after the miscalculations and setbacks experienced by Bering and Chirikov on their memorable voyage in 1741.

Appendix 1

Bering's Accounts
of His First Voyage

BERING AUTHORED THREE accounts of his first voyage. Only one of them has been published in its entirety, though it was the last to be written. This is his "Short Account of the Siberian expedition on which Your Imperial Majesty's humble servant Fleet Captain V. I. Bering was sent" (*Kratkaia reliatsiia o sibirskoi ekspeditsi v kotoruiu posylan byl Vashego Imperatorskogo Velichestva nizhashi rab ot Flota Kapitan V. I. Bering*) which he submitted to the Empress Anna in Moscow in April 1730. In it he narrates both the journey across Siberia to Okhotsk and Kamchatka and the voyage from the Kamchatka River to 67° 18′ north latitude and back. According to Andreev, the account was first published in its Russian text in 1824 by Prince Lobanov-Rostovskii, who owned the original manuscript, but Andreev does not say where it was published (1943e, p. 41, n. 1). (Golder [1922, p. 9, n. 11], and Pokrovskii [*EB*, p. 59n] located a copy, if not the original, in the Russian state archives as organized before World War I and World War II, respectively.) It was published again in 1847 in *Zapiski Voennotopograficheskago depo* (10:69–75), the appearance most frequently cited. It was published still again by Vakhtin in his *Russkie truzheniki moria* (pp. 86–96), and most recently in *Ekspeditsiia Beringa* (pp. 59–68). In this last appearance two lists accompanying the account are included: a list of towns found on the expedition's map and a table of distances between points on the route of the expedition.

Non-Russian versions of this account appeared in the eighteenth century. Though not labeled as translations, for most practical purposes they are. Too, though these versions were styled as Bering's journal, comparison of them with the "Short Account" makes it clear that this was the document used, not a journal kept by Bering in the course of his expedition. Two of the versions are in French. The first is that which appears in Du Halde's *Description géographique, historique, chronologique, politique, et physique de l'empire de la Chine et de la Tartarie chinoise* (4:452–58), accompanied by the expedition's map and titled "Relation succincte du voyage du Capitaine Beerings dan la Sibérie," published in 1735. It is a slightly abridged version and a close paraphrasing rather than a literal translation of the "Short Account." Bering is referred to in the third person, not in the first as in the "Short Account"; and Chirikov, Spanberg, and others are not mentioned by name. The two lists at the end of the Russian text are omitted. Du Halde states that he received a copy of Bering's account and map from the King of Poland; but Albert Isnard (1916, p. 48) tells us that the Russian Academy suspected Joseph N. Delisle of having provided the map and document for the "Relation succincte" and expressed its displeasure by removing him from the office he then held in the academy. The second French version is found in the French edition of Strahlenberg's work on north and east Russia, *Description historique de l'empire russien* (2:264–94) under the title "Relation du voyage fait par le Capitaine Beering au Kamtschatka depuis 1725 jusqu'en 1730; ou abrégé de son journal." It appeared in 1757. This too is only somewhat abridged and is a close paraphrasing of the "Short Account." How the unnamed translator obtained a copy of the "Short Account" is not said, unless he rephrased the account in Du Halde's work.

A third version, an English counterpart of the two French versions, was published in 1748 in the second edition of John Harris' *Navigantium atque itinerantium bibliotheca* (2:1018–22). This was the work of the editor, Dr. John Campbell, who revised and greatly expanded Harris' original work published in 1705. He added a section on Russian discoveries in the north in which he incorporated a free translation, with a few interpolations, of the "Short Account," including the two lists at the end. He specifies "a copy of Bering's original journal" and map as his sources without saying how he gained access to them. One possible explanation is provided by Lord Hyndford, British minister at St. Petersburg. On 21 November 1747 he wrote the Earl of Chesterfield, secretary of state for the northern department, that he had procured "a copy of the journal and map of the famous Captain Bearing [*sic*], who took a survey of the coast of Kamchatka and the islands towards Japan, which I hope to be able to send to your lordship by the next courier, but this must be kept a secret, for, if Czernishew [Russian minister at London] comes to the knowledge of it, some people may be sent to finish their days in that country" (Imperatorskoe russkoe istoricheskoe obshchestvo, 1897, p. 452). Though the year is 1747, six years after Bering's voyage to Alaska, and there is reference to exploration of the islands toward Japan, the fact that in 1747 the journal and map of Bering's second voyage were still in Siberia and had not been received by the Admiralty College (Andreev 1959, pp. 5, 6) makes it most likely that the documents relate to

Bering's first voyage. These most likely are the copies to which Campbell had access. Efforts by correspondence to ascertain their fate or present whereabouts have been fruitless.

Two English translations of the "Short Account" have been made since the publication of the Russian text. The first, by William H. Dall, appeared in 1891 in "A Critical Review of Bering's First Expedition, 1725–1730. . . ," (*The National Geographic Magazine*, 2:135–44) and includes the first list. The second translation, by Frank A. Golder, appeared in 1922 in his *Bering's Voyages* (1:9–20); it omits both lists.

Bering's second account is a "Report" of his voyage which he submitted to the Admiralty College under date of 10 March 1730. Andreev mentions this *raport*, saying that it contains several details different from or not found in the "Short Account." He dates it incorrectly, however, as of 10 February 1730 (1943a, p. 9, n. 1). Belov, in a letter to me of 19 June 1973, corrects Andreev's dating to 10 March, gives the archival location of the "Report" (TsGA VMF, *f.* 216, *opis'* 1, *d.* 110, *ll.* 98–100 *ob.*), and reproduces a part of it, summarizing the rest. The March date is confirmed in a document prepared in the Admiralty College, a long account (*otchet*) to date of the Second Kamchatka Expedition, dated 5 October 1738 and reproduced in *Ekspeditsiia Beringa* (pp. 85–120). The "Report" appears near the beginning of the long account, taking the form of a summary (*spravka*; *EB*, pp. 86–87). It begins: "On 10 March 1730 Bering arrived in St. Petersburg and delivered a map and journal and protocol and at the same time declared the following. . . ." What follows is what Belov reproduced in his letter as the "Report," Bering's first person being changed to the third person and the questions and answers of the meeting on 20 August 1728 with the forty Chukchi interpolated. The date 10 March 1730 may be taken as the date of the "Report," but not of Bering's arrival in St. Petersburg, which is stated in the "Short Account" as 1 March. From this Admiralty College account the "Report" appears to be a deposition taken from Bering by admiralty officials. Andreev chided Pokrovskii, editor and compiler of *Ekspeditsiia Beringa*, for reprinting the "Short Account" already twice published, instead of the "Report" not yet published. Evidently Andreev overlooked the fact that part or all of the "Report" had been incorporated in the Admiralty College's account (1943c, p. 62). Nevertheless publication of the "Report" by Pokrovskii in its original form would have left no uncertainties as to its extent and content.

Bering's third account is the journal he kept on the voyage. It is, however, scarcely used and infrequently mentioned in the literature on the voyage. In fact so little seems to be known about it that one questions whether it is a third account or is another name for Bering's "Report" or Chaplin's journal. Kushnarev (1976, p. 74) claims that Bering kept no journal, and Andreev tells us nothing specific about Bering's journal in his discussion of archival materials relating to the Kamchatka expeditions (1965, p. 48). He writes only that the ships' journals (*sudovye zhurnaly*) of both Kamchatka expeditions are in the archives and parts of the Russian texts of two of them, those of Chaplin and Chirikov, have been published. Such evidence as there is that Bering kept a journal comes from three sources. The first is the "Report" in the Admiralty College document of 5 October 1738, the opening sentence of which says that Bering delivered a journal to the college, but whether it was his or someone else's, such as Chirikov's, is not said. The second is Pokrovskii. In the *po spravke* as reproduced in *Ekspeditsiia Beringa* (p. 87) there is an editorial note accompanying the entry for 5 June 1729, which begins: "In the journal of Captain Commander Bering there is written for June 9, 1729. . . ." A logbook type of entry dealing with wind conditions and compass directions follows, one of the few samples we have as to the nature of the journal's contents. The third source is Polonskii. On reaching the point in his narrative of the First Kamchatka Expedition when the *Sviatoi Gavriil* started its run down the Kamchatka River to the open sea on 13 July 1728, Polonskii turns to primary sources and makes the narrative of the voyage almost wholly a succession of quotations from them. At this point he appends a note to the entry for 13 and 14 July in which he explains himself in these words: "Excerpt from Bering's journal." But then he goes on to say: "The following account of the voyage is taken from Bering's report (*donesenie*) in the Admiralty College; the gaps are filled in from the journals of Chirikov and Chaplin and others" (1851, p. 18 and n.). Unfortunately, this statement introduces an element of confusion. The second part of the statement seems at variance from the first, leaving the reader to wonder if Polonskii's use of the word "journal" is in fact a reference to the "Report" of 10 March. In answer we can point to the facts that the entry for 13 July in the "Report" (*EB*, p. 86)—there is none for 14 July—is worded differently from that in the journal quoted by Polonskii and that he is explicit in saying that the entry for 16 August 1728 comes from Bering's journal (1851, pp. 18, 21). With so little evidence to go on, we are left in the dark as to whether the information in the journal is confined to navigational data and also as to why Bering's journal has not been published when extensive excerpts from Chaplin's journal have. One would like to know more about the journal.

Appendix 2

Kirilov's Memorandum
on the Kamchatka Expedition

IN THE PRESENT prosperous reign of our sovereign empress, by God's mercy and the fates, by her own good fortune two undertakings are developing, not only of great and immortal glory, but for the expansion of the empire and for inexhaustible wealth: the first [and] well-known one is the Siberian and Kamchatka expeditions; the second [and] still not disclosed one, is the Kirghiz-Khazakh and Karakalpak expedition. When they are successfully carried out, begging God's help, this will give hope that more will be added to the many Russian possessions and that there will be increased income for the reduction of taxes.

First: The Siberian and Kamchatka expeditions are already known to everyone, but not everyone is aware of the useful expectations from them. These will be mentioned in particular below.

Their beginning occurred in the time of Peter the Great by virtue of the fact that when it pleased His Majesty to be in France [1717] the local Academy of Sciences wished to find out (through sending people from Siberia) whether or not Siberia is joined to America, for they knew that there was no other nearby sovereign or any volunteer for this inquiry except His Majesty. Although this was the wish of His Majesty, wartime and the lower [Caspian] campaign did not permit it to be carried out. Meanwhile, in 1722, when His Majesty chose to go to Persia, there appeared in Kazan the geodesist Evreinov, who, having been in Kamchatka on the western side of Kamchatka and the sixteen islands lying toward Japan, described them and made a map, which he presented to His Majesty. He was ordered to wait for [His Majesty's] return, but actually he soon died. Then when the dispute

*From Prilozhenie no. 1 in Andreev 1943a, pp. 35–36, and Document no. 4, Prilozhenie in Efimov 1950, pp. 288–92. Regarding its date and first publication, see chapter 6, note 17 above.

arose between the Russian and Chinese courts over the Mongol defectors and the establishment of the boundary, His Majesty, while in the Senate in December 1724, wished to see a map of the Siberian lands; whereupon I had the temerity to report that there were no Siberian maps with which His Majesty would be satisfied, but that there were Chinese maps printed in Peking on which the Siberian boundary places were in part indicated. This offer to His Majesty proved acceptable, which emboldened [me] to mention also Evreinov's map of Kamchatka, according to which Kamchatka was much farther away than Japan. This became incredible to His Majesty. Nevertheless, he ordered that the Kamchatka and Chinese maps be combined and placed on one sheet and that it be stated that this was according to His Majesty's wish. I drew [the map] in the course of one night with my own hand and declared that he deigned to take it for himself (and when I was in Moscow I saw it in the possession of Field-Marshall Count Brius, who declared that he had received it from His Majesty for copying). At the beginning of 1725, at the time of the sovereign's death, in accordance with an ukaz written in his own hand, Captain Bering was sent [to Kamchatka], for whom nothing else actually than exploration was prescribed, as explained above. When he returned, he added the eastern side of Kamchatka to the map, and there were shown more than thirty degrees of longitude nearer America beyond previous information.

Meanwhile, I saw from the sending of Bering that he would bring back only the one item of information, whether America is joined or is not joined [with Asia], but [that one should] expect nothing from him about the current interest. I [sought] by whatever means to arouse someone to a search thence for new lands and other useful matters. It so happened that there appeared the cossack head Shestakov, who arrived from Iakutsk with a report (some had good things to say about him, but others called him a knave) asking to go with a party to Kamchatka to pacify and conquer the local hostile natives and to seek new lands and islands for subjection. Having inquired sufficiently of him about the local places, I was eager to get things going. When his proposal reached the Senate, an adequate presentation was made by the Senate to the then existing Supreme Council, from which approval was received. Shestakov was sent with Captain Pavlutskii and a detachment. With them [was sent] the foreigner Gardebol', who knows something about assaying ores (I induced him [to go] so far away and called [him] son). Pavlutskii and Gardebol' are there now, but Shestakov was killed by the Chukchi. What they did during their visit there is stated in the Senate's report to Her Imperial Majesty concerning the despatch again of Bering.

So in 1731 I entrusted to the procurator-general Count Iaguzhinskii (for I had no reason to be at court), for the best outcome of this useful undertaking, the project drafted by me concerning the local places and benefits—and the fact that there is now no other closer route than through Okhotsk—with a statement of sufficient reasons. When he announced Her Majesty's confirmation in the Senate, then there really began to be results in Kamchatka and Okhotsk concerning the establishment of good order, the increase in population, and introduction of grain and cattle, etc. The exile Pisarev was sent as commander because no one else there was adjudged more capable than he for this position.

Although Captain Bering, who had returned from the first expedition, had his proposals, they were without effect until last year, 1732; then in that year it was ordered by Her Majesty's special ukaz again to send Bering to Kamchatka and Pisarev to return [sic]. Zeal and industry were added to a guiding God in this matter, in the sending of Bering and especially the academic professors and students and artists with all manner of supplies, so that the Senate coöperated with the Admiralty College and the Academy of Sciences, seeking thereby to attain in full the desired benefits (besides which it worked as much as possible at its [regular] duties). Full confirmation of the Senate's report of December 28 of that year was received from Her Imperial Majesty, and Bering and the others were provided with useful instructions.

This sending of an important expedition, the like of which there has never been before, consists of various investigations: (1) to find out for certain whether it is possible to pass from the Arctic Ocean to the Kamchatka or Southern Ocean sea (I hope ultimately in light of the investigations of several people that this is so); (2) to reach from Kamchatka the very shores of America at some unknown place about 45 degrees of longitude [sic]; (3) to go from Kamchatka to Japan, between which the distance is only ten degrees of north latitude; (4) on that voyage and everywhere to search for new lands and islands not yet conquered and to bring them under subjection; (5) to search for metals and minerals; (6) to make various astronomical observations both on land and sea and to find accurate longitude and latitude; (7) to write a history of the old and the new, as well as natural history, and other matters.

The benefit to be expected is that from the eastern side Russia will extend its possessions as far as California and Mexico, although it will not immediately receive the rich metals which the Spanish have there. However, without preparing for war we can in time acquire [them] through kindness though I know that the Spanish will not be pleased. Besides, the local people are greatly embittered against the Spanish and for that reason have to escape to unknown places farther away (and it appears that there are no other places but closer to us). Here on our side it is firmly established not to embitter such people (I wrote about this in particular in the full instructions to the Kamchatka commander, which applies to all native peoples). To the south all the islands as far as Japan do not really belong to anyone, and already four islands have been brought under subjection by Pavlutskii's command. The same has to be reckoned about Esso and the land called "Company," [i.e.,] that they can not escape Russian possession if only assistance for the present beginning does not slacken in the future. Although God will nowhere disclose in any way what wealth the Japanese have, nonetheless the Japanese will not reject trade here for it is better for them to buy needed goods from us directly than to purchase them through the Chinese at higher cost. There are good signs in this respect. This can be better believed when there is brought here a stout young man from among the Japanese cast ashore on Kamchatka, with whom a Moscow merchant lived for a while.

Russia is especially endowed by God with natural resources for the development of this new eastern trade, since all through Siberia there are natural canals: that is, the great rivers are close to one another, along which vessels with goods can readily go, and only in three places are there overland portages, and these are not lengthy. Okhotsk, the most essential route in that area, will expand quickly when the chief commander goes there to live. If the direct sea route from the town is finally judged to be inconvenient, there will, nevertheless, still be enough other rivers.

Here we have a great advantage over the Europeans who sail to the East and West Indies for it is not necessary [for us] to go to the equator and suffer from intense heat. Also there will be no fear of the Algerians and other pirates; and besides, what is paid en route at foreign ports will all become useful to our subjects.

This will be an advantage in case the Chinese should rupture the peace. It would be possible to approach them by sea from Okhotsk to Korea itself, in galleys or other vessels, or to win over the Koreans to our side, who have a special ruler and are opposed to and distrustful of the Chinese now and who have a rich and populous land, and to force the Chinese to do what Russia wishes. Earlier, when the Chinese took Albazin from a few persons, their strength was terrifying; but now, it seems, they can not cope with the Kontaisha and must ask Kalmyk assistance.

However, I stop writing in detail about the benefits and Her Imperial Majesty's interests dependent upon this [enterprise]. But when, with God's help, the despatched persons arrive and get started according to their instructions, we will enjoy frequent reports. In the Senate there is being worked out the establishment of a rapid transmission of letters, of a postal service through which letters may arrive from Kamchatka in fewer than three months, and when it becomes a regular practice, in much less time. . . .

Works and Articles Cited

Abbreviations used:

AN SSSR   Akademiia nauk Soiuza sovetskikh sotsialisticheskikh respublik

VGO   Vsesoiuznoe geografícheskoe obshchestvo (Geograpfícheskoe obshchestvo SSSR), Leningrad

AN SSSR, Institut etnografii

   Atlas   *Atlas geografícheskikh otkrytii v Sibiri i v severo-zapadnoi Amerika XVII–XVIII vv.* [Atlas of the geographical discoveries in Siberia and northwestern America in the seventeenth and eighteenth centuries], A. V. Efimov, ed. Moscow: Nauka, 1964.

Alekseev, Aleksandr I.

   1961   *Uchenyi Chukcha Nikolai Daurkin* [Chukchi scientist Nikolai Daurkin]. Magadan: Magadanskoe knizhnoe izdatel'stvo.

Amburger, Erik

   1966   *Geschichte der Behördenorganisation Russlands von Peter dem grossen bis 1917.* Leiden: Brill [Studien zur Geschichte Osteuropas, 10].

Andreev, Aleksandr I.

   1943a   "Ekspeditsii V. Beringa" [The expeditions of V. Bering], *Izvestiia VGO* 75, no. 2(March–April):3–44.

   1943b   "Pervaia russkaia ekspeditsiia XVIII v. v severnom okeane" [The first Russian expedition in the eighteenth century in the northern ocean], *Izvestiia VGO* 75, no. 2(March–April):57–58.

   1943c   Review of A. A. Pokrovskii, ed., *Ekspeditsiia Beringa: Sbornik dokumentov* (Moscow, 1941), *Izvestiia VGO* 75, no. 2(March–April): 60–64.

   1943d   "N'iuton i russkaia geografiia XVIII v." [Newton and Russian geography in the eighteenth century], *Izvestiia VGO* 75, no. 3(May–June):3–12.

   1943e   "Russkie otkrytiia v tikhom okeane v pervoi polovine XVIII veka" [Russian discoveries in the Pacific ocean in the first half of the eighteenth century], *Izvestiia VGO* 75, no. 3(May–June):35–52.

   1944a   "Vtoraia kamchatskaia ekspeditsiia, 1733–43 gg." [The Second Kamchatka Expedition, 1733–1743], *Izvestiia VGO* 76, no. 1(January–February):56–58.

1946   "Ekspeditsii na vostok do Beringa (v sviazi s kartografiei Sibiri pervoi chetverti XVIII veka)" [Expeditions to the east before Bering (in connection with the cartography of Siberia in the first quarter of the eighteenth century)] in *Trudy Istoriko-arkhivnogo instituta*, A. I. Andreev, ed. Moscow, 2:183–202.

1947   "Osnovanie Akademii nauk v Peterburge" [The founding of the academy of sciences in St. Petersburg] in *Petr veliki: Sbornik statei* [Peter the great: a collection of articles], A. I. Andreev, ed. Moscow: AN SSSR, 1:283–333.

1959   "Trudy G. F. Millera o vtoroi kamchatskoi ekspeditsii" [The works of G. F. Müller about the Second Kamchatka Expedition], *Izvestiia VGO* 91,no. 1(January–February):3–16.

1960   *Ocherki po istochnikovedeniiu Sibiri* [Outlines of source materials for Siberia], vol. 1: XVII vek [seventeenth century], 2d ed. Moscow and Leningrad: AN SSSR.

1965   *Ocherki po istochnikovedeniiu Sibiri*, vol. 2: XVIII vek (pervaia polovina) [eighteenth century (first half)]. Moscow and Leningrad, AN SSSR.

Andreev, Aleksandr I., ed.

1944b   *Russkie otkrytiia v tikhom okeane i severnoi Amerike v XVIII–XIX vekakh* [Russian discoveries in the Pacific ocean and North America in the eighteenth and nineteenth centuries]. Moscow and Leningrad: AN SSSR.

1948   *Russkie otkrytiia v tikhom okeane i severnoi Amerike v XVIII veke* [Russian discoveries in the Pacific Ocean and North America in the eighteenth century]. Moscow: Ogiz.

1952   *Russian Discoveries in the Pacific and in North America in the Eighteenth and Nineteenth Centuries: A Collection of Materials*, trans. from the Russian by Carl Ginsburg. Ann Arbor, Mich.: J. W. Edwards.

Atlas of the World

n.d.   A Collection of Eighteenth Century Maps (Mainly by J. B. Homann) of Various Dates, Bound Together without Title Page or Table of Contents. University of California, Los Angeles: University Research Library, Department of Special Collections.

Baddeley, John F.

1919   *Russia, Mongolia, China.* . . , 2 vols. London and New York: Macmillan.

Baer, Karl E. von

1849   "Zaslugi Petra velikago po chasti rasprostraniia geograficheskikh poznanii" [The services of Peter the Great in the spread of geographical knowledge], *Zapiski Imperatorskago geograficheskago obshchestva* (St. Petersburg) 3:217–53; 4(1850):260–83.

1872   *Peter's des grossen Verdienste um die Erweiterung der geographischen Kenntnisse.* St. Petersburg: Kaiserliche Akademie der Wissenschaften [Beiträge zur Kenntniss des russischen Reiches und der angrenzenden Länder Asiens, 16].

Bagrow, Leo

1947 "Sparwenfeld's Map of Siberia," *Imago Mundi* (Stockholm) 4:65–70.

1952 "The First Russian Maps of Siberia and Their Influence on the West European Cartography of N. E. Asia," *Imago Mundi* (Leiden) 9:83–93.

1954 "Semyon Remezov—a Siberian Cartographer," *Imago Mundi* (Leiden) 11:111–26.

1955a "A Few Remarks on the Amur, Tartar Strait, and Sakhalin," *Imago Mundi* (Leiden) 12:127–36.

1955b "The First Map Printed in Russia," *Imago Mundi* (Leiden) 12:152–56.

1975 *A History of Russian Cartography up to 1800*. Ed. by Henry W. Castner. Wolfe Island, Ont.: The Walker Press.

Baker, John N. L.

1937 *A History of Geographical Discovery and Exploration*. Boston and New York [pref. 1931]; new ed. rev., London: Harrap; reprinted, 1945.

Bakhrushin, Sergei V.

1955 *Izbrannye raboty po istorii Sibiri XVI–XVII vv.* [Selected studies of the history of Siberia in the sixteenth and seventeenth centuries]. Vol. 3 of *Nauchnye trudy* [Scholarly works], 4 vols. Moscow: AN SSSR.

1959 *Ocherki po istorii krasnoìarskogo uezda v XVII v.* [Outlines of the history of Krasnoiarsk uezd in the seventeenth century]. Vol. 4 of *Nauchnye trudy* [Scholarly works].

Bancroft, Hubert H.

1886 *History of Alaska, 1730–1885*. San Francisco: A. L. Bancroft [Works, 33].

Bartenev, Petr, ed.

1900 "Graf Vladislavich o Kitae v XVIII veke" [Count Vladislavich on China in the eighteenth century], *Russkii arkhiv* (Moscow) bk. 2:572–80.

Baskin, Semen I.

1949 "Bol'shoi chertezh kamchadalskoi zemli" [The great sketch-map of the Kamchatka land], *Izvestiia VGO* 81, no. 2(March–April):226–38.

1952 "Puteshestvie Evreinova i Luzhina v kuril'skii arkhipelag (1719–22)" [The journey of Evreinov and Luzhin to the Kurile archipelago (1719–22)], *Izvestiia VGO* 84, no. 4(July–August):363–79.

Belov, Mikhail I.

1948 *Semen Dezhnev, 1648–1948: K trekhsotletiiu otkrytiia proliva mezhdu Aziei i Amerikoi* [Semen Dezhnev, 1648–1948: commemorating the tricentennial of the discovery of the strait between Asia and America]. Moscow and Leningrad: Glavsevmorput'.

1949 "Istoricheskoe plavanie Semena Dezhneva" [The historical voyage of Semen Dezhnev], *Izvestiia VGO* 81, no. 5(September–October):459–72.

1952 *Russkie morekhody v ledovitom i tikhom okeanakh: Sbornik dokumentov o velikikh russkikh geograficheskikh otkrytiiakh na severo-vostoke Azii v XVII veke* [Russian seafarers in the Arctic and Pacific oceans: a collection of documents concerning the great Russian geographical discoveries in northeastern Asia in the seventeenth century]. Moscow and Leningrad: Glavsevmorput'.

1955 *Semen Dezhnev*. 2d ed. rev. Moscow: Morskoi transport.

1956   *Arkticheskoe moreplavanie s drevneishikh vremen do serediny XIX veka* [Arctic seafaring from ancient times to the middle of the nineteenth century]. Ia. Ia. Gakkel', A. P. Okladnikov, and M. B. Chernenko, eds. Moscow: Morskoi transport [Istoriia otkrytiia i osvoeniia severnogo morskogo puti, 1].

1957   "Russkie pokhody na Kamchatku do Atlasova" [Russian expeditions to Kamchatka before Atlasov], *Izvestiia VGO* 89, no. 1(January–February):25–35.

1965   "Daniia i Vitus Bering" [Denmark and Vitus Bering] in *Puteshestviia i geograficheskie otkrytii v XV–XIX vv.* [Journeys and geographical discoveries in the fifteenth to nineteenth centuries], M. I. Belov, ed. Leningrad: Nauka, pp. 46–56.

1973   *Podvig Semena Dezhneva* [The exploit of Semen Dezhnev]. Moscow: Mysl'. [3d ed. rev. of *Semen Dezhnev*. Moscow, 1948; 1955.]

Belov, Mikhail I., ed.

1964   *Russkie arkticheskie ekspeditsii XVII–XX vv. Voprosy istorii izucheniia i osvoeniia Arktiki* [Russian Arctic expeditions of the seventeenth to twentieth centuries. Historical questions of the exploration and mastering of the Arctic]. Leningrad: Arkticheskii i antarkticheskii nauchno-issledovatel'skii institut.

Berg, Lev S.

1942   "Ekspeditsiia Beringa" [Bering's expedition], *Izvestiia VGO* 74[only issue for that year]:5–15.

1943   "Pervye karty Kamchatki" [The first maps of Kamchatka], *Izvestiia VGO* 75, no. 4(July–August):3–7.

1946   *Otkrytie Kamchatki i ekspeditsii Beringa, 1725–41* [The discovery of Kamchatka and Bering's expeditions, 1725–41], 3d ed. Moscow and Leningrad: AN SSSR.

1948   "300-letie otkrytiia Semenom Dezhnevym beringova proliva (1648–1948)" [The tricentennial of the discovery of Bering Strait by Semen Dezhnev (1648–1948)], *Vestnik AN SSSR* (Leningrad) no. 10(October): 57–64; "The Three-hundredth Anniversary of the Discovery of Bering Strait by Semyon Dezhnev (1648–1948)," *Soviet Press Translations* (Seattle) 4, no. 6(14 March, 1949):178–84.

Bering, Vitus J.

1847   "Donesenie Flota Kapitana Beringa ob ekspeditsii ego k vostochnym beregam Sibiri" [Report of fleet captain Bering on his expedition to the eastern shores of Siberia], [*Zapiski Voenno-topograficheskago depo* (Voennoe ministerstvo, Glavnoe upravlenie general'nago shtaba, St.. Petersburg), 10:69–75.

Berkh, Vasilii N.

1823a   *Pervoe morskoe puteshestvie rossiian, predpriniatoe dlia resheniia geograficheskoi zadachi: Soediniaetsia li Aziia s Amerikoiu? i sovershennoe v 1727, 28 i 29 godakh po nachal'stvom Flota kapitana 1-go ranga Vitus Beringa. S prisovokupleniem kratkago biograficheskago svedeniia o Kapitana Beringa i byvshikh s nim ofitserov* [The first Russian maritime voyage, undertaken to decide the geographical question: Is Asia joined to America? and completed in 1727, 1728, and 1729 under the command of fleet captain of the first rank Vitus Bering. With the addition of brief biographical information about captain Bering and officers who were with him]. St. Petersburg: Imperatorskaia akademiia nauk.

1823b   *Khronologicheskaia istoriia otkrytiia aleutskikh ostrovov ili podvigi ros-siiskago kupechestva, s prisovokupleniem istoricheskago izvestiia o mekhovoi torgovle* [A chronological history of the discovery of the Aleutian Islands or the exploits of the Russian merchantry, with the addition of historical information about the fur trade]. St. Petersburg: N. Grech.

1974   *A Chronological History of the Discovery of the Aleutian Islands; or, The Exploits of the Russian Merchants, with a Supplement of Historical Data on the Fur Trade*, Dmitri Krenov, trans., and Richard A. Pierce, ed. Kingston, Ont.: Limestone Press.

Blackwell, William L.

1968   *The Beginnings of Russian Industrialization, 1800–60.* Princeton, N.J.: Princeton University Press.

Bodnarskii, Mitrofan S.

1926   *Velikii severnyi morskii put': Istoriko-geograficheskii ocherk otkrytiia severo-vostochnogo prokhoda* [The great northern sea route: an historical-geographical outline of the discovery of the northeastern passage]. Supplement by A. E. Nordenshel'd [Nordenskiöld], *Vokrug Evropy i Azii na parakhode "Vega" v 1878–80 gg.* (v izvlecheniiakh) [Around Europe in the steamship "Vega," 1878–80 (a summary)]. Moscow and Leningrad: Gosudarstvennoe izdatel'stvo.

1947   *Ocherki po istorii russkogo zemlevedeniia* [Outlines of the history of Russian geography], vol. 1. Moscow: AN SSSR [Nauchno-populiarnaia seriia AN SSSR].

Breitfuss, L.

1939   "Early Maps of Northeastern Asia and the Lands around the North Pacific," *Imago Mundi* (London) 3:87–99.

Brooks, Alfred H.

1953   *Blazing Alaska's Trails*, Burton L. Fryxell, ed. College, Alaska: University of Alaska, and Washington, D.C.: Arctic Institute of America.

Burney, James

1818   "A Memoir on the Geography of the North-eastern Part of Asia, and on the Question Whether Asia and America Are Contiguous, or Are Separated by the Sea," *Philosophical Transactions of the Royal Society of London* 108, pt. 1:9–23.

1819   *A Chronological History of the North-eastern Voyages of Discovery; and of the Early Navigations of the Russians.* London: Payne and Foss; reprinted, Amsterdam: Nico, Israel, 1969.

Cahen, Gaston

1911   *Les cartes de la Sibérie. Essai de bibliographie critique.* Paris: Imprimerie nationale [Nouvelles archives des missions scientifiques et littéraires, 19, nouvelle série, fasc. 1].

1912   *Histoire des relations de la Russie avec la Chine sous Pierre le grand (1689–1730)*. Paris: Alcan.

Charlevoix, Pierre F. X. de

1754   *Histoire du Japon. . .* , new and rev. ed., 6 vols. Paris: Rollin.

Chukovskii, Nikolai K.

1961   *Bering; biografiia* [Bering; a biography]. Moscow: Molodaia gvardiia.

Clark, Henry W.

1930   *History of Alaska*. New York: Macmillan.

Cook, James

1967   *The Voyage of the "Resolution" and "Discovery," 1776–80*, J. C. Beaglehole, ed., 2 vols. Cambridge, Eng.: The Hakluyt Society, [The Journals of Captain James Cook on His Voyages of Discovery, 3, pts. 1 and 2].

Cook, James, and James King

1784   *A Voyage to the Pacific Ocean. Undertaken by Command of His Majesty, for Making Discoveries in the Northern Hemisphere, to Determine the Position and Extent of the West Side of North America; Its Distance from Asia; and the Practicability of a Northern Passage to Europe. Performed under the Direction of Captains Cook, Clerke, and Gore, in His Majesty's Ships the* Resolution *and* Discovery, *in the Years 1776, 1777, 1778, 1779, and 1780*. Vols. I and II written by Captain James Cook, F.R.S., vol. III by Captain James King, L.L.D. and F:R.S. . . . Published by order of the Lords Commissioners of the Admiralty, 3 vols. London: G. Nicoll & T. Cadell.

Cook, Warren L.

1973   *Flood Tide of Empire: Spain and the Pacific Northwest, 1543–1819*. New Haven and London: Yale University Press, [Yale Western Americana Series, 24].

Dall, William H.

1890   "A Critical Review of Bering's First Expedition, 1725–30, Together with a Translation of His Original Report on It" (with a map), *The National Geographic Magazine* (Washington, D.C.) 2(1890 [1891]):111–66.

1891   "Notes on an Original Manuscript Chart of Bering's Expedition of 1725–30, and on an Original Manuscript Chart of His Second Expedition; Together with a Summary of a Journal of the First Expedition, Kept by Peter Chaplin, and Now First Rendered into English from Bergh's Russian Version," *Report of the Superintendent of the U.S. Coast and Geodetic Survey Showing the Progress of the Work during the Fiscal Year Ending with June, 1890*. App. no. 19 (1890), pp. 759–74. Washington: Government Printing Office.

Delisle, Joseph N.

1752   *Explication de la carte des nouvelles découvertes au nord de la mer du sud*. Paris: Desaint and Saillant. An English translation is in Müller 1754, pp. 60–71.

The Dictionary of National Biography . . . from the Earliest times to 1900. . . , Sir Leslie Stevens and Sir Sidney Lee, eds., 22 vols. London: Milford, [1921–22].

Divin, Vasilii A.

1953   *Velikii russkii moreplavatel' A. I. Chirikov* [The great Russian navigator A. I. Chirikov]. Moscow: Gos. izd-vo geogr. lit-ry.

1956   *K beregam Ameriki; plavaniia i issledovaniia M. S. Gvozdeva, pervootkryvatelia severo-zapadnoi Ameriki* [To the shores of America; the navigations and explorations of M. S. Gvozdev, the first discoverer of northwestern America]. Moscow: Gos. izd-vo geogr. lit-ry.

1957   "Vtoraia sibirsko-tikhookeanskaia ekspeditsiia i voprosy khoziaistvennogo osvoeniia dal'nego vostoka" [The second Siberian-Pacific Ocean expedition and the question of the economic integration of the far east], *Letopis' severa* (Moscow: Gos. izd-vo geogr. lit-ry) 2:156–75 [AN SSSR, Komissiia po problemam severa].

1971   *Russkie moreplavaniia na tikhom okeane v XVIII veke* [Russian seafaring on the Pacific Ocean in the eighteenth century]. Moscow: Mysl'.

Dobrosmyslov, A. I., ed.

1900   *Materialy po istorii Rossii. Sbornik ukazov i drugikh dokumentov, kasaiushchikhsia upravleniia i ustroistva orenburgskago kraia* [Material for the history of Russia. A collection of ukazes and other documents concerning the administration and organization of the Orenburg region], 2 vols. Orenburg: F. B. Sachkov [Orenburgskii gubernskii statisticheskii komitet].

Donnelly, Alton S.

1968   *The Russian Conquest of Bashkiria, 1552–1740: A Case Study of Russian Imperialism.* New Haven and London: Yale University Press.

Du Halde, Jean B.

1735   *Description géographique, historique, chronologique, politique, et physique de l'empire de la Chine et de la Tartarie chinoise,* 4 vols. Paris: P. G. Lemercier.

1736   *The General History of China, Containing a Geographical, Historical, Chronological, Political and Physical Description of the Empire of China, Chinese-Tartary, Corea and Thibet. Including an Exact and Particular Account of Their Customs, Manners, Ceremonies, Religion, Arts and Sciences. . . .* Done from the French . . . by Richard Brookes, 4 vols. London: J. Watts.

Efimov, Aleksei V.

1948   *Iz istorii russkikh ekspeditsii na tikhom okeane (pervaia polovina XVIII veka)* [History of Russian expeditions on the Pacific Ocean (first half of the eighteenth century)]. Moscow: Voennoe izdatel'stvo Ministerstva vooruzhennykh sil SSSR.

1949   *Iz istorii velikikh russkikh geograficheskikh otkrytii* [History of the great Russian geographical discoveries]. Moscow: Gos. uchebno-pedagog. izd-vo.

1950   *Iz istorii velikikh russkikh geograficheskikh otkrytii v severnom ledovitom i tikhom okeanakh XVII-pervaia polovina XVIII v.* [History of the great Russian geographical discoveries in the Arctic and Pacific oceans in the seventeenth and first half of the eighteenth centuries]. Moscow: Gos. izd-vo geogr. lit-ry.

1971 *Iz istorii velikikh russkikh geograficheskikh otkrytii* [History of the great Russian geographical discoveries], rev. ed. of 1950. Moscow: Nauka.

Ekspeditsiia Beringa: Sbornik dokumentov

EB [Bering's expedition: a collection of documents], A. A. Pokrovskii, ed. Moscow: Glavnoe arkhivnoe upravlenie NKVD SSSR, 1941.

Entsiklopedicheskii slovar' [Encyclopedia]

 F. A. Brockhaus and I. E. Efron, eds., 41 vols. in 82. St. Petersburg: Semenovskaia tipo-lit, 1890–1904.

Evteev, O. A.

1950 *Pervye russkie geodezisty na tikhom okeane* [The first Russian geodesists on the Pacific Ocean]. Moscow: Gos. izd-vo geogr. lit-ry.

Fel', Sergei E.

1960 *Kartografiia Rossii XVIII veka* [Russian cartography of the eighteenth century]. Moscow: Geodezicheskaia literatura.

Fisher, Raymond H.

1943 *The Russian Fur Trade, 1550–1700*. Berkeley and Los Angeles: University of California Press; reprinted, Millwood, N.Y.: Kraus Reprint Co., 1974 [University of California Publications in History, 31].

1956 "Semen Dezhnev and Professor Golder," *Pacific Historical Review* (Berkeley and Los Angeles) 25, no. 3(August):281–92.

1969 "Kerner, Bering, and the Amur," *Jahrbücher für Geschichte Osteuropas* (Osteuropa-Institut, Munich), neue folge, 17, heft 3(September):397–407.

1973 "Dezhnev's Voyage of 1648 in the Light of Soviet Scholarship," *Terrae Incognitae* (Society for the History of Discoveries; Amsterdam), 5:7–26.

Florovsky, Anthony

1951 "Maps of the Siberian Route of the Belgian Jesuit, A. Thomas (1690)," *Imago Mundi* (Leiden) 8:103–8.

Forster, Johann R.

1786 *History of the Voyages and Discoveries Made in the North*, trans. from the German. London: G. G. J. and J. Robinson.

Ger'e [Guerrier], Vladimir I.

1870 "Otnosheniia Leibnitsa k Petru velikomu" [The relations of Leibnitz to Peter the Great], *Zhurnal Ministerstva narodnago prosveshcheniia* (St. Petersburg) 147(January):1–48; 147(February):345–415; 148(April):308–90.

Gmelin, Johann G.

1751 *Reise durch Sibirien, von den Jahr 1733 bis 1743*, 4 vols. Göttingen: A. Vandenhoecks, 1751–52 [Sammlung neuer und merkwürdiger Reisen zu Wasser und zu Land, 4–7].

Gnucheva, Vera F.

1946 *Geograficheskii departament Akademii nauk XVIII veka* [The geographical department of the academy of sciences in the eighteenth century]. A. I. Andreev, ed. Moscow: AN SSSR [Trudy arkhiva AN SSSR, 6].

Gnucheva, Vera F., ed.

  1940   *Materialy dlia istorii ekspeditsii Akademii nauk v XVIII i XIX vekakh.*
           Khronologicheskie obzory i opisanie arkhivnykh materialov [Materials for
           the history of the expeditions of the academy of sciences in the eighteenth
           and nineteenth centuries. A chronological survey and description of ar-
           chival materials]. Moscow: AN SSSR [Trudy arkhiva AN SSSR, 4].

Gol'denberg, Leonid A.

  1965   *Semen Ul'ianovich Remezov: Sibirskii kartograf i geograf, 1642-posle*
           1720 gg. [Semen Ul'ianovich Remezov: Cartographer and geographer,
           1642 to 1720 and later]. Moscow: Nauka [AN SSSR, Nauchno-
           biograficheskaia seriia].

Golder, Frank A.

  1914   *Russian Expansion on the Pacific, 1641–1850: An Account of the Earliest*
           and Later Expeditions Made by the Russians along the Pacific Coast of
           Asia and North America, Including Some Related Expeditions to the Arc-
           tic Regions. Cleveland: Arthur H. Clark; reprinted, Gloucester, Mass.:
           Peter Smith, 1960.

  1922,   *Bering's Voyages: An Account of the Efforts of the Russians to Learn the*
  1925   *Relation of Asia and America*, 2 vols. New York: American
           Geographical Society; reprinted, New York: Octagon Books, 1968 [Re-
           search series, 1–2].

Gorin, P., ed.

  1935   "Iz istorii osvoeniia severnogo puti" [From the history of the mastering of
           the northern route], *Krasny arkhiv* (Tsentrarkhiv SSSR and RSFSR,
           Moscow and Leningrad) 71, no. 4:137–69; 72, no. 5:160–81.

Grekov, Vadim I.

  1956   "Naibolee rannee pechatnoe izvestie o pervoe kamchatskoi ekspeditsii
           (1725–30 gg.)" [The earliest printed information about the First Kam-
           chatka Expedition (1725–30)], *Izvestiia AN SSSR, seriia geograficheskaia*
           (Moscow) no. 6(November–December):108–12.

  1960   *Ocherki iz istorii russkikh geograficheskikh issledovanii v 1725–65 gg.*
           [Outlines of the history of Russian geographical exploration, 1725–65].
           Moscow: AN SSSR.

Grimsted, Patricia K.

  1972   *Archives and Manuscript Repositories in the USSR, Moscow and Lenin-*
           grad. Princeton, N.J.: Princeton University Press.

Harris, John

  1705   *Navigantium atque Itinerantium Bibliotheca; or, a Compleat Collection of*
           Voyages and Travels: Consisting of Above Four Hundred of the Most
           Authentick Writers . . . in the English, Latin, French, Italian, Spanish,
           Portuguese, German or Dutch Tongues. . . , 2 vols. London: T. Bennet.

  1744,   *Navigantium atque Itinerantium Bibliotheca. Or, a Complete Collection of*
  1748   *Voyages and Travels. Consisting of Above Six Hundred of the Most*
           Authentic Writers . . . by John Harris. . . Now Carefully Revised, with
           Large Additions, and Continued down to the Present Time; Including

Particular Accounts of Manufactures and Commerce of Each Country, by John Campbell, 2 vols. London: T. Woodward.

Hulley, Clarence C.
 1953   *Alaska, 1741–1953*. Portland, Ore.: Binford and Mort.

Ianikov, G. V.
 1949   *Velikaia severnaia ekspeditsiia* [The great northern expedition]. Moscow: Gos. izd-vo geogr. lit-ry.

Imperatorskoe russkoe istoricheskoe obshchestvo
 1884   *Diplomaticheskaia perepiska frantsuzskikh poslannikov i agentov pri russkom dvore, 1719–23 g.* [Diplomatic correspondence of the French ministers and agents at the Russian court, 1719–23]. G. F. Shtendman, ed., pt. 2. Vol. 40 of *Sbornik* [Collection]. . . . , 148 vols. St. Petersburg: n.p., 1867–1914.

 1897   *Diplomaticheskaia perepiska angliiskikh poslannikov pri russkom dvore, s 1746 po 1748 g. Soobshchena iz angliiskago gosudarstvennago arkhiva Ministerstva inostrannykh del* [Diplomatic correspondence of the English ministers at the Russian court, from 1746 to 1748. From the English state archive of the ministry of foreign affairs], pt. 13. Vol. 103 of *Sbornik* [Collection].

 1898   *Bumagi Kabineta ministrov imperatritsy Anny Ioannovny 1731–40 gg.* [Papers of the cabinet of ministers of the Empress Anna Ioannovna, 1731–40], A. N. Filippov, ed., tom 1:1731–32. Vol. 104 of *Sbornik* [Collection].

 1899   *Bumagi Kabineta ministrov imperatritsy Anny Ioannovny 1731–1740 gg.*, A. N. Filippov, ed., tom 2:1733. Vol. 106 of *Sbornik* [Collection].

Isnard, Albert
 1916   "Joseph-Nicolas Delisle, sa biographie et sa collection de cartes géographique à la Bibliotheque nationale," *Bulletin de la Section de géographie du Comité des travaux historiques et scientifiques* (Paris: Imprimerie nationale) 30(anné 1915):34–164.

Kerner, Robert J.
 1931   "Russian Expansion to America: Its Bibliographical Foundations," *Papers of the Bibliographical Society of America* (New York) 25:111–29.

Keuning, Johannes
 1954   "Nicolaas Witsen as a Cartographer," *Imago Mundi* (Leiden) 11:95–110.

Kliuchevskii, Vasilii O.
 1961   *Peter the Great*, trans. from the Russian by Liliana Archibald. New York: Random House.

Krasheninnikov, Stepan P.
 1949   *Opisanie zemli Kamchatki, s prilozheniem raportov, donesenii i drugikh neopublikovannykh materialov* [Description of Kamchatka, with an appendix of reports, communications and other unpublished materials]. Moscow: Glavsevmorput' [AN SSR, Institut geografii i Geograficheskoe obshchestvo SSR, Institut etnografii].

 1972   *Exploration of Kamchatka, 1735–41*, trans. with an introduction and notes by E. A. P. Crownhart-Vaughan. Portland, Ore.: Oregon Historical Society.

Kushnarev, Evgenii V.

1964   "Nereshennye voprosy istorii pervoi kamchatskoi ekspeditsii" [Unresolved questions of the history of the First Kamchatka Expedition], *Russkie arkticheskie ekspeditsii XVII–XX vv.*, M. I. Belov, ed. Leningrad: Arkticheskii i antarkticheskii nauchno-issledovatel'skii institut, pp. 5–15.

1976   *V poiskakh proliva: Pervaia kamchatskaia ekspeditsiia, 1725–1730* [In search of a strait: The First Kamchatka Expedition, 1725–30]. Leningrad: Gidrometeoizdat, 1976.

Kuskov, V. P.

1966   "Byl li Fedot Popov na reke Kamchatke?" [Was Fedot Popov on the Kamchatka River?], *Voprosy geografii Kamchatki* (Kamchatskii otdel, Geograficheskoe obshchestvo SSSR, Petropavlovsk-Kamchatskii), no. 4:94–100.

Lantzeff, George V.

1943   *Siberia in the Seventeenth Century: A Study of the Colonial Administration*. Berkeley and Los Angeles: University of California Press; reprinted, New York: Octagon Books, 1972 [University of California Publications in History, 30].

Lantzeff, George V., and Richard A. Pierce

1973   *Eastward to Empire: Exploration and Conquest on the Russian Open Frontier, to 1750*. Montreal and London: McGill-Queen's University Press.

Lauridsen, Peter

1889   *Vitus Bering: The Discoverer of Bering Strait*, rev. by the author and trans. from the Danish by Julius O. Olson. Chicago: S. C. Griggs and Co.

Lebedev, Dmitrii M.

1950   *Geografiia v Rossii petrovskogo vremeni* [Geography in Russia in Petrine times], Moscow and Leningrad: AN SSSR.

1951   *Plavanie A. I. Chirikova na paketbote "Sv. Pavel" k poberesh'iam Ameriki, s prilozheniem sudago zhurnala 1741 g.* [The voyage of A. I. Chirikov on the packetboat "St. Paul" to the shores of America, together with the ship's journal of 1741]. Moscow: AN SSSR.

1957   *Ocherki po istorii geografii v Rossii XVIII v. (1725–1800 gg.)* [Outlines of the history of geography in Russia in the eighteenth century (1725–1800)]. Moscow: AN SSSR, Institut geografii.

Lebedev, Dmitrii M., and Vasilii A. Esakov

1971   *Russkie geograficheskie otkrytiia i issledovaniia s drevnykh vremen do 1917 goda* [Russian geographical discoveries and explorations from ancient times to 1917]. Moscow: Mysl'.

Lebedev, Dmitrii M., and Vadim I. Grekov

1967   "Geographical Explorations by the Russians," *The Pacific Basin. . . ,* Herman R. Friis, ed. New York: The American Geographical Society, pp. 170–200.

Lensen, George A.
1959   *The Russian Push toward Japan: Russo-Japanese Relations, 1697–1875*. Princeton, N.J.: Princeton University Press.

Lomonosov, Mikhail V.
1952   *Trudy po russkoi istorii, obshchestvenno-ekonomicheskim voprosam i geografii, 1747–65 g.* [Complete collection of works. . . . Works on Russian history, socio-economic questions and geography, 1747–65]. Vol. 6 of *Polnoe sobranie sochinenii*. Moscow: AN SSSR.

Makarova, Raisa V.
1968   *Russkie na tikhom okeane vo vtoroi polovine XVIII v.* [The Russians on the Pacific Ocean in the second half of the eighteenth century]. Moscow: Nauka.

1975   *Russians on the Pacific, 1743–99*, trans. from the Russian and ed. by Richard A. Pierce and Alton S. Donnelly. Kingston, Ont.: Limestone Press [Materials for the Study of Alaska History, 6].

Masterson, James R., and Helen Brower, eds.
1948   *Bering's Successors, 1745–80: Contributions of Peter Simon Pallas to the History of Russian Exploration toward Alaska*. Seattle: University of Washington Press. Reprinted from *Pacific Northwest Quarterly*, 38, no. 1(January 1947):35–83; no. 2(April 1947):109–55.

Materialy dlia istorii russkago flota, 17 vols. St. Petersburg: Morskoe ministerstvo, 1865–1905.

Mazour, Anatole G.
1958   *Modern Russian Historiography*, 2d ed. Princeton, N.J.: Princeton University Press.

Messerschmidt, Daniel G.
1968   *Tagebuchaufzeichnungen, February–November 1725*, E. Winter, G. Uschmann, and G. Jarosch, eds. Vol. 4 of *Forschungsreise durch Sibirien, 1720–27*, E. Winter and N. A. Figurovskii, eds. Berlin: Akademie-Verlag, 1962–68 [Deutsche Akademie der Wissenschaften zu Berlin. Institut für Geschichte Osteuropas, 8].

Miliukov, Pavl N.
1905   *Gosudarstvennoe khoziaistvo Rossii v pervoi chetverti XVIII stoletiia i reforma Petra velikago*, 2d ed. St. Petersburg: M. M. Stasiulevich.

Miliukov, Pavl N., Charles Seignobos, and L. Eisenmann
1968   *History of Russia*, Charles L. Markmann, trans., 2 vols. New York: Funk and Wagnalls.

Mirzoev, Vladimir G.
1970   *Istoriografiia Sibiri* [Historiography of Siberia]. Moscow: Mysl'.

Monas, Sidney
1961   *The Third Section: Police and Society in Russia under Nicholas I*. Cambridge, Mass.: Harvard University Press [Russian Research Center Studies, 42].

Müller, Gerhard F.
        Lettre d'un officier de la marine russienne à un seigneur de la cour concernant la carte des nouvelles découvertes au nord de la mer du sud et le

mémoire qui y sert d'explication, publié par M. de l'Isle à Paris en 1752.
Traduite de l'original russe. . . . Berlin: Hande and Spener, 1753.

1753 "Lettre. . . ," *Nouvelle bibliotheque germanique, ou histoire litteraire de l'Allemagne, de la Suisse, et des pays du nord* (Amsterdam), 13, première partie (July, August, and September):46–87.

1754 *A Letter from a Russian Sea-officer, to a Person of Distinction at the Court of St. Petersburgh, Containing His Remarks on Mr. de l'Isle's Chart and Memoir, Relative to the New Discoveries Northward and Eastward from Kamtschatka. Together with Some Observations on That Letter by Arthur Dobbs, Esq., Governor of North Carolina. To Which Is Added, Mr. de l'Isle's Explanatory Memoir on His Chart Published at Paris. . . ,* trans from the French. London: A. Linde.

1758a *Nachrichten von Seereisen, und zur See gemachten Entdeckungen, die von Russland aus längst de Küsten des Eismeeres und auf dem östlichen Weltmeere gegen Japon und America geschehen sind. Zur Erläuterung einer bey der Akademie der Wissenschaften verfertigten Landkarte.* St. Petersburg: Kaiserliche Academie der Wissenschaften [Sammlung russischer Geschichte, 3].

1758b "Opisanie morskikh puteshestvii po ledovitomu i po vostochnomu moriu s rossiiskoi storony uchenennykh" [Description of the ocean voyages made in the Arctic and Pacific oceans from the Russian side], *Sochineniia i perevody, k pol'ze i uveseleniiu sluzhashchiia* (Imperatorskaia akademiia nauk, St. Petersburg) 7(January):3–27, (February):99–120, (March):195–212, (April):291–325, (May):387–409; 8(July):9–32, (August):99–129, (September):195–232, (October):309–36, (November):394–424.

1761 *Voyages from Asia to America, for Completing the Discoveries of the Northwest Coast of America. To Which Is Prefixed a Summary of the Voyages Made by the Russians on the Frozen Ocean. Serving As an Explanation of a Map of the Russian Discoveries, Published by the Academy of Sciences at Petersburgh,* trans. from the High Dutch of S[taatsrath?] Muller. . . . London: Thomas Jefferys; 2d ed., 1764; reprinted, Amsterdam: Nico Israel, 1967.

1766 *Voyages et découvertes faites par les Russes le long des côtes de la mer Glaciale & sur l'océan Oriental, tant vers le Japon que vers l'Amérique. On y a joint l'Historie du fleuve Amur et des pays adjacens, depuis le conquête des Russes. . . ,* trans. from the German . . . by C. G. F. Dumas. . . , 2 vols. Amsterdam: M. M. Rey.

1890 *Istoriia Akademii nauk G.-F. Millera, s prodolzheniiami I.-G. Shtrittera (1725–43)* [G. F. Müller's history of the academy of sciences, with a continuation by J. G. Stritter (1725–43)]. St. Petersburg [Imperatorskaia akademiia nauk, Materialy dlia istorii Imperatorskoi akademii nauk, 6].

1937 *Istoriia Sibiri* [History of Siberia], 2 vols. Moscow and Leningrad: AN SSSR, 1937–41.

Nartov, Andrei K.

1891 *Razskazy Nartova o Petre velikom* [Nartov's stories about Peter the

Great], L. N. Maikov, ed. St. Petersburg: Imperatorskaia akademiia nauk. Also in *Zapiski Imperatorskoi akademii nauk*, vol. 47 (1892), supplement no. 6 (1891).

Navrot, M. I.

1971 "Novoi variant itogovoi karty Pervoi Kamchatskoi Ekspeditsii" [A new variant of the complete map of the First Kamchatka Expedition] in *Letopis' severa*, (Sovet po izucheniiu proizvoditel'nykh sil pri Gosplane SSSR, Mezhduvedomstvennaia komissiia po problemam Severa, Moscow), 5:173–79.

Nordenskiöld, [Nils] Adolf E.

1881 *The Voyage of the "Vega" round Asia and Europe with a Historical Review of Previous Journeys along the North Coast of the Old World.* Trans. from the Swedish by Alexander Leslie, 2 vols. London: Macmillan.

Novlianskaia, Mariia G.

1964 *Ivan Kirilovich Kirilov; geograf XVIII veka* [Ivan Kirilovich Kirilov; geographer of the eighteenth century]. Leningrad: Nauka.

1966 *Filip Ioann Stralenberg; ego raboty po issledovaniiu Sibiri* [Philip Johann Strahlenberg; his works on Siberia]. Moscow: Nauka.

Nunn, George E.

1929 *Origin of the Strait of Anian Concept.* Philadelphia: privately printed.

Ogloblin, Nikolai N.

1890 *Semen Dezhnev (1638–71 gg.), (Novyia dannyia i peresmotr starykh)* [Semen Dezhnev (1638–71), (New data and a re-examination of the old)]. St. Petersburg: V. S. Balashev. Also in *Zhurnal Ministerstva narodnago prosveshcheniia* (St. Petersburg) 272(December 1890), Sec. 2:249–306.

1891 "Dve 'skazki' Vl. Atlasova ob otkrytii Kamchatki" [Two 'stories' of Vladimir Atlasov about the discovery of Kamchatka], *Chteniia v Imperatorskom obshchestve istorii i drevnostei rossiiskikh pri Moskovskom universitete*, 157, bk. 3, [pt.] 1:1–18.

Ogryzko, I. I.

1948 "Ekspeditsiia Semena Dezhneva i otkrytie Kamchatki" [The expedition of Semen Dezhnev and the discovery of Kamchatka], *Vestnik Leningradskogo universiteta* 3, no. 12(December):36–47.

1953 "Otkrytie kuril'skikh ostrovov" [Discovery of the Kurile Islands] in *Iazyki i istoriia narodnostei krainego severa SSSR*, pp. 167–207 [Uchenye zapiski Leningradskogo gosudarstvennogo universiteta, 157. Seriia Fakul'teta narodov severa, no. 2].

Okun', Semen B.

1935 *Ocherki po istorii kolonial'noi politiki tsarizma v kamchatskom krae* [Outlines of the history of the colonial policy of tsarism in the Kamchatka region]. Leningrad: Ogiz—Sotsekgiz, Leningradskoe otdelenie.

Orlova, N. S., comp.

1951 *Otkrytiia russkikh zemleprokhodtsev i poliarnykh morekhodov XVII veka na severo-vostoke Azii: Sbornik dokumentov* [Discoveries of the Russian land and polar sea farers of the seventeenth century: a collection of documents], A. V. Efimov, ed. Moscow: Gos. izd-vo geogr. lit-ry [Tsentral'nyi gosudarstvennyi arkhiv drevnikh aktov SSSR].

Pekarskii, Petr P.

1870   *Istoriia Imperatorskoi akademii nauk v Peterburge* [History of the imperial academy of sciences in St. Petersburg], 2 vols. St. Petersburg: Imperatorskaia akademiia nauk, 1870–73.

Perevalov, V. A.

1949   *Lomonosov i Arktika; iz istorii geograficheskikh nauk i geograficheskikh otkrytii* [Lomonosov and the Arctic; from the history of the geographical sciences and geographical discoveries]. Moscow and Leningrad: Glavsevmorput'.

Perry, John

1716   *The State of Russia, under the Present Czar.* . . . London: Benjamin Tooke.

Petersen, Josef

1947   *Vitus Bering, der Seefahrer*, trans. from the Danish by H. Kurtzweil. Hamburg: Hoffmann and Campe.

Polevoi, Boris P.

1962a   "O mestopolozhenii pervogo russkogo poseleniia na Kolyme" [The location of the first Russian settlement on the Kolyma]. *Doklady Instituta geografii Sibiri i Dal'nego Vostoka* (AN SSSR, Irkutsk), no. 2:66–75.

1962b   "Nakhodka podlinnykh dokumentov S. I. Dezhneva o ego istoricheskom pokhode 1648 g." [The finding of the original documents of S. I. Dezhnev about his historical journey of 1648], *Vestnik Leningradskogo gosudarstvennogo universiteta* 17, no. 6(June):145–52 [Seriia geologii i geografii, no. 1].

1964a   "Glavnaia zadacha pervoi kamchatskoi ekspeditsii po zamyslu Petra I. (O novoi interpretatsii instruktsii Vitusu Beringu 1725 g.)" [The principal task of the First Kamchatka Expedition according to the intent of Peter the Great. (A new interpretation of the instructions of 1725 to Vitus Bering)], *Voprosy geografii Kamchatki* (Kamchatskii otdel, Geograficheskoe obshchestvo SSSR, Petropavlovsk-Kamchatskii), no. 2:88–94.

1964b   "Zabytyi pokhod I. M. Rubtsa na Kamchatku v 60-kh gg. XVII veka" [The forgotten journey of I. M. Rubets to Kamchatka in the sixties of the seventeenth century], *Izvestiia AN SSSR, seriia geograficheskaia* (Moscow) no. 4(July–August):130–35.

1964c   "K istorii formirovaniia geograficheskikh predstavlenii o severo–vostochnoi okonechnosti Azii v XVII v. (Izvestie o 'kamennoi peregrade'. Vozniknovenie i dal'neishaia metamorfoza legendy o 'neobkhodimon nose')" [Contribution to the history of the formation of the geographical ideas about the northeastern extremity of Asia in the seventeenth century. (Information about the 'rocky barrier'. Origin and subsequent metamorphosis of the legend of the 'impassable cape'.)] *Sibirskii geograficheskii sbornik* (Institut geografii Sibiri i Dal'nego Vostoka, Sibirskoe otdelenie AN SSSR, Moscow) 3:224–70.

1965a   "O tochnom tekste dvukh otpisok Semena Dezhneva 1655 goda" [Concerning the exact text of Semen Dezhnev's two despatches of 1655], *Izvestiia AN SSSR, seriia geograficheskaia* (Moscow) no. 2(March–April):101–11.

1965b   "Vodnyi put' iz ledovitogo okeana v tikhii; zabytyi nakaz A. A. Vinius 1697 goda" [The water route from the Arctic Ocean to the Pacific; a forgotten instruction of A. A. Vinius in 1697], *Priroda* (AN SSSR, Leningrad) no. 5:94.

1965c   "Semen Remezov i Vladimir Atlasov (k utocheniiu datirovki rannykh chertezhei Kamchatki)" [Semen Remezov and Vladimir Atlasov (toward a precise dating of the earliest sketch-maps of Kamchatka)], *Izvestiia AN SSSR, seriia geograficheskaia* (Moscow) no. 6(November–December):92–101.

1965d   "Novoe o nachale istoricheskogo plavaniia S. I. Dezhneva 1648 g." [A new datum on the beginning of S. I. Dezhnev's historical voyage of 1648], *Izvestiia Vostochno–sibirskogo otdela Geograficheskogo obshchestva SSR* (Irkutsk) 63:51–57.

1966   "Nakhodka chelobit'ia pervootkryvatelei Kolymy" [The finding of the petition of the first discoverers of the Kolyma], *Ekonomika, upravlenie i kul'tura Sibiri XVI–XIX vv.* (Novosibirsk: Nauka), pp. 285–91. [Materialy po istorii Sibiri. Sibir' perioda feodalizma, no. 2.]

1967   "Iz istorii otkrytiia severo-zapadnoi chasti Ameriki (ot pervogo izvestii sibirskikh zemleprokhodtsev ob Aliaske do petrovskogo plana poiska morskogo k Amerike)" [From the history of the discovery of the north-western part of America (from the first information of Siberian land farers about Alaska to Peter's plan for a maritime search for America], *Ot Aliaski do ognennoi zemli . . .* , I. R. Grigulevich, ed. Moscow: Nauka, pp. 107–20.

1969   "Geograficheskie chertezhi posol'stva N. G. Spafariia" [The geographical sketch-maps of the mission of N. G. Spafarii], *Izvestiia AN SSSR, seriia geograficheskaia* (Moscow) no. 1(January–February):115–24.

1970a   "O karte 'Kamchadalii' I. B. Gomana" [J. B. Homann's map of 'Kamchadaliia'], *Izvestiia AN SSSR, seriia geograficheskaia* (Moscow) no. 1(January–February):99–105.

1970b   "Soobshchenie S. I. Dezhneva o 'bol'shom kamennom nose' i proiskhozhdenie ego lozhnogo tolkovaniia" [S. I. Dezhnev's communication about the 'great rocky cape' and the origin of its false meaning], *Izvestiia AN SSSR, seriia geograficheskaia* (Moscow) no. 6(November–December):150–57.

1970c   "O 'Pogyche'-Pokhache" [Concerning the 'Pogycha'-Pokhacha], *Voprosy geografii Kamchatki* (Kamchatskii otdel, Geograficheskoe obshchestvo SSSR, Petropavlovsk-Kamchatskii) no. 6:82–86.

1971   "Commemorating the Three Hundredth Anniversary of the 'Godunov Map' of Siberia," James R. Gibson, trans., *The Canadian Cartographer* (Toronto) 8, no. 1(June):19–26.

1975   "Kolumby russkie (k 250-letiiu ekspeditsii Vitusa Beringa)" [Russian Columbuses (commemorating the 250th anniversary of Vitus Bering's expedition)], *Dalnyi vostok* (Khabarovsk) no. 1:127–32.

Polonskii, Aleksandr S.

1850a   "Pokhod geodezista Mikhaila Gvozdeva v beringov proliv, 1732 goda" [The journey of geodesist Mikhail Gvozdev into the Bering Strait, 1732], *Morskoi sbornik* (St. Petersburg) 4, no. 11:389–402.

1850b   "Pervaia kamchatskaia ekspeditsiia Beringa, 1725–29 goda" [Bering's first Kamchatka expedition, 1725–29], *Zapiski Gidrograficheskago departamenta* (Morskoe ministerstvo, St. Petersburg) 8, sec. 4:535–56.

1851   "Pervaia kamchatskaia ekspeditsiia Beringa, 1725–29 goda," *Otechestvennyia zapiski* (St. Petersburg), [ser. 3], 75, sec. viii:1–24.

1871   "Kurily" [The Kuriles], *Zapiski Imperatorskago russkago geograficheskago obshchestva po otdeleniiu etnografii* (St. Petersburg) 4:367–576.

Riabchikov, Petr A.

1959   *Morskie suda: Istoriia razvitiia i sovremennye tipy sudov* [Ocean vessels: Historical development and types of vessels], 2d ed. Moscow: Transport.

Russia. Arkheograficheskaia kommissia

DAI   *Dopolneniia k aktam istoricheskim* [Supplement to Historical acts], 12 vols. St. Petersburg: Vtoroe otdelenie Sobstvennoi EIV kantseliarii, 1846–72; index, 1875.

PSI   *Pamiatniki sibirskoi istorii XVIII v.* [Memorials of Siberian history in the eighteenth century], 2 vols. St. Petersburg: Ministerstvo vnutrennykh del, 1882–85.

Russia. Sobstvennaia ego imperatorskago velichestva kantseliariia

PSZ   *Polnoe sobranie zakonov rossiiskoi imperii s 1649 goda* [Complete collection of laws of the Russian empire since 1649], 44 vols. St. Petersburg: Sobstvennaia ego imperatorskago velichestva kantseliariia, 1830.

Samoilov, Viacheslav A.

1945   *Semen Dezhnev i ego vremia. S prilozheniem otpisok i chelobitnykh Semena Dezhneva o ego prokhodakh i otkrytiiakh* [Semen Dezhnev and his times. With an appendix of the despatches and petitions of Semen Dezhnev about his journeys and discoveries]. Moscow: Glavsevmorput'.

Sgibnev, A. S.

1868   "Bol'shoi kamchatskii nariad (ekspeditsiia Elchina)" [The Great Kamchatka Command (Elchin's expedition)], *Morskoi sbornik* (St. Petersburg) 99, no. 12(December):unofficial sec., 131–39.

1869a   "Popytki russkikh k zavedeniiu torgovykh snoshenii s Iaponiei v XVIII i nachale XIX stoletii" [Russian attempts to establish trade relations with Japan in the eighteenth and at the beginning of the nineteenth century], *Morskoi sbornik* (St. Petersburg) 100, no. 1(January):sec. 2, 37–72.

1869b   "Istoricheskii ocherk glavneishikh sobytii v Kamchatke 1650–1856" [Historical outline of the principal events in Kamchatka, 1650–1856], *Morskoi sbornik* (St. Petersburg) 101, no. 4(April):65–142 [1650–1742]; 102, no. 5(May):53–84 [1742–59]; no. 6(June):37–69 [1759–72]; 103, no. 7(July):1–129 [1772–1816]; no. 8(August):33–110 [1816–56].

1869c   "Materialy dlia istorii Kamchatki: ekspeditsiia Shestakova" [Material for the history of Kamchatka: Shestakov's expedition], *Morskoi sbornik* (St. Petersburg) 100, no. 2(February):unofficial sec., 1–34 [65–83].

Sokolov, Aleksandr P.

1851a   "Pervyi pokhod russkikh k Amerike, 1732" [The first Russian journey to America, 1732], *Zapiski Gidrograficheskago departamenta* (Morskoe ministerstvo, St. Petersburg), 9:78–107.

1851b   "Severnaia ekspeditsiia, 1733–43 goda" [The northern expedition, 1733–43], *Zapiski Gidrograficheskago departamenta*, 9:190–468.

Solov'ev, Sergei M.

1894–   *Istoriia Rossii s drevneishikh vremen* [The history of Russia from ancient
96[?]   times], 2d ed., 6 bks. St. Petersburg: "Obshchestvennaia pol'za".

Stejneger, Leonhard

1936   *Georg Wilhelm Steller, the Pioneer of Alaskan Natural History.* Cambridge, Mass.: Harvard University Press.

Strahlenberg, Philipp Johann Tabbert von

1730   *Das nord und östliche Theil von Europa und Asia, in so weit solches das gantze russische Reich mit Sibirien und der grossen Tatarei in sich begreisset, In einer historisch-geographischen Beschreibung der alten und neuern Zeiten, und vielen andern unbekannten Nachrichten vorgestellet. . . .* Stockholm: the author.

1738   *An Historico-geographical Description of the North and Eastern Parts of Europe and Asia; but More Particularly of Russia, Siberia, and Great Tartary; Both in the Ancient and Modern State. . . .* Now faithfully translated into English. London: W. Innys and R. Manby; reprinted, New York: Arno Press, 1970.

1757   *Description historique de l'empire russien*, trans. from the German, 2 vols. Amsterdam: Desaint and Saillant.

Sykes, Godfrey

1915   "The Mythical Straits of Anian," *Bulletin of the American Geographical Society of New York* 67, no. 3:161–72.

Titov, Andrei A.

1890   *Sibir' v XVII v. Sbornik starinnykh russkikh statei o Sibiri i prilezhashchikh k nei zemliakh* [Siberia in the seventeenth century. A collection of old Russian articles about Siberia and the lands adjacent to it]. Moscow: L. and A. Snegirev.

Tompkins, Stuart R.

1945   *Alaska: Promyshlennik and Sourdough.* Norman, Okla: University of Oklahoma Press.

Tompkins, Stuart R., and Max L. Moorhead

1949   "Russia's Approach to America. Part I: From Russian Sources, 1741–61," *British Columbia Historical Quarterly* (Victoria, B.C.) 13, no. 2(April):55–66; "Russia's Approach to America. Part II: From Spanish Sources, 1761–75," ibid., nos. 3–4(July–October):231–55.

Trisman, V. G.

1951   "Russkie istochniki v monografii N. Vitsena 'Severnaia i vostochnaia

Tatariia' " [Russian sources in N. Witsen's 'Northern and eastern Tartary'], *Kratkie soobshcheniia Instituta etnografii AN SSSR* (Moscow),
13:15–19.

United States Hydrographic Office

1952   *Sailing Directions, East Coast of Siberia. Mys Otto Shmidta to
Sakhalinskiy Zaliv (Sakhalin Gulf)*, 2d ed., 1951. Washington: Government Printing Office [H. O. Pub. No. 122a].

Vakhtin, Vasilii V.

1890   *Russkie truzheniki moria. Pervaia morskaia ekspeditsiia Beringa dlia resheniia voprosa, soediniaetsia li Aziia s Amerikoi* [Russian toilers of the
sea. Bering's maritime expedition to decide the question whether Asia is
joined to America]. St. Petersburg: Morskoe ministerstvo.

Varep, Endel F.

1959   "O kartakh, sostavlennykh russkimi, v atlase I. B. Gomana, 1725 g."
[Concerning the maps composed by Russians in J. B. Homann's atlas of
1725], *Izvestiia VGO* 91, no. 3 (May–June):290–98. "Über einige Karten
Russlands in J. B. Homanns Atlas von 1725," *Petermanns Geographischen
Mitteilungen* (Gotha) 1963, no. 4:308–11.

Vdovin, Innokentii S.

1965   *Ocherki istorii i etnografii Chukchei* [Outlines of the history and ethnography of the Chukchi]. Moscow and Leningrad: Nauka.

Vernadsky, George

1969   *The Tsardom of Moscow, 1547–1682*, 2 pts. New Haven and London:
Yale University Press [A History of Russia, 5].

Vize, Vladimir Iu.

1948   *Russkie poliarnye morekhody iz promyshlennykh, torgovykh i sluzhilykh
liudei XVII–XIX vv. Biograficheskii slovar'* [Russian promyshlenniki,
traders and service men of the seventeenth to nineteenth centuries as
polar seafarers. A biographical dictionary]. Moscow and Leningrad: Glavsevmorput'.

1949   "Novye svedeniia o russkom arkticheskom moreplavanii v XVII veke"
[New information about Russian Arctic navigation in the seventeenth
century], *Letopis' severa* (Moscow and Leningrad: Glavsevmorput'), 1:78–93.

Vladislavich, Sava L.

1842   "Sekretnaia informatsiia o sile i sostoianii kitaiskago gosudarstva, i o
protchem" [Secret information about the strength and condition of the
Chinese state and about other matters], *Russkii vestnik* (St. Petersburg)
no. 2(February):180–243; no. 3(March):281–337.

Wagner, Henry R.

1937   *The Cartography of the Northwest Coast of America to the Year 1800*, 2
vols. Berkeley: University of California Press; reprinted, 2 vols. in 1,
Amsterdam: Nico Israel, 1968.

Waxell, Sven

1940   *Vtoraia kamchatskaia ekspeditsiia Vitusa Beringa* [The Second Kamchatka Expedition of Vitus Bering], trans. from the German by Iu. I. Bronshtein; A. I. Andreev, ed. Leningrad and Moscow: Glavsevmorput'.

1952   *The American Expedition*, trans. from Johan Skalberg's Danish version, with an introduction and note by M. A. Michael. Edinburgh: William Hodge, and New York: Macmillan; reprinted.: *The Russian Expedition to America*. New York: Collier Books, 1962.

Weber, Friedrich C.

1727?   *Nouveaux mémoires sur l'état present de la grande Russie, ou Moscovie. . . ,* 2 vols. [Paris: Pissot?].

Witsen, Nicolaas C.

1785   *Noord en oost Tartaryen: behelzende eene beschryving van versheidene tartersche en nabuurige gewesten, in de noorder en oostelykste deelen van Aziën en Europa; zedert naauwkeurig onderzoek van veele jaaren, en eigen ondervinding ontworpen, beschreven, geteekent en in 't licht gegeven. . . .* [North and east Tartary: containing a description of several Tartar and adjacent regions in the northern and easternmost parts of Asia and Europe; designed, described, drawn up, and published on the basis of many years of research and personal experience. . . .] Nieuwe uitgaa. . . , 2 vols. Amsterdam: M. Schalekamp.

Wroth, Lawrence C.

1944   *The Early Cartography of the Pacific*. New York. [Papers of the Bibliographical Society of America, 38, no. 2(April, May, June).]

Zhdanko, M.

1916   "Raboty russkikh moriakov v okhotskom more" [The work of Russian mariners in the Sea of Okhotsk], *Zapiski po gidrografii* (Glavnoe gidrograficheskoe upravlenie, Morskoe ministerstvo, Petrograd), 40, no. 5.

Znamenskii, S.

1929   *V poiskakh Iaponii. Iz istorii russkikh geograficheskikh otkrytii i morekhodstva v tikhom okeane* [In search of Japan. From the history of Russian geographical discovery and seafaring in the Pacific Ocean]. Vladivostok: Knizhnoe delo.

Zubov, Nikolai N.

1954   *Otechestvennye moreplavateli-issledovateli morei i okeanov* [The fatherland's mariner-explorers of the seas and oceans]. Moscow: Gos. izd-vo geogr. lit-ry.

Index

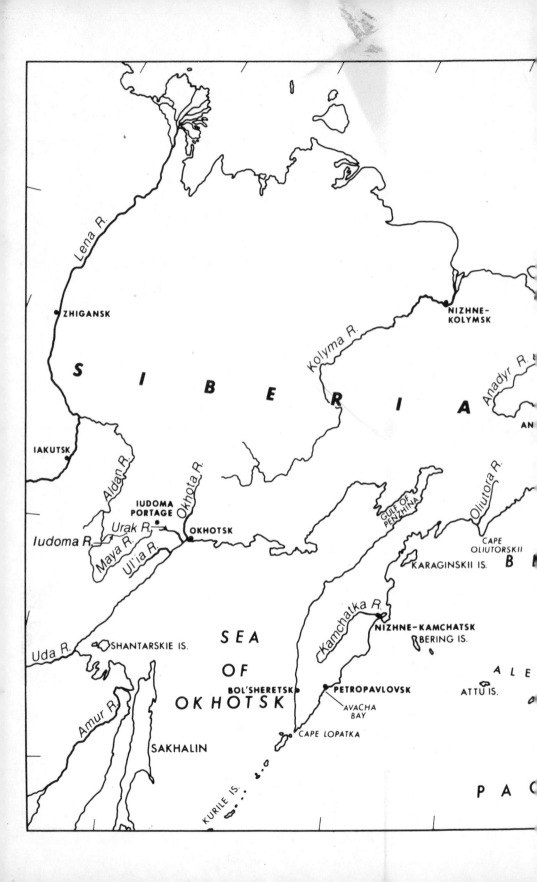